Historical Chinese
Letter Writing

Historical Chinese
Letter Writing

Dániel Z. Kádár

continuum

Continuum International Publishing Group
The Tower Building   80 Maiden Lane
11 York Road   Suite 704
London SE1 7NX   New York NY 10038

www.continuumbooks.com

British Library Cataloguing-in-Publication Data
A catalogue record for this book is available from the British Library.

ISBN: 978-1-4411-8036-0   (PaperBack)

Library of Congress Cataloging-in-Publication Data
Kádár, Dániel Z., 1979-
Historical Chinese letter writing / Dániel Z. Kádár.
  p. cm.
Summary: Collected letters from the Qing Dynasty era (1644-1911), with
English translation.
ISBN 978-1-4411-8036-0
1. Chinese language–Readers–Correspondence. 2. Chinese
letters–Translations into English. I. Title.
PL1117.5.L48K33 2009
491.7–dc22   200903484

Typeset by Newgen Imaging Systems Pvt Ltd, Chennai, India
Printed and bound in Great Britain by the MPG Books Group

Contents

Contents

List of Illustrations

Acknowledgements

I would like to express my gratitude to the following colleagues who helped me enormously in the writing of this book. I am grateful to Professor Andrew Kirkpatrick (Hong Kong Institute of Education) and Professor Hongyin Tao (UCLA) for their kind support during the early stages of this project. I am also very much indebted to Dr. Huba Bartos (Research Institute for Linguistics, Hungarian Academy of Sciences) for his comments on some technical aspects of this book. My sincere thanks to Ms. Mei-hua Ni for kindly reviewing the Chinese translations and texts and to Mr. Ben Mousley for his English style-review. I am grateful to the editorial team of the Continuum International Publishing Group, in particular Gurdeep Mattu, Colleen Coalter, Luke Roberts, P. Muralidharan and Rathna Maria Muthayya for their kind and expert support in the course of publishing this volume. Last but not least, I am greatly indebted to the two anonymous referees whose invaluable comments strongly aided me to develop the manuscript. All the remaining errors are the responsibility of the author.

I am grateful to the City of Vancouver Archives for allowing me to reprint illustrative materials from the so-called Yip Sang Correspondence (葉生信件). This recently discovered correspondence of the Canadian businessman 葉生 Yip Sang (1845–1927) and his employees contains late imperial and early Republican business and family correspondence, predominantly written in Classical Chinese. I would also like to express my sincere thanks to Mrs. Deborah Blumer for permitting to reprint an early Republican Chinese official letter and its envelope, which was found in the papers of Rev. George Oliver Lillegard (1888–1965), a renowned Chinese missionary.

I am extremely grateful to the following two organizations for their kind support, without which the present work could have never been completed. The Hungarian Scientific Research Fund ('OTKA'), whose three-year Postdoctoral Research Grant (PD 71628) made it possible for me to devote my time to the research of historical Chinese letters and write the present work; and The Chiang Ching-Kuo Foundation for International Scholarly Exchange (CCKF), whose long-term Research Grant (RG003-U-07) provided the necessary financial backing for fieldtrips and book acquisitions, which were fundamental in the completion of this book.

Preface

古人尺牘，短祇數行，長不越幅，
以其用筆遒峭，敘事簡潔。

The men of ancient times wrote short letters of a few lines,
and even their long epistles exceeded not a page;
they selected their words with skill
and expressed themselves in a succinct manner.

龔未齋 Gōng Wèizhāi (1738–1811)

Introduction

Letter writing is a universally important medium of communication in historical written cultures: before the electronic age it was the main channel of written discourse. Therefore, when one ventures into the study of a historical culture, sooner or later (s)he will unavoidably encounter letters. Epistolary genres are not only relevant to experts in historical linguistics, communication and rhetoric who approach them as a corpus, but also to those in other fields, such as history, literature and sociology, as sources.

In Chinese studies we have to cope with an epistolary corpus that can justifiably be claimed to be immense. By the Hàn Dynasty the Chinese had already formed the basis of an epistolary tradition – labelled here as 'historical Chinese letter writing' – which was in use until around the middle of the 20th century and still strongly influences written communication (in particular in non-mainland communities, such as Taiwan). Although diachronic changes can be observed when one studies historical Chinese letters, it is a relatively homogenous corpus, and so historical Chinese letter writing is arguably the diachronically longest monolingual epistolary tradition.

Despite the importance of letters for the student of sinology and the huge Chinese epistolary corpus, until now there has not been any educational work published on historical Chinese letter writing. This is not that surprising, considering that at first sight letter writing may seem to be rather a 'dry' genre compared with, for example, Chinese novels. Also, letters are generally understudied in sinological literature, which may be another reason for this. Finally, it may appear evident that someone who has a skill in reading basic Classical Chinese texts will also be able to read historical Chinese letters without difficulty, due to the fact that letters do not differ grammatically from other historical genres.

However, in reality this is not the case: not only do Chinese letters utilize unique stylistic and lexical elements, which may differ across the different epistolary genres, but also historical Chinese letter writing has its own communicational-rhetorical features. It is not a coincidence that the Chinese themselves, especially during the Míng and the Qīng Dynasties, regarded letter writing as an *art form*. For example, as the introductory sentence – written by a famous epistolary expert (see Chapter 6) on the "art of letter writing" (尺牘之道 *chǐdú-zhī-dào*) – demonstrates, proper letter writing was an idealized skill associated with ancient masters. In sum, letter writing is a unique corpus within historical Chinese corpora, and its reading necessitates preliminary study.

The goal of this book is to fill this gap and act as an introduction to historical Chinese private[1] letter writing. It is a textbook for *advanced* students of sinology, that is readers who have actively studied at least three or four semesters of Classical and modern Chinese. Thus, the reader should be able to translate simple Classical Chinese texts with the aid of dictionaries, to have a basic command of Classical Chinese grammar, to possess a basic vocabulary of around 1,500–2,000 words, and also to be able to interpret vernacular or colloquial grammatical forms and lexical items that frequently occur in letters. The book is designed in a way that it will not only aid the reader to learn the special features of historical Chinese letter writing, but also be able to independently read letters.

It should be noted that this textbook primarily focuses on the communicational and rhetorical norms as well as the sociocultural features of historical letters, rather than on strict-sense grammar. It is assumed that readers are advanced students of sinology, and so grammar is not discussed nor are simpler lexical items included in the glossaries of the chapters. Instead, the present work focuses on issues that *differentiate* letter writing from other historical Chinese genres, that is its aforementioned communicational, rhetorical and sociocultural features.

The present book studies Qīng Dynasty texts. This period has been chosen because from a stylistic and rhetorical perspective historical Chinese letter writing reached its peak during this time. Considering the fact that the Chinese epistolary corpus is a relatively homogenous one, it can be argued that the linguistic and communicational features we study in this book represent historical Chinese letter writing in general. Furthermore, the letters used in the present work are selected from some of the most renowned individual epistolary collections, written by Qīng Dynasty authors of different social status, personal interests and discursive goals, and from this perspective the texts used in the present work are also representative. In a nutshell, after the successful study of this book the reader should be able to understand letters from other periods, as well.

How To Use This Book

This book can be used either as a course book, or individually by advanced students of Classical Chinese. In what follows, this section will focus on the needs of individual readers and give some tips on how to use this work individually.

The chapters of this book have the following structure: Every chapter begins with a brief section that introduces the author studied and his epistolary work, and ends with a brief section, 'Further Reading', where the reader can find a list of suggested additional material. Further information relevant to specific portions of the text in each chapter is provided in the 'Notes' section at the end of the book. The chapters contain three texts (except Chapter 7 that contains one long letter), which are followed by glossaries and then translations; although the translations follow the original Chinese texts to a degree, they are literary and not word-by-word, and often explanatory sections are included, denoted within square brackets. In order to facilitate the translation of the texts, they are separated into sections. After each text, there is a 'Brief summary' section, which discusses the importance of the given letter either from historical or other perspectives. This is followed by a detailed section titled 'Rhetorical, pragmatic[2] and sociocultural features', which aids the reader to interpret the contents of the work, and also to get to grips with the general communicational features of historical Chinese letter writing. Finally, the examination of a given letter ends with some exercises and, in the initial four chapters, question-answer tasks.

When starting a chapter, the reader is advised first to translate the texts without relying either on the translation or on the 'Rhetorical, pragmatic and sociocultural features' section. Although it is necessary to try to read the texts alone, the reader should not devote too much energy to this, that is if a section or a text type proves to be too difficult on the first try, (s)he is recommended to consult the translation and the explanatory section. It should be emphasized that if one is unable to individually translate the texts in the beginning it does not mean that (s)he does not have the necessary command of Chinese to use this book – as letters are rather specific texts, such a problem in the beginning is quite natural.

If lexical or grammatical difficulties emerge during the translation of the texts, the reader should not hesitate to make use of reliable Classical Chinese dictionaries, as well as Classical Chinese grammars, such as Edwin G. Pulleyblank's *Outline of Classical Chinese Grammar* (1996, Vancouver: University of British Columbia Press). Further, the reader may need to make use of modern Chinese dictionaries, due to the fact that the style of some epistolary genres, such as family letters, is not strictly 'Classical', that is they contain different colloquial structures and lexical items.

After translating a text, the reader is advised to go through the 'Rhetorical, pragmatic and sociocultural features' section, which explains some communicational and cultural aspects of the given letter and often puts them in perspective as regards historical Chinese letter writing in general. Thus, this section explains certain communicational and cultural issues in order to train the reader to become able to individually translate Chinese letters, and so its use necessitates some active work, that is the reader is supposed to reread (and, if necessary, reinterpret) the text in light of what is discussed. A recurring theme in the 'Rhetorical, pragmatic and sociocultural features' sections is the given letter's chain of thought, which is the perhaps most difficult aspect of understanding Chinese letters. It should be noted that in these notes the traditional Chinese rhetorical (修辭 *xiūcí*) vocabulary and its Western counterpart are not applied, and the notes are termed in a rather lay manner, in order to make them accessible to readers without previous training in this field.

The 'Rhetorical, pragmatic and sociocultural features' section is followed by an 'Exercise' section, which also aims to train the reader to individually translate Chinese letters. While the previous section deals with socio-pragmatic and other linguistic features of letters, this one primarily focuses on calligraphic and typographical issues, as well as textual ones, which are distinctive and difficult features of historical Chinese letters. In fact, letter writing was (and continues to be) an artistic genre in that the authors used different forms of calligraphy; furthermore, many letters are available only in an original unpunctuated form (the Chinese did not usually punctuate texts until modern times). Thus, in order to be able to work with the Chinese epistolary corpus the reader also needs to become familiar with calligraphic and unpunctuated texts. Therefore, the basic task in the 'Exercise' sections, along with some minor tasks in some chapters, is to reread some part of the text studied, printed in an unpunctuated form and by using various calligraphic/archaic font types. Another basic, (con)textual, form of exercise is to reread some part of the text studied, printed in an incomplete form – that is some characters are missing from the text. The practice of reading incomplete texts is essential because one unavoidably meets cases when some characters of a letter are missing or unreadable due to dilapidation. It should be noted that the number of the missing characters in these exercises is relatively large in comparison with the average in 'real' texts; this is in order to aid the reader to become accustomed to this phenomenon and to be able to interpret missing sections by means of contextual information. Finally, the 'Exercise' section is followed by a brief Q & A section in the first four chapters, which will require the reader to think about some issues raised in the given letter, thus becoming familiar with the logic of historical Chinese letter writers. The reader is advised to devote some time to these sections, in particular to 'Exercise', because these are crucial in order to develop competence in working with the Chinese epistolary corpus.

It should be noted that this book becomes more and more difficult as one progresses and the reader will have more and more individual work as (s)he proceeds. As well as the complexity of the texts (this issue will be discussed in detail in the following section) the exercises will become more difficult. Furthermore, the calligraphic features and typography will gradually move towards the original calligraphic style and layout. In the first two chapters the typography of the texts is relatively easy: the texts in Chapter 1 are printed in a Western (from left-to-right) order, they are punctuated, and the proper names are underlined; those of Chapter 2 are slightly more difficult, the only difference is that they are printed in the traditional Chinese (vertical and from right-to-left) order. The exercises of these chapters rely on the texts studied and the main tasks are to punctuate some parts cited from these works, printed using calligraphic characters, and to reread some parts of the text containing 'missing' characters. The texts of Chapters 3 and 4 are printed in a more difficult way. The texts of Chapter 3 are punctuated but proper names are not underlined any more in them, that is it will be the reader's task to find proper names when translating these letters. The texts of Chapter 4 are punctuated in a way that was popular particularly in early Republican editions, that is the texts are only punctuated by dots and no other punctuation mark occurs, that is it will be the reader's task to define sentence endings. In Chapters 3 and 4, although the reader will still have to punctuate and interpret some calligraphic citations, and also to deal with texts of 'missing' characters, (s)he will also have to individually translate some brief letter-citations in Chapter 3, as well as some brief letters in Chapter 4. The citations and short letters in these chapters will be punctuated and written by standard (non-calligraphic) characters. The texts of Chapters 5 and 6 are printed in an unpunctuated form and by standard characters; in the joint exercise of these chapters the reader will have to translate two relatively long letters printed in a similar fashion, that is these exercises will also be typographic (but not calligraphic) in nature. Finally, the last chapter of the book is an exercise in itself, that is the reader will have to translate an unpunctuated long letter written using calligraphic 行書/行书 *xíng-shū* ('running style', i.e. Semi-cursive Script) characters. If one meets any problem in punctuation of a text in Chapter 5–7, one may consult Appendix I, which contains every text studied in this book in a punctuated and standardized form.[3]

Along with devoting time to the exercises, the reader is advised to try to memorize some words and expressions listed in the glossaries of the chapters. Yet, the lexicon of the present work should be approached in a different way from introductory Classical Chinese textbooks: not only are simpler words not included in the glossaries but also in some cases the authors studied use some rare and obscure lexical items. Therefore, it is the reader's task to decide which word (s)he finds useful enough to memorize. Generally speaking, it is recommended to learn formulaic expressions and idioms, as well as epistolary technical terms and honorifics because they will be needed for one's individual work with the Chinese epistolary corpus. Epistolary expressions and honorifics, along with some grammatical words that are generally used in historical Chinese letters, can be found in alphabetical order in the Glossary.

Contents

The chapters of this book are arranged into the following four parts: 'Family Letter Writing', '"Specialized" Epistolary Discourse', 'Non-family "Social" Letter Writing' and 'Political Letter Writing'. These parts represent the different aspects of historical Chinese letter writing, even if truly comprehensive coverage cannot be given in such a concise introduction.

Letter writing is usually divided into family and non-family domains; this dichotomy is represented by Part I vs. Parts II–IV. Within non-family letter writing, the label 'specialized' epistolary discourse covers letters on some abstract topics, such as scholarly activities and literary ideas, instead of conveying social goals in a similar way to 'ordinary' letters. On the other hand, non-family 'social' letters are 'ordinary' in that they have a social purpose such as the enforcement of an interpersonal relationship, and/or to carry out discursive acts such as a request or apology. Finally, political letter writing refers to the most 'official' domain of private letter writing, that is letters in which Chinese statesman and intellectuals address governmental and political issues.

These parts, as well as the chapters and sections within these parts, are arranged so that the level of difficulty increases as one progresses. Non-family correspondence, which is covered in Part II–IV, usually necessitates the application of a large number of honorific forms, elaborate politeness strategies, and other refined discursive epistolary tools, compared with the family letters in Part I, which have a more direct and intimate style (even though the style of family letters can greatly differ, too, as shown in Chapter 2). Within non-family letters, perhaps the simplest category is 'specialized' discourse, which does not usually have a social goal and so politeness, honorifics, and other epistolary social communicational tools do not play an important role within it. However, 'specialized' letters are usually more difficult to read than family ones, due to the fact that they make in-depth discourse on different abstract topics. The third category of non-family 'social' letters is relatively complex, due to the fact that this genre necessitates the application of a wide array of politeness strategies, honorifics and rhetorical tools, and so even letters written to friends have a rather formal style. Finally, 'political letters' is the most difficult genre, due to the fact that besides being formal it raises interpretational difficulties, that is the reader must cope with the fact that a political letter may serve different hidden purposes, and is also subject to political, ideological or scholarly debates.

Within the aforementioned division the chapters are also arranged in order of difficulty, either on a linguistic or topical basis. This in some cases overrides other aspects, for example, the diachronic order of the date of the authors' lives in Chapters 5 and 6. Furthermore, the texts within every chapter become increasingly longer and/or difficult.

The present work includes 21 main texts from 7 authors; the label 'main text' is used here due to the fact that 5 brief letters and 2 letter-fragments are also included in different parts of this book. The authors, introduced at the beginning of each chapter, have been chosen primarily due to their representative nature. It should be noted that this book's choice of authors is somewhat in contrast with literary historical studies on letter writing (see more in Postscript), such as 趙樹功 Zhào Shùgōng's otherwise outstanding monograph 中國尺牘文學史 *Zhōng-guó chǐdú wénxuéshǐ* (*History of Chinese Epistolary Literature*, 1999, Shijia-zhuang, 河北人民出版社 Hebei renmin chubanshe), which often evaluate Chinese epistolary sources and authors by means of ideological and moral principles. That is, this book has developed from a linguistic-stylistic perspective, without placing too much emphasis on ideological or other issues. For instance, it is often argued that 許葭村 Xǔ Jiācūn's letters are 'decadent' due to the fact that they represent the artistic interactions of a limited circle of intellectuals; however, for this book Xǔ's letters are suitable not only because from the linguist's perspective labels such as a 'decadent corpus' do not exist, but also because from the perspective of Chinese letter writing Xǔ's letters have prominent rhetorical and stylistic features.

Part I

Family Letter Writing

Chapter 1

Family Letter Writing I:
Letters of Zhèng Bǎnqiáo 鄭板橋

In this chapter we begin the study of historical Chinese family letter writing by analyzing three letters, written by the Qīng Dynasty painter and man of letters Zhèng Bǎnqiáo 鄭板橋/郑板桥 (1693–1765; Bǎnqiáo's birth name was 鄭燮/郑燮 Zhèng Xiè). Zhèng was one of the most renowned painters of the Qīng Dynasty. He began his life in poverty but after successfully passing the official examinations he was promoted to high official rank; however, after 12 years as an official he resigned and devoted his time to painting and became one of the so-called Eight Eccentrics of Yángzhōu (揚州八怪/扬州八怪 Yángzhōu-bā-guài), a group of famous painters.

Zhèng's collected family letters – 鄭板橋家書/郑板桥家书 *Zhèng Bǎnqiáo jiāshū* (*The Family Letters of Zhèng Bǎnqiáo*) – is one of the most representative and renowned sources of historical Chinese family letter writing. This collection of 60 letters supposedly became popular partly due to Zhèng's simple yet artistic style, and partly due to the philosophical and emotive ways in which Zhèng approaches every topic. The collection was published by Zhèng himself in 1749. Most of the letters in the collection are addressed to his younger paternal cousin 鄭五橋/郑五桥 Zhèng Wǔqiáo (his birth name was 鄭墨/郑墨 Zhèng Mò, his exact dates are unknown) with whom Zhèng had a very close relationship. In most of the letters written to Wǔqiáo, Zhèng instructs his cousin in the way of the life of men of letters in order to aid his career.

The three letters studied in the present chapter do not belong to the most renowned works of Zhèng Bǎnqiáo. They are addressed to Zhèng's maternal younger cousin 郝 Hǎo (his full name and dates of life are unknown), with whom Zhèng rarely exchanged letters: in fact, among Zhèng Bǎnqiáo's family letter corpus only the three letters studied are addressed to Cousin Hǎo, and so these epistles constitute an independent group within the Zhèng-corpus. From the aspect of this textbook, an important joint characteristic of these works is that they are 'practical' family letters, that is they were written in order to attain certain practical in-family goals, rather than to educate the addressee in a similar way to most of the family letters written to recipients who are younger than the authors (see, for example Letter 4 in the next chapter and Zhèng's other family letters). Thus, these letters not only have a relatively 'practical' lexicon (including business vocabulary), but also they do not touch on complex philosophical or social issues and therefore provide a relatively easy corpus with which to start learning historical Chinese letter writing.[1]

Letter 1

Section 1

范縣署中寄郝表弟

墓地風水，原屬堪輿家藉以惑人利己之言，不足取徵者也。語云：「墓地好，不如心地好。」苟子孫心地惡，祖宗雖葬好地，不興發，子孫心地好，祖宗葬壞地，亦得興發。故范文正公見五絕之地，不忍遺禍他人，安葬其父母，竟得飛黃騰達，位至宰相，足見好心地可以移轉惡風水。於其登山涉水，踏破鐵鞋，覓不到牛眠善地，不如清夜捫心，自省方寸間之心地，對於父母無愧怍，對於自己無暴棄，對於世人無欺詐，即可將父母之靈魂安葬心田，其遺骸盡可隨意處置，但求入土為安。故先嚴先慈之遺柩，即葬於刹院寺老墳。

New words/expressions

1. 堪輿家 (堪輿家) *kānyújiā*: professional geomancer

2. 藉以/借以 *jièyǐ*: by means of; for the purpose of

3. 五絕之地 (五绝之地) *wǔjué-zhī-dì*: a land of unfortunate geomantic properties (*wǔjué* is a *fēngshuǐ* technical term for 'unlucky and harmful')

4. 飛黃騰達 (飞黄腾达) *fēihuáng-téngdá*: to rise like a meteor in one's career (formulaic expression)

5. 於其 (于其) / 與其 (与其) *yúqí*: rather than

6. 登山涉水 *dēngshān-shèshuǐ*: to scale mountains and cross rivers (idiomatic expression)

7. 踏破鐵鞋 (踏破铁鞋) *tàpò-tiěxié*: to search painstakingly everywhere (idiomatic expression)

8. 牛眠善地 *niúmián-shàndì*: a lucky spot for grave (a technical term used in *fēngshuǐ*; see also *niúmián* in Section 2)

9. 清夜捫心 (清夜扪心) *qīngyè-ménxīn*: to examine one's heart in the stillness of the night (idiomatic expression)

10. 方寸 *fāngcùn*: heart

11. 愧怍 *kuìzuò*: to feel ashamed

12. 暴棄 (暴弃) *bàoqì*: indolent, lackadaisical

13. 欺詐 (欺诈) *qīzhà*: to swindle

14. 先嚴 (先严) *xiānyán*: lit. 'former-strict [person]', one's own deceased father (honorific expression)

15. 先慈 *xiāncí*: lit. 'former-kind [person]', one's own deceased mother (honorific expression)

16. 遺柩 (遗柩) *yíjiù*: lit. 'coffin with corpse in it', coffin

Proper names

1. 范縣 (范县) Fàn-xiàn: Fàn County, located in Hénán Province

2. 郝 Hǎo: Zhèng Bǎnqiáo's younger cousin

3. 范文正公 Fàn Wénzhèng-gōng: that is Fàn Zhòngyān 范仲淹 (989–1052), a renowned Chinese politician and man of letters; 文正公 Wénzhèng-gōng is a posthumous title issued by the imperial court to men of letters with the most excellent skill (see also Chapter 2)

4. 刹院寺 (刹院寺) Chàyuàn-sì: a Buddhist temple

Translation

A letter written to younger cousin Hǎo from my post in Fàn County

The [good or evil] geomancy of a burial ground is only the assertion of professional geomancers, by means of which they deceive others and earn profit; it should not be believed. As the saying goes: "the excellence of a burial ground cannot be compared with the excellence of moral character." If the morality of the younger generations of a family is corrupted, the family shall not prosper even if the ancestors are buried at a proper place; if the morality of the younger generations of a family is appropriate, the family shall attain prosperity even if the ancestors are buried at an improper site. This is why Fàn Zhòngyān – who found a plot which had unfortunate geomantic properties and, as he did not want others to suffer, buried his [own] parents there – rose [in rank] like a meteor and reached the [highest] position of chancellor. This testifies that good moral character can overcome evil geomancy. [One can] scale mountains and cross rivers and undertake a painstaking search, without finding a site with perfect geomantic properties. This will be inferior to examining his conscience in the stillness of the night, meditating on the morality within his heart, [and determining whether he should] not feel ashamed [of his actions] towards his parents, was not lackadaisical in his own [progress], and was not unjust to others. It is enough if one inters the soul of his parents in his heart; he can then place their remains where he chooses, only that they should be laid to rest. Therefore, I laid the coffins of my deceased sire and late mother in the old [family] tomb in the Chàyuàn Temple.

Section 2

貴莊舊有墓田一塊。先嚴生前滿擬購置，旋因田
中有孤墳一座，不忍平人之塚以作己塚，因是中
止。然而此地既主出售，價值十二兩，又極克
己。世人未必盡若先嚴，都存不忍鏟墓之心，必
然貪廉爭購，至今未識有主與否？如未賣去，願
出十二金得之，以作愚夫婦之壽穴。留此孤墳一
角，以作牛眠常伴。生前預結鬼鄰，死後不虞寂
寞，亦屬狂生之韻事。當自撰碑記，刻石示子

孫，於祭掃時，多備 一份卮酒麥飯，奠此孤墳，
永著爲例，以竟先君仁厚之意。

New words/expressions

1. 貴莊 (贵庄) *guìzhuāng*: lit. 'precious-hamlet', respected village (honorific addressee-elevating expression)

2. 滿擬 (满拟) *mǎnnǐ*: to have the intention of

3. 購置 (购置) *gòuzhì*: to purchase

4. 旋 *xuán*: soon; thereupon

5. 克己 *kèjǐ*: economic, frugal, to be of friendly price

6. 鏟 (铲) *chǎn*: to shovel; shovel

7. 廉 *lián*: to be of underestimated price

8. 爭購 (争购) *zhēnggòu*: to rush to purchase

9. 愚夫婦 (愚夫妇) *yú-fūfù*: lit. 'stupid husband and wife', myself and my wife (honorific self-denigrating expression)

10. 壽穴 (寿穴) *shòuxué*: grave bought and prepared before one's death

11. 牛眠 *niúmián*: a euphemistic reference to the author's grave, derived from the *fēngshuǐ* technical term 牛眠地 *niúmián-dì* ('a lucky spot for a grave')

12. 鬼鄰 (鬼临) *guǐlín*: 'neighbour in death'

13. 虞 *yú*: to worry about

14. 狂生 *kuángshēng*: lit. '[this] crazy person' (honorific self-denigrating expression)

15. 韻事 (韵事) *yùnshì*: self-indulgent pastime, refined pastime

16. 卮酒麥飯 (卮酒麦饭) *zhījiǔ-màifàn*: roughly: 'some cups of wine and wheat and rice', here: sacrificial drink and food

17. 先君 *xiānjūn*: lit. 'former lord', deceased father (honorific elevating expression)

Translation

In your respected village there had long been a burial site. My late sire in his life-time had the intention of purchasing [this land] but as there was a lone grave [re-maining] on this burial site [my sire] was unable to endure [the thought that] he would make the grave of another person his own, and for this reason abandoned [his plan]. However, this land now is offered for sale, at 12 ounces [of silver] – and this is extremely cheap. Others may not be akin to my late sire, possessed of a heart unable to endure the destruction of a grave; inevitably [some] will desire [that land] because of its price and [will] hasten to buy it. I wonder [in fact] whether the land already has an owner? If it has not yet been sold, I am willing to pay 12 ounces to obtain it, in order to make it a grave prepared for my humble self and my wife. I shall preserve that one lonely grave and make it our eternal graveyard companion. Preparing to form a relationship with our neighbour in the afterlife – in order that we shall not have to be afraid of loneliness after our death – is a self-indulgent pastime of my humble self. I must record [this matter] on a stone tablet and show this stele to my descendants [in order] that whenever they clean and offer sacrifices at our ancestral tomb they should also prepare an extra portion of sacrificial wine and food and offer it at the lonely tomb. By recording [this matter] I will make it an ever-lasting practice, [and so] I will be able to fulfil the benevolent and generous intentions of my late sire.

Section 3

專此拜託，佇盼復音。

New words/expressions

1. 專此 (专此) *zhuāncǐ*: sending this, hereby . . . (letter closing formula)
2. 拜託 (拜讬) / 拜托 *bàituō*: lit. 'to prostrate and rely on', to request some-body to do a favour (honorific epistolary form)
3. 佇盼 (伫盼) *zhùpàn*: lit. 'standing for long and spying the distance', to await (honorific epistolary form)
4. 復音 (复音) *fùyīn*: lit. 'answer voice', letter of response

Translation

I send this [letter] and humbly ask you to do me the service [of checking the status of that land] and I will eagerly await your letter of response.

Brief overview

This letter, written in 1742, is the first in a correspondence between Zhèng Bǎnqiáo and his cousin on the purchase of a burial site for Zhèng and his wife. In this letter, Zhèng asks his cousin to make enquiries regarding the availability of the land.

Rhetorical, pragmatic and sociocultural features

1. In order to understand the message of a letter, the pragmatic goals of the author should be considered. The author's chain of thought is as follows:

Section 1: Discussion on and critique of the geomantic *fēngshuǐ* beliefs.

Section 2: Introduction of the plan of the author's late father → Introduction of the father's reason for abandoning this plan (out of respect for the lonely grave) → Enquiry about the present status of the land (indirect request to the recipient to aid the author by checking the availability of this land) → Discussion on the author's plan as regards how to use this land in order to comply with his late father's wish to treat the extant grave with respect, in accordance with the requirement of filial piety.

Section 3: A more direct request to the recipient, 'wrapped' in the closing formulaic sentence.

Seemingly, the present letter has several messages because the author (i) makes a practical request to the recipient, (ii) criticizes the beliefs of geomancers and (iii) introduces his own plan for the land that he wishes to acquire. However, the letter has one 'main message', that is it requests that the recipient enquire as to the availability of the burial site. Perhaps the most difficult rhetorical issue in this letter is the pragmatic relationship between Section 1 and Section 2; they seem to be unrelated. But, in fact they are pragmatically linked: in Section 2 the author describes his intention to buy a burial site in order to realize his late father's intention of respecting the existing grave, albeit by buying and protecting it rather than simply letting it be, and Section 1 constructs a *foundation* for this request. That is, in Section 1 the author describes his negative view on geomancy in order to implicitly validate the claim in Section 2 that his intention to buy the land is based solely on his desire to act in accordance with his father's wish to respect the existing grave, rather than personal greed.

2. The last sentence of Section 1 may be somewhat ambiguous to the reader. This sentence can be interpreted as meaning that the author buried the bodies of his parents in a place that has negative geomantic properties and hence defied *fēngshuǐ* values; in this way the author's deed could be compared to that of Fàn Zhòngyān, mentioned previously in the text, who, for humane reasons, chose an unfortunate

place as a grave for his parents and thus protected others from buying this land. However, as becomes evident from the author's following letter, he buried his parents in a site which had positive geomantic properties. Therefore, the rhetorical goal of this sentence is to support the author's previous argument that he did not "scale mountains and cross rivers, undertaking a painstaking search everywhere" for a land of special geomantic properties but simply buried his parents in an appropriate place (in reality, Zhèng had little choice due to his relative poverty).

3. A typical argumentative feature of historical Chinese letters is that authors make references to historical persons and deeds in order to support a certain argument. The Chinese traditionally respect historical figures, hence the popularity of such references in historical letters. Thus, the author's reason for referring to Fàn Zhòngyān in the first section of the letter is to support his own reluctance to follow *fēng-shuǐ* when buying the burial site.

Exercise 1

1. Historical Chinese letter writers – not unlike their European counterparts – preferred to use longer sentences when relating a complex issue or story. In such long sentences 'narrative subsentences' are often used in order to introduce relevant information. A typical narrative subsentence in the present letter is the following:

故范文正公見五絕之地，不忍遺禍他人，安葬其父母 ...

This is why Fàn Zhòngyān – who found a plot which had unfortunate geomantic properties and, as he did not want others to suffer, buried his [own] parents there . . .

Here the author's main message is that Fàn Zhòngyān buried his parents in a place that had unfortunate geomantic properties, and he adds a narrative subsentence in order to briefly explain Fàn's reason for doing so, that is he did not want anyone else to suffer by buying such a plot.

Task: Read the letter again and try to find other examples of narrative subsentences.

2. Chinese texts were originally unpunctuated and their punctuation depends in many cases on the translator's interpretation.

Task: Reread and punctuate the text below, which is printed in a more calligraphic style than the 'main' text above, and also without punctuation, in a similar way to which historical Chinese letters were originally written and printed.

墓地風水原屬堪輿家藉以惑人利己之言不足取徵
者也語云墓地好不如心地好苟子孫心地惡祖宗雖
葬好地不興發子孫心地好祖宗葬壞地亦得興發故
范文正公見五絕之地不忍遺禍他人安葬其父母竟
得飛黃騰達位至宰相足見好心地可以移轉惡風水
於其登山涉水踏破鐵鞋覓不到牛眠善地不如清夜
捫心自省方寸間之心地對於父母無愧怍對於自己
無暴棄對於世人無欺詐即可將父母之靈魂安葬心
田其遺骸盡可隨意處置但求入土為安故先嚴先慈
之柩即葬於剎院寺老墳

If the reader's punctuation differs from that of this book, it does not necessarily mean that (s)he misunderstood the text: maybe (s)he has simply interpreted some parts of the text in a different way to the author of this work. If you prepared a different punctuation, try to give a grammatical or rhetorical explanation.

3. In the course of epistolary research, especially when working with original texts, one unavoidably meets cases when some characters of a text are missing or unreadable due to dilapidation.

Task: Interpret the text below, which unlike the 'main' text above contains several 'missing' characters, and define the 'missing' characters (denoted with squares):

貴莊舊有墓田一塊。先嚴生□滿擬購置，旋因
田中有孤墳一座，不忍平人之塚以作己塚，因
是中止。然而此地既主出售，價值十二兩，又
極克己。世□未必盡若先嚴，都存不忍鏟墓之
心，□然貪廉爭購，至今未識有主與否？如未
賣□，願出十二金得之，以作愚夫婦□壽穴。
留此孤墳一角，以作牛眠常伴。生前預結鬼
鄰，死後不虞寂寞，亦屬狂生之韻事。當自撰

碑記，刻石示子孫，於祭掃時，多備一份卮
酒麥飯，奠此孤墳，永著爲例，以竟
先□仁厚之意。

It is no problem if the reader's substitution of some 'missing' characters differs from the original text, provided that the new character makes sense in the given context.

Questions

1. When reading Chinese letters it is important to be aware of the relationship between the author and the recipient. Was the relationship in this letter hierarchical or equal? Was it close or distant?

2. The following sentence is arguably self-mocking:

生前預結鬼鄰，死後不虞寂寞，亦屬狂生之韻
事。

Preparing to form a relationship with our neighbour in the afterlife – in order that we shall not have to be afraid of loneliness after our death – is a self-indulgent pastime of my humble self.

What could be the author's reason for mocking himself?

3. Why might the existing grave have stopped the father from buying the land?

Answers

1. The letter suggests a relatively equal and not particularly close relationship (that is not to say that it was weaker than a typical maternal cousin relationship[2] – in fact, they were on good terms). Not only has the author avoided authoritative expressions despite his higher rank (older age implies higher rank in a Chinese family), but also several honorific expressions are used in the text, which would look unusual in letters written to lower-ranking closer family members. Furthermore, the author could be considered inconsistent in his application of honorific expressions: those used in this text are non-familiar (but in his other letters to Cousin Hǎo he uses familiar ones, see the

next letter). For example, 狂生 *kuángshēng* is typically used as a self-referential expression in letters written to recipients who do not belong to the author's family.

2. The author's reason for self-mockery could have been that he intended to reinforce the polite message of the sentence, already conveyed by the honorific self-denigrating expression *kuángshēng*. It should be noted that in historical Chinese letters where a request, refusal or other 'face-threatening act' is made, as in the case of the present one, authors often use self-mockery in order to reinforce self-denigration and hence mitigate the face-threatening content of the given message.

3. It is probable that the author's father did not buy the land out of respect for the existing grave, not wanting to force himself upon the incumbent as a "neighbour" (the author makes a reference to this belief in the letter).

Letter 2

Section 1

范縣署中寄郝表弟

台駕不來，好音先至，亦足以稍慰予懷。墓田既被捷足者先得，誠屬愚兄疏忽之咎。

New words/expressions

1. 台駕 (台驾) *táijià*: your honour (honorific addressee-elevating expression)

2. 好音 *hǎoyīn*: good news

3. 捷足者 *jiézúzhě*: lit. 'quick footed person', that is a customer who snapped up something before the author

4. 愚兄 *yúxiōng*: lit. 'stupid elder brother', this humble person (honorific self-denigrating expression)

Translation

A letter written to younger cousin Hǎo from my post in Fàn County

You, my honoured friend, have not [yet] arrived, but the good news [of your plan to come hither] has reached me, and this is sufficient to slightly comfort my [troubled] heart. The burial site has been obtained by a swifter customer, and this is certainly the fault of your humble elder brother's carelessness.

Section 2

至於該田風水，四面環河，後靠土山，不等堪輿家言，一望而知爲牛眠佳地。我本不信風水，自先父母安葬後，閱三年即登賢書，成進士，出宰此邑，殊令人不能不信風水之得力也。

New words/expressions

1. 至於 (至于) *zhìyú*: as to, as regards

2. 等 *děng*: to wait; here: to wait for the opinion of . . . , that is to consult

3. 賢書 (贤书) *xiánshū*: lit. 'list of the wise', that is list of successful graduates for the Second Official Degree (舉人/举人 *jǔrén*); the expression 登賢書 *dēng-xiánshū* (lit. 'to ascend to the list of the wise') means that the author was included in the list of successful graduates, that is he gained the rank *jǔrén*

4. 得力 *délì*: to benefit from

Translation

Regarding this land, it is surrounded by water on all sides and at the back it rests on a hill. One does not even need to consult a geomancer to see at first glance that it is a plot of beneficial geomantic properties. I did not previously believe in geomancy. Yet, having buried my parents [at an appropriate site, only] three years passed and I attained the Second Degree, [then] passed the Highest Imperial Examination [and was finally] promoted to govern this district. [These occurrences] certainly make me unable to dismiss the beneficial power of geomancy.

Section 3

貴莊墓田，既爲農家所得，至今仍事種植，固可設法收買。但田價須溢出兩倍，比較舊時價格，雖覺昂貴，然而物價早晚不同，何況相隔已閱十餘年，滄海桑田，變遷無定，漲價又屬居奇慣例。既目爲奇貨而卻得之，三十六金自不能短期分毫。

New words/expressions

1. 昂貴 (昂贵) *ángguì*: expensive

2. 相隔 *xiānggé*: after a lapse of; to be separated by

3. 滄海桑田 (沧海桑田) *cānghǎi-sāngtián*: lit. 'blue sea and plantation of mulberry trees', time brings great changes (idiomatic expression)

4. 漲價 (涨价) *zhǎngjià*: rise in price

5. 居奇 *jūqí*: to keep certain goods/rare commodities for higher prices

6. 短期分毫 *duǎnqī-fēnháo*: lit. 'short-term iota', few, underestimated (formulaic expression)

Translation

The burial site in your respected village has already been purchased by a peasant family. [They] still [merely] use it to grow plants, and certainly there should be a way of purchasing it. The current price of this land must be at least double [the original]. Although one feels that this is overtly expensive in comparison to the original price, land prices are always in flux. This is all the more [understandable] as more than ten years have passed [since my sire wished to purchase this land]: time brings great changes and circumstances alter, and such an increase in price belongs to [i.e. illustrates] the way in which rare goods held on to increase in value. Thus, if one regards [this land] as a rare commodity and [intends to] acquire it [despite the price], [an offer of] 36 ounces of [silver] cannot be [regarded as] ungenerous.

Section 4

老表弟既有來范之約，請挈同田主偕來，當場敘
券。倘田主吝惜川資，即煩老表與之立券交易，
墊款容後歸趙。

New words/expressions

1. 挈同 *qiètóng*: to take along, to carry

2. 券 *quàn*: contract

3. 吝惜 *lìnxī*: to lack; to be miserly

4. 川資 (川资) *chuānzī*: travel expenses

5. 墊款 (垫款) *diànkuǎn*: advance money to be paid back later

6. 容後 (容后) *rónghòu*: soon afterwards

7. 歸趙 (归赵) *guī-Zhào*: lit. 'to return to Zhào', that is to return something to its rightful owner (idiomatic expression)

Translation

You, my venerable cousin, plan to come to Fàn County: I beg you to bring along the owner of the land so that I can discuss the [matter of] the contract with him on the spot. If the owner is unable to cover his travel expenses, then I would like to trouble you, venerable cousin, to settle [i.e. sign] the contract and make the transaction [with him], and soon I shall return any sum you pay on my behalf.

Section 5

拜託拜託。

Translation

I humbly beg you for your aid!

Brief overview

This is the second letter written by Zhèng Bǎnqiáo to his cousin on the purchase of a burial site of beneficial geomantic properties. In this letter, Zhèng makes a request to his cousin to aid him to purchase this site by making a generous offer to the peasant family that bought it, and either to arrange a meeting where Zhèng can personally sign the contract with the owner or to carry out the transaction on Zhèng's behalf.

Rhetorical, pragmatic and sociocultural features

1. This is a typical family business letter: the author makes a request to his cousin to aid him in a financial transaction. The author's chain of thought is as follows:

Section 1: Reference to the recipient's planned visit → Introduction of the situation (the author's failure to purchase the burial site).

Section 2: Reference to the burial site's excellent geomantic properties → Discussion of the reason(s) for the author's belief in geomancy.

Section 3: Mentioning the fact that the burial site was bought by a peasant family with practical purpose and that the purchase of the land can still be negotiated (due to the fact that it is not used as a burial site) → Discussion of the author's opinion that this land should now cost more than twice of the original undervalued price → Overview of the reason for this rise in price: the burial land has become a "rare commodity" → Introduction of the sum offered (thirty six ounces of silver, which is three times more than the original price).

Section 4: Request to the recipient either to bring along the landowner when he visits the author and thus the author can make the transaction, or to make the transaction on the author's behalf.

Section 5: Confirmation of this request by using a formulaic closing.

Perhaps the most problematic rhetorical feature of this letter is the role of Section 2 where the author first discusses the excellent geomantic properties of the burial site and then introduces his own reason for believing in geomancy. Seemingly, this section does not have a direct relationship with Section 3 where the practical price-issue is discussed. But in fact the description in Section 2 functions as an *indirect* statement that the purchasing of this land is important for the author, and hence it functions as a foundation for the author's request made later in the text.

2. It may be problematic for the reader that in this letter the author explicitly contradicts himself: in his previous letter he denied the validity of *fēngshuǐ* beliefs while in the present writing he states that he in fact believes in geomancy. When one reads historical Chinese letters such contradictions may occur: business letter writing (as well as some other 'practical' forms of social letter writing) is typically an 'applied' genre, that is it often serves the attainment of practical objectives; also, it is a 'situated' genre, that is letters are written to certain readers in specific circumstances. Therefore, the authors of business letters are not necessarily consistent

in the discussion of certain philosophical ideas. In the previous and the present letter the purpose of the author is to purchase a burial site, and so the argument for or against the validity of geomancy merely serves a practical goal, namely, the introduction of the author's requests to the recipient.

3. When reading this letter for the first time it may be difficult to interpret the meaning of the expression 好音 *hǎoyīn* ('good news') in the first section because it is not explicitly mentioned what *hǎoyīn* refers to. In order to properly interpret such expressions of 'problematic' reference, it should be noted that letter writing is a situated genre in which the authors refer to certain facts that are evident to them and their (circle of) recipients, without explaining them (unlike the authors of more 'literary' genres); thus, such expressions should be examined either in (i) a narrower or (ii) a wider interactional context. In the case of *hǎoyīn* the narrower interactional context is the sentence in which one finds:

台駕不來，好音先至，亦足以稍慰予懷。

> You, my honoured friend, have not [yet] arrived, but the good news [of your plan to come hither] has reached me, and this is sufficient to slightly comfort my [troubled] heart.

From this sentence it becomes evident that although the recipient did not come, there is "good news" that has already *preceded* him (先至 *xiān zhì*, lit. 'first arrive'); thus, logically the meaning of 台駕不來 *táijià bù lái* should be that the recipient has not arrived *yet*, and the meaning of 好音 *hǎoyīn* should be the 'good news of his *plan to come*'.

The wider interactional context is the text of the letter: if one further reads the letter it becomes evident in Section 4 that the recipient in fact plans to come to Fàn County.

When reading historical Chinese letters arguably the best approach is from (i) to (ii), that is first try to interpret a reference in the narrower interactional context on a logical-contextual basis, and if this does not work read the whole text. It should be noted that 'wider interactional context' is not necessarily limited to the text studied: one often finds cases when information on a certain reference can be obtained only from different sources. For example, in the section

何況相隔已閱十餘年

> This is all the more [understandable] as more than ten years have passed [since my sire wished to purchase this land]

it becomes possible to interpret the reference of "more than ten years have passed" only if one knows the antecedents of the transaction documented in the previous Letter 1.

4. The closing formulaic honorific expression 拜託 *bàituō* ('to request somebody to do a favour') is repeated in order to emphasize its deferential meaning. Such repetition of honorific forms often occurs in historical Chinese letters.

Exercise 2

1. **Task**: Reread and punctuate the text below, which is printed in a more calligraphic style than the 'main' text above, and also without punctuation, in a similar way to which historical Chinese letters were originally written and printed. Furthermore, the text is printed in the traditional vertical, right-to-left fashion.

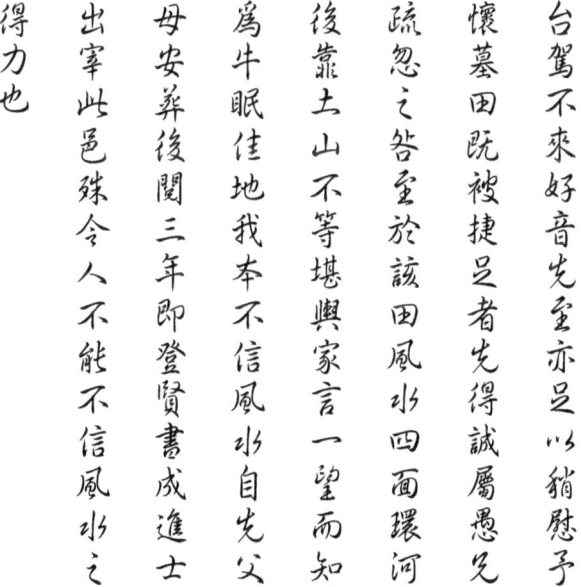

台駕不來好音先至亦足以稍慰予
懷墓田既被捷呈者先得誠屬愚兄
疏忽之咎至於該田風水四面環河
後靠土山不等堪興家言一望而知
爲牛眠佳地我本不信風水自先父
母安葬後閱三年即登賢書成進士
出宰此邑殊令人不能不信風水之
得力也

2. **Task:** Interpret the text below, which unlike the 'main' text above contains several 'missing' characters, and define the 'missing' characters (denoted with squares); this text, in a similar fashion with that of Exercise 1, is printed in the traditional vertical, right-to-left fashion.

貴莊墓□，既爲農□所得，至今仍事種植，固可設法收買。□田價須溢出兩倍，比較舊□□□，雖覺昂貴，□而物價早晚不同，何況相隔已閱十餘年，滄海桑田，□遷無定，漲價又屬居奇慣例。既目□奇貨□卻得之，三十六金自不能短期分毫。

Questions

1. Does the present letter differ in rhetorical style from modern business letters in English? If yes, could you define why?

2. Why are there more honorifics in this letter than in the previous one?

Answers

1. The rhetorical structure of the present letter definitely differs from the ways in which Anglo-Saxon business handbooks or letter manuals approach business letter writing. They stress the importance of directness and clarity, whereas the present letter is circumspect in approaching the main theme, that is the author's request. Further, it is of interest to consider the indirect and vague way in which the amount of payment is introduced: the author applies an impersonal and seemingly hypothetical description.

2. The author here makes a larger request than in the previous letter by asking the recipient not simply to enquire about the availability of the land but also to aid him in the practical negotiation and transaction. Therefore, he makes a more 'face-threatening' act than in the previous letter.

Letter 3

Section 1

<u>范縣</u>署中寄郝表弟

<u>范</u>縣風俗惇厚，四民各安其業，不喜干涉閒事，因此訟案稀少。衙署多暇，閒來唯有飲酒看花，醉後擊桌高歌，聲達戶外。一般皀隸聞之，咸竊竊私相告語，謂：「主人殆其傎乎！」語爲雛婢所聞，奔告内子，旋來規勸曰：「曆來只有狂士掃生，未聞有狂官。請勿再萌故態，滋騰物議。從此杯中物，必待黃昏退食，方得略飲三壺。」受此壓制，殊令人不耐。繼思勸我少飲，是屬善意，遂與之相約，每晚罄十壺而後睡。次晨宿醒已解，從政自無妨礙矣。然而較之在<u>焦山</u>讀書時，每飯必得暢飲，其苦樂迥不相同。所以古人不肯爲五斗米折腰，良有以也。我今直視靴帽如桎梏，奈何，奈何！

New words/expressions

1. 惇厚/敦厚 *dūnhòu*: sincere and honest

2. 干涉 *gānshè*: to interfere, to intervene

3. 閒事/閑事 *xiánshì*: other people's business

4. 訟案 (讼案) *sòng'àn*: lawsuit

5. 稀少 *xīshǎo*: few, scarce

6. 飲酒看花 (饮酒看花) *yǐnjiǔ-kànhuā*: lit. 'drink alcohol and watch flowers', to spend one's time with leisure activities (formulaic expression)

7. 皂隸 (皂隶) *xiānglì*: servant

8. 私相告語 (似相告语) *sīxiāng-gàoyǔ*: to have talks in secret (formulaic expression)

9. 傎 *diān*: to go crazy

10. 雛婢 (雏婢) *chúbì*: young servant girl

11. 內子 *nèizǐ*: lit. 'inner person', my humble wife (self-denigrating honorific expression)

12. 狂士掃生 (狂士扫生) *kuángshì-sǎoshēng*: lit. 'conceited scholar scallywag', roughly: unemployed scholars behaving in extravagant ways

13. 萌 *méng*: lit. to sprout, here: to start to be addicted to an old (bad) habit

14. 故態 (故态) *gùtài*: one's former habit

15. 滋騰 (滋腾) *zīténg*: to generate

16. 物議 (物议) *wùyì*: criticism from the people

17. 杯中物 *bēizhōngwù*: lit. 'the thing in the cup', that is wine

18. 罄 *qìng*: to exhaust

19. 宿醒 *sùchéng*: hangover

20. 暢飲 (畅饮) *chàngyǐn*: to drink one's fill

21. 迥不相同 *jiǒng-bù-xiāngtóng*: to be considerably different (formulaic expression)

22. 五斗米折腰 *wǔ-dǒu-mǐ-zhéyāo*: lit. 'five pecks of rice bending waist' (i.e. humiliating oneself for five pecks of rice, which originally was the salary for officials), to compromise one's principle for some trifle (historical reference, see more below)

23. 有以 *yǒuyǐ*: to be reasonable

24. 直視 (直视) *zhíshì*: to look steadily at; here: to regard something as it was . . .

25. 靴帽 *xuēmào*: lit. 'boot and cap', that is official clothes

26. 桎梏 *zhìgù*: shackles

Proper names

焦山 Jiāoshān: a mountain in Zhènjiāng 鎮江/镇江 City, Jiāngsū Province

Translation

A letter written to younger cousin Hǎo from my post in Fàn County

It is a custom [of the people here] in Fàn County to be sincere and honest; all the four classes [i.e. scholars, peasants, artisans and merchants] of people peacefully [carry out their] duties, and do not like to interfere with other people's business, and thus there are very few lawsuits. In the tribunal I have a good deal of leisure time, and previously when free I would drink and admire the flowers, and when drunk would beat the table and sing lustily, my voice carrying out of my room. The ordinary servants heard this and they all secretly whispered together, saying: "The master is on the verge of insanity!" They were overheard by a young maid-servant who ran to tell this to my humble wife. Then she came to me and admonished me with these words: "Hitherto it was only unemployed scholars who behaved in such extravagant ways and I had never heard that extravagant officials existed. I beg you not to become addicted again to your former manner [of drinking a lot] and thus provoke criticism from the people. From now on [when drinking] wine, you should wait until you retire for your evening meal and only then drink around three bottles." Accepting such hard regulations would indeed make me unable to bear [the situation]. Yet, then I thought that [my wife] advised me to drink less with good intentions, and so I made an agreement [with her] that every evening I would drink ten bottles and then [go to] sleep. Next morning when my hangover had already dissolved I [was able to] focus on administrative matters in an unperturbed manner. Yet, if I compare this [mirthless period] with the time when I studied at Jiāoshān, when it was a must to drink one's fill, the sorrow and joy of these [times] greatly differ. This is why the men of old did not agree to compromise their principles for some trifle, and they were right indeed! I now look upon my official garments as if they were shackles – what should I do, what should I do!?

Section 2

老表是我酒友，惠然肯來，欣甚慰甚，當下榻相迎，共謀痛飲也。

New words/expressions

1. 惠然肯來 (惠然肯来) *huìrán-kěnlái*: lit. '[one] agrees to come due to his benevolent nature', be so kind as to come (honorific formula)

2. 欣甚慰甚 *xīnshèn-wèishèn*: lit. 'to enjoy extremely, to be comforted extremely', to be extremely gratified (formulaic epistolary expression)

3. 下榻相迎 *xiàtà-xiāngyíng*: lit. 'to get up from one's couch and welcome somebody', to personally greet as an honoured guest (formulaic expression)

4. 共謀 (共谋) *gòngmóu*: to collaborate, to collude

5. 痛飲 (痛饮) *tòngyǐn*: to drink to one's heart's content

Translation

You, venerable cousin, are my drinking companion, if you would be so kind as to come I would be extremely gratified; I would personally greet you as my honoured guest, and would join you to drink to our hearts' content.

Section 3

臨穎不勝佇望之至。

New words/expressions

1. 臨穎 (临颖) *línyǐng*: lit. 'copying [words by using] the writing brush', while writing these words . . . (epistolary expression)

2. 佇望 (伫望) *zhùwàng*: lit. 'to stand still and spy the distance', to wish to see someone (epistolary form)

3. 之至 *zhīzhì*: extremely

Translation

While writing these words I am unable to suppress my wish to see you.

Brief overview

In this letter, written from Zhèng Bǎnqiáo's post in Fàn County similar to the previous epistles, Zhèng invites his cousin to visit him at his official post. The present letter was supposedly written in the same year as the previous ones.

Rhetorical, pragmatic and sociocultural features

1. This is a typical historical Chinese informal letter of invitation. For the Western reader its most difficult rhetorical feature is perhaps the author's indirect approach to the act of invitation: he describes his situation in detail first, and only then does he invite the addressee. The author's chain of thought is as follows:

Section 1: Description of the reason why the author must endure a restriction on his drinking → Description of the present situation of the author → Comparison of this situation with the author's student life → Lamentation for the difficult life as an official.

Section 2: Invitation to the recipient to join the author in drinking.

Section 3: Reinforcement of this invitation by means of formulaic honorific closing expressions.

The main message of this letter can be found in Section 2, and Section 1 serves as an introduction for Section 2. It should be noted that such lengthy introductions are typical properties of historical Chinese letters of invitation: the authors usually prefer to discuss certain situations or their emotions/states of mind and use these discussions as a 'pretext' for the invitation extended to the recipient.

It should be noted that the author's lamentation on his difficult life as an official is also part of the aforementioned rhetorical strategy, and so it primarily serves practical communicational goals rather than being an autotelic description of the author's state of mind. This is all the more valid because lamentation on the difficulties of official life is a *stereotypical* discursive topic in historical Chinese letters.

2. It is a common phenomenon in historical Chinese letters that authors – when citing a certain person's words – use colloquial speech forms; these are sometimes difficult to understand if one is not experienced in vernacular texts. In the present letter a potentially difficult vernacular structure is

歷來只有 A … 未聞有 B …

hitherto there was only A . . . [I] have not heard that there is B . . .

This structure means that only A is possible and B is impossible or improper. It is used here by the author's wife in order to admonish the author, and in the present text it expresses that the author, being in the state of B (i.e. he is an imperial official) should not behave in an A-like manner (i.e. the extravagance displayed by unemployed scholars).

If a difficult vernacular structure like this one occurs in a Chinese letter, the best way to interpret it is to consider the discursive situation in which it is used.

As in the present letter it is made clear by the author that his wife admonished him, it is evident that the above structure should refer to the way in which the author behaves.

3. As mentioned previously in historical Chinese letters authors often make historical references with different pragmatic goals. In the present text the author makes a historical reference in order to emphasize the negative nature of official life; this reference differs from Letter 1 in that it is an *indirect* reference, that is the author refers to a certain story without mentioning the name of the person and presupposes that the recipient has the necessary cultural background to interpret the given reference. In the case of the present text, the expression 五斗米折腰 *wǔ-dǒu-mǐ-zhéyāo* ('humiliating oneself for five pecks of rice', which originally was the salary for officials) is a historical reference to 陶潛/陶潜 Táo Qián or Táo Yuānmíng 陶淵明 (365–427), a renowned poet. The 陶潛傳/陶潜传 *Táo Qián-zhuàn* (*The Biography of Táo Qián*) chapter of the 晉書/晋书 *Jìnshū* (*History of the Jìn Dynasty*) records the following words of Táo Yuānmíng:

吾不能爲五斗米折腰，拳拳事鄉裡小人邪！

I am unable to humiliate myself, just in order to gain an official salary, and sincerely serve worthless people in the countryside!

Such indirect historical references are quite popular in historical Chinese letters. This is because by using these references the author not only invites the recipient to participate in an 'intellectual game' but also politely presupposes that the recipient has a strong command of Chinese literacy.

If one comes across such a reference it is not always necessary to find the background story in order to interpret it. The quickest and most efficient way to find the given expression's origin is to use internet search engines. Although the internet is criticized by some expert sinologists as a too simplistic means of retrieve information, I believe that it is a viable resource, and students of sinology should not hesitate to make use of it. However, the internet is still not as reliable a source as books are, and so one's internet sources should be cross-references for accuracy and if in doubt one should refer to a book.

Exercise 3

1. As mentioned previously, one needs to rely on context when reading Chinese letters.

Task: Read the citations below, without consulting the translation, and interpret the sections framed:

(i) 請勿 ⟦再萌故態⟧，滋騰物議。

What kind of former manner or habit might the author's wife be referring to?

(ii) 繼思勸我少飲，是屬善意，遂與 ⟦之⟧ 相約 ...

Who does the pronoun 之 *zhī* refer to?

2. **Task**: Read and punctuate the text below.

語為雛婢所聞奔告內子旋來規勸曰曆來
只有狂士掃生未聞有狂官請勿再萌故態
滋騰物議從此杯中物必待黃昏退食方得
略飲三壺受此壓制殊令人不耐繼思勸我
少飲是屬善意遂與之相約每晚罄十壺而
後睡次晨宿醒已解從改自無妨礙矣然而
較之在焦山讀書時每飯必得暢飲其苦樂
迴不相同所以古人不肯為五斗米折腰良
有以也

3. **Task:** Interpret the text below, which unlike the 'main' text above contains several 'missing' characters, and define the 'missing' characters (denoted with squares):

然而較□在焦山讀書時，每飯
必得暢飲，其□□迥不相同。
所以□人不肯爲五斗米折腰，
良有以也。我今直視靴帽如桎
梏，□□，□何！
老□□我酒友，惠然肯
□，欣□慰甚，□下榻相迎，
共謀痛飲也。

Questions

1. The three letters in this chapter have the same title. What may be the reason for this?

2. The author refers to the servants who heard him singing as 一般皀隸 *yībān-xiānglì*, that is '*ordinary* servants'. Why is 'ordinary' emphasized here?

Answers

1. Due to the fact that these are *edited* letters prepared for publication, their original superscriptions and other 'paratextual' features (such as texts written on envelopes) have been cut and replaced by titles, which usually describe the place where the given epistle was written and the recipient. In these letters the place and the recipient are identical, and hence the titles are the same. It should be noted that Zhèng's other family letters written from the same place to an identical recipient are usually numbered (first letter from . . . to . . ., second letter from . . . to . . .), but supposedly due to the fact that only three letters addressed to Cousin Hǎo are included in the collected letters of Zhèng, these three works are unnumbered.

2. *Yībān* is mentioned here in order to differentiate these 'regular' servants from the 'young maidservant' (*chúbì* 雛婢) of the author's wife.

Further Reading

For readers with interest in Zhèng Bǎnqiáo's letters, an essential work is *Bǎnqiáo jiāshū* 板橋家書 (*Family Letters of Banqiao*), a bilingual edition of Zhèng's letters made by the renowned literary historian, linguist, and writer 林語堂 Lín Yǔtáng (1895–1976). This book is available in many larger Western libraries due to the fact that it was recently reprinted (in 2002) by 百花文艺出版社 Baihua wenyi chubanshe (Beijing). Lín's is an excellent translation, and its only shortcoming is its brevity: it only includes 11 of Zhèng Bǎnqiáo's 60 family letters.

A literary historical description of Zhèng Bǎnqiáo's epistolary activity can be found in 趙樹功 Zhào Shùgōng's monograph 中國尺牘文學史 *Zhōngguó chǐdú wénxuéshǐ* (*History of Chinese Epistolary Literature*, 1999, Shijiazhuang, 河北人民出版社 Hebei renmin chubanshe, 526–533).

For those who intend to read the letters of Zhèng Bǎnqiáo in Chinese, the most reliable modern edition is that of 廣文書局 Guangwen shuju (1994, Taipei). An excellently edited reprint edition of the selected letters of Zhèng was published by 岳麓書社 Yuelu shushe (2003, Changsha).

Chapter 2

Family Letter Writing II:
Letters of Zēng Guófān 曾國藩

In this chapter we continue our enquiry into historical Chinese family letter writing by analyzing three letters, written by the renowned Qīng Dynasty statesman Zēng Guófān 曾國藩/曾国藩 (1811–1872). Zēng was one of the most prominent political figures of Qīng China. He started an amazing career at a young age and later became the chief advisor to the Qīng Court, which in the 1850s and 1860s struggled with both the colonizing Western powers and the so-called Tàipíng (太平) Rebellion. It was primarily due to Zēng's effort that the Qīng Dynasty successfully put down the rebellion, and also Zēng was the first important initiator of the adoption of Western warfare and techniques with which to oppose the colonizing powers.

Zēng's collected family letters – 曾國藩家書/曾国藩公家书 *Zēng Guófān jiā-shū* (*The Family Letters of Zēng Guófān*) – is arguably the most representative source of historical Chinese family letter writing. This extensive corpus was published first in 1879 under the title 曾文正公家書全集/曾文正公家书全集 *Zēng Wénzhèng-gōng jiāshū quánjí* (*The Collected Family Letters of Zēng Wénzhèng-gōng*[1]), and it had a strong impact on premodern Chinese thinking. The letters in the collection represent practically every aspect of Chinese familiar letter writing, due to the fact that Zēng had intensive epistolary interaction with his large family. Furthermore, this corpus is also of interest because Zēng's letters were preserved in a relatively untouched form, unlike many other epistolary collections where editors removed the superscriptions and subscriptions.

The three letters studied in the present chapter have been chosen as they represent the three main hierarchical relationships between author and recipient in historical Chinese family letters. That is, the first work written to Zēng's nephew represents letters where the author is more powerful than the recipient, the second one to his wife represents a case when the power difference between the author and the recipient is insignificant, while in the third work to his parents the author is less powerful than the recipients. Therefore, these letters will aid the reader to gain insight into the communicational and rhetorical norms of historical Chinese letter writing in different settings.

Letter 4

Section 1

諭紀瑞　十二月四日

字寄紀瑞侄左右：

前接吾侄來信，字跡端秀，知近日大有長進。紀鴻奉母來此，詢及一切，知侄身體業已長成，孝友謹慎，至以爲慰。

New words/expressions

1. 諭（谕）*yù*: to inform a lower-ranking person (formulaic expression, often used in the titles of family letters written to younger relatives)

2. 字寄 *zì-jì*: lit. 'words sent to' (letter opening formula, used before names)

3. 左右 *zuǒyòu*: deferential epistolary expression used either after the recipient's name or as an independent form of address

4. 字跡/字迹 *zìjì*: handwriting, style of calligraphy

5. 端秀 *duānxiù*: proper and delicate

6. 業已 (业已) *yèyǐ*: already

7. 謹愼/謹慎 (谨慎) *jǐnshèn*: cautious

Proper names

1. 紀瑞 (纪瑞) Jìruì: that is Zēng Jìruì 曾紀瑞 (1872–1942), nephew of Zēng Guófān and son of Zēng's younger brother Zēng Guóquán 曾國荃/曾国荃 (1824–1890)

2. 紀鴻 (纪鸿) Jìhóng: that is Zēng Jìhóng 曾紀鴻 (1848–1881), son of Zēng Guófān

Translation

Letter to Jìruì   On the 3rd Day of the 12th Lunar Month

These are my words sent to my revered nephew Jìruì:

    I previously received your letter, nephew, and I found your calligraphy proper and delicate, and noted that recently you have made incredible progress. [When] Jìhóng escorted his mother hither I enquired about all matters [at home], and knew [i.e. was informed that] my nephew had already grown up, he [observes] filial piety and brotherly love and he is cautious [in his deeds], [and this news] was of great comfort to me.

Section 2

吾家累世以來，孝弟勤儉。

輔臣公以上吾不及見，竟希公、星岡公皆未明即起，竟日無片刻暇逸。竟希公少時在陳氏宗祠讀書，正月上學，輔臣公給錢一百，爲零用之需，五月歸時，僅用去二文，尚餘九十八文還其父。其儉如此！星岡公當孫入翰林之後，猶親自種菜收糞。吾父竹亭公之勤儉，則爾等所及見也。

New words/expressions

1. 累世 *lěishì*: for many generations

2. 勤儉 (勤俭) *qínjiǎn*: hard-working and frugal

3. 暇逸 *xiáyì*: relaxation

4. 零用 *língyòng*: allowance; to use some money in small sums

5. 收糞 (收粪) *shōufèn*: to tend a plot of land

Proper names

1. 輔臣公 (辅臣公) Fǔchén-gōng: lit. 'Lord Fǔchén', that is Zēng Fǔchén 曾辅臣/曾辅臣 (1721–1776), an ancestor of Zēng Guófān

2. 竟希公 Jìngxī-gōng: that is Zēng Jìngxī 曾竟希 (1745–1811), the great-grandfather of Zēng Guófān

3. 星岡公 (星冈公) Xīnggāng-gōng: that is Zēng Xīnggāng 曾星岡/曾星冈 (1772–1848; his personal name was 玉屏 Yùpíng), the grandfather of Zēng Guófān

4. 陳氏宗祠 (陈氏宗祠) Chén-shì-zōngcí: 'The Ancestral Temple of the Chén Clan'; a temple and Confucian school where several members of the Zēng family were educated

5. 竹亭公 Zhútíng-gōng: that is Zēng Zhútíng 曾竹亭 (1790–1857, Zhútíng's personal name was 麟書/麟书 Línshū), the father of Zēng Guófān

6. 紀澤 (纪泽) Jìzé: that is Zēng Jìzé 曾紀澤 (1839–1890), son of Zēng Guófān

Translation

Our family [has followed] filial piety and brotherly love for many generations and [has been] hard-working and frugal. I did not see [the generations] before Lord Fǔchén, but Lord Jìngxī and Lord Xīnggāng all rose before dawn and rested not a moment during the day. Lord Jìngxī in his younger days studied at the Ancestral Temple of the Chén Clan, and when he left to study in the First Lunar Month, Lord Fǔchén gave him one hundred [silver] coins as an allowance; when he returned in the Fifth Month he had only spent two coins and gave back the remaining ninety-eight [pieces] to his father. He was that frugal! Lord Xīnggāng, upon his grandson's [i.e. the author's] induction into the Imperial Academy, even grew vegetables and tended land himself [in order to cover his grandson's study costs]. And the hard-working and frugal [nature of] my father Lord Zhútíng, you all had opportunity to see personally.

Section 3

今家中境地雖漸寬裕，姪與諸昆弟切不可忘卻先世之艱難，有福不可享盡，有勢不可使盡。「勤」字工夫，等一貴早起，等二貴有恆。「儉」字工夫，等一莫著華麗衣服，等二莫多用僕婢雇工。凡將相無種，聖賢豪傑亦無種，衹要人肯立志，都可以做得到的。姪等處最順之境，當最富之年，明年又從最賢之師，但須立定志向：何事不可成？何人不可做？願吾姪早勉之也。蔭生尚算正途功名，可以考御史。待姪十八九歲，即與|紀澤|同進京應考。然姪此際專心讀書，宜以八股試帖爲要，不可專恃蔭生爲基，總以鄉試會試能到榜前，益爲門戶之光。

New words/expressions

1. 境地 *jìngdì*: circumstances; territory

2. 寬裕 (宽裕) *kuānyù*: comfortably-off

3. 昆弟 *kūndì*: elder and younger brothers

4. 艱難 (艰难) *jiānnán*: difficulty

5. 有恆 (有恒) *yǒuhéng*: to persevere

6. 雇工 (雇工) *gùgōng*: to hire labour, hired labourer

7. 種 (种) *zhǒng*: lit. 'seed'; here: 'to have seeds', that is to bequeath a rank to subsequent generations

8. 志向 *zhìxiàng*: ambitions, ideal

9. 蔭生 (荫生) *yìnshēng*: a student who was admitted to the Imperial College in recognition of the distinguished services of his father/ancestors

10. 功名 *gōngmíng*: scholarly honour and official rank

11. 御史 *yùshǐ*: imperial censor

12. 此際 (此际) *cǐjì*: for the time being

13. 八股 *bāgǔ*: eight-part essay (a compulsory genre in the imperial examinations)

14. 試帖 (试帖) *shìtiě*: poetry composed in the imperial examinations

15. 恃 *shì*: to rely on

16. 鄉試 (乡试) *xiāngshì*: triennial provincial civil-service examination

17. 會試 (会试) *huìshì*: the highest metropolitan examination

18. 榜 *bǎng*: a list of candidates who successfully took the imperial examinations

Proper names

1. 紀澤 (纪泽) *Jìzé*: Zēng Jìzé 曾紀澤 (1839–1890), the eldest son of Zēng Guófān

Translation

Although the [financial] state of our family is gradually improving nowadays, my nephew and the elder and younger brothers in his generation should not forget the difficulties of the previous generations, and even if one has wealth one should not squander it, even if one has influence one should not exhaust it. [When learning] the art of the character 'hard-working' the most important [thing] is to get up early and the second is [to] persevere. [When learning] the art of the character 'frugality' the first [thing] to avoid is the wearing of mag-nificent clothes and the second is the employment of too many servants. The ranks of General and Minister cannot be inherited, nor can [the status of] men of virtue and heroes be passed on: one needs to be determined and only then can he attain these [positions]. Although my nephew and all the others [in the generation] now enjoy the fairest circumstances, living in our richest year to date, and from next year will study at the feet of the best tutors, it is necessary for you to forge your ideals, [and consider questions, such as:] What will pre-vent success? What sort of man will not succeed? I hope my nephew will achieve diligence in his youth. Being a *yìnshēng* student [who will be admitted to the Imperial College in recognition of the distinguished services of his father to which my nephew is entitled] still counts as a proper rank – [a *yìnshēng* can apply for the rank of] Imperial Censor through examination. My nephew should wait until he becomes eighteen or nineteen and then with Jìzé should proceed to the capital to take the examinations. Yet, for the time being you, nephew, should concentrate all your efforts on learning; [practising the con-struction of] eight-part essays and examination poems should be priorities for you. You should not solely rely on the basis [i.e. fact] that you can become a *yìnshēng* but should [rather] always [strive to attain] a leading position on the list of candidates who successfully take the triennial provincial civil-service examinations and the highest metropolitan examinations, and thus increase the glory of our family.

Section 4

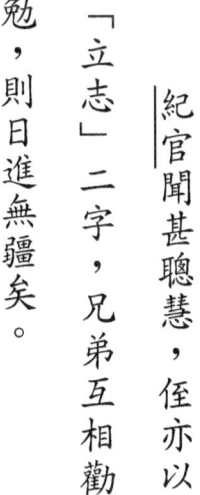

紀官聞甚聰慧，侄亦以「立志」二字，兄弟互相勸勉，則日進無疆矣。

New words/expressions

1. 日進 (日近) *rìjìn*: to improve with each passing day

2. 無疆 (无疆) *wújiāng*: endless, boundless

Proper names

1. 紀官 (纪官) Jìguān: that is Zēng Jìguān 曾紀官 (1852–1881), the younger
    brother of the recipient

Translation

Jìguān [as I] heard is very intelligent, my nephew and he should mutually discuss the two characters 'making ideal', and hence endlessly improve themselves with every passing day.

Section 5

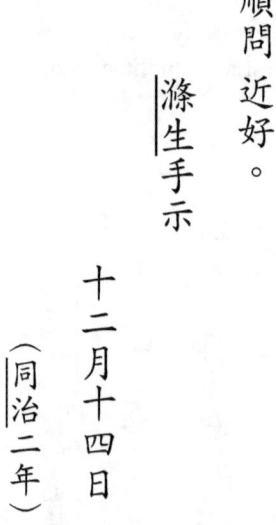

New words/expressions

1. 順問 (顺问) *shùnwèn*: hereby wish … (formulaic letter closing expression)

2. 近好 *jìnhǎo*: lit. 'the approach of good', blessing (formulaic letter closing
    expression)

3.   手示 *shǒushì*: lit. 'personally written instructions' (formulaic expression used after the author's name in family letter written to a younger and less powerful family member)

Proper names

1.   滌生 (涤生) Díshēng: the literary name of Zēng Guófān

Translation

Hereby I wish you blessing.

Díshèng wrote this instructive letter on the 14th Day of the 12th Month (the Second Year of Tóngzhì [1863 in the Christian calendar])

Brief overview

This letter, written in 1863, represents the typical way in which Zéng Guófān educated his younger relatives: he discusses certain principles that his nephew should observe in order to attain success and thus "increase the glory" of the family. Typically, these moral principles are approached in a way illustrated by the present letter, that is Zēng discusses certain 'characters' (字 *zì*) of moral implication, such as 儉 *jiǎn* ('frugality'), and their practical application.

Rhetorical, pragmatic and sociocultural features

1. The author's chain of thought is as follows:

Section 1: Intertextual reference to the recipient's letter → Appraisal of the recipient's good calligraphy → Reference to Zēng Jìhóng's positive report on the recipient, that is the recipient observes 'filial piety' and 'brotherly love'.

Section 2: Reference to the previous generations of the Zēng family who were hardworking and frugal → Detailed description of the hardworking and frugal deeds of ancestors.

Section 3: Reference to the generation of the recipient who enjoys good circumstances due to the hardwork of the ancestors and the author's generation → Warning that this situation can only be maintained if the recipient and his generation continues to preserve the morality of the ancestors → Practical advice on the way in which these morals can be preserved → This is necessary because the ancestor's ranks and positions cannot be inherited, and so the recipient and his generations have to form and attain their life ideals instead of just enjoying their pleasant situation → Personal advice to the recipient: although he can automatically attain some rank due to his father's merits, he should work hard and attain some rank through his own effort.

Section 4: Reference to the recipient's younger brother who is talented in a similar way to the recipient → Encouraging the recipient to be diligent and form his ideals for life together with his brother.

Section 5: Closing formulaic expression → Signature → Date.

In Section 2 the author's sudden switch of topic (addressee → ancestors) may be confusing for the reader. This is a typical example of the Chinese rhetoric strategy that could be defined as 'instructive praising', that is the author simultaneously praises and instructs the recipient by pointing out certain aspects of his (already good) personality, which should be further developed. Thus, in the present letter the author first praises the addressee for observing filial piety and brotherly love, and then he switches topic and describes the ancestors who were also hardworking and frugal; the recipient's instruction as to how these morals should be attained is the central message of the letter.

2. This letter, in a similar way to other letters of Zēng Guófān, is preserved in a full form, that is it includes (i) (parts of)[2] the original envelope inscription, (ii) formulaic openings, and (iii) formulaic closings. When reading Chinese letters that contain such sections one should be aware that these parts utilize a special terminology that usually not only fulfils the goal of formally opening and closing a text, but also defines the social relationship and power hierarchy between the author and the recipient. For example, in the present letter both the envelope inscription and the closing contain forms that 'frame' the recipient as a lower-ranking person than the author (this is due to his younger age); see, for example, 諭 *yù* ('to inform a lower-ranking person') and 手示 *shǒushì* ('personally handwritten instructions'). In fact, some epistolary expressions like this are included in Classical Chinese dictionaries. However, there are so many of them that the reader may come across some unknown epistolary expressions. Perhaps the best method of interpreting them is to examine the social relationship between the author and the recipient and then reread the paratextual parts in which they occur.

It should be noted that in the present letter the 'title' (諭紀瑞 *Yù Jìruì*) and the date below (十二月四日 *Shièr-yuè sì-rì*) are parts of the envelope inscription. It may be confusing for the reader that this date occurs twice in the 'text', and so one should be aware that its first occurrence is paratextual.

3. In the present letter the author refers to some older members of the Zēng Clan by modifying their personal names with the honorific suffix *gōng* 公 (lit. 'lord'). For example, he refers to his father Zēng Línshū 曾麟書/曾临书

(1790–1857) as 竹亭公 Zhútíng-gōng, which literally means 'Lord Zhútíng' (Zhútíng is Línshū's so-called adult name or 字 zi). The use of personal name – in contrast with that of the family name – has some intimate implication and in the present context it supposedly emphasizes the fact that both the author and the recipient are members of the same clan, while the intimacy of this form of address is somewhat counterbalanced by the honorific *gōng*.

Exercise 4

1. **Task:** Reread and punctuate the text below.

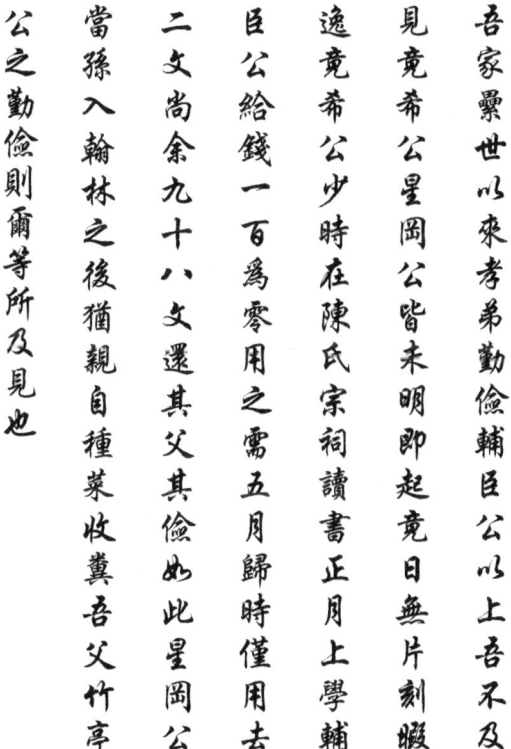

公之勤儉則爾等所及見也

當孫入翰林之後猶親自種菜收糞吾父竹亭

二文尚余九十八文還其父其儉如此星岡公

臣公給錢一百爲零用之需五月歸時僅用去

逸竟希公少時在陳氏宗祠讀書正月上學輔

見竟希公星岡公皆未明即起竟日無片刻暇

吾家纍世以來孝弟勤儉輔臣公以上吾不及

2. **Task:** Interpret the text below, which unlike the 'main' text above contains several 'missing' characters, and define the 'missing' characters (denoted with squares):

今家□境地雖漸寬裕，侄與諸昆弟切□可忘卻先世之艱

難，有福□可享盡，有勢不可使盡。「勤」字工夫，等一

貴早起，等二貴有恆。「儉」字工夫，等一莫著華麗衣

服，等二莫多用僕婢雇□。凡將相無種，聖□□傑亦無

種，祇要人肯立志，都可以做得到的。侄等處最順之境，

當最富之年，明年又從最賢之師，但須立定志向：何□不

可成？何人不可做？願吾侄早勉之也。蔭生尚算正途功

名，可以考御史。待侄十八九歲，即與紀澤□進京應考。

然侄此際專心讀書，宜以八股試帖爲要，不可專恃蔭生爲

基，總以鄉試會□能到榜前，益爲門□□光。

Questions

1. Is this a 'personal letter' in, for example, the modern Anglo-Saxon sense of the phrase?

2. It must have been evident to the recipient that the grandfather of the author with humble origins in fact lived from the land. What could be the reason for the author nevertheless emphasizing this fact in Section 2?

Answers

1. This, in a similar way with many other Chinese didactic family letters written to younger family members (but unlike, for example, the letters in the previous chapter), is not a personal letter. In fact, the author seems to address the whole generation by using plural forms such as 爾等 *ěrděng*. In historical China family letters of this kind, especially in large families such as the Zēng Clan, were not written to the recipient only.

2. The author discusses here the importance of being hard-working and frugal, and the emphasis is on 親自 *qīnzì* ('personally'), that is he emphasizes that his grandfather did not rely on *others* but *personally* worked in the fields in order to support the author's learning.

Letter 5

Section 1

致歐陽夫人　　五月初五日午刻

歐陽夫人左右：

自余回金陵後，諸事順遂。惟天氣亢旱，雖四月二十四、五月初三日兩此甘雨，稻田尚不能栽插，深以爲慮。科一出痘，非常危險，幸祖宗神靈庇佑，現已全癒發體，變一結實模樣。十五日滿兩個月後，即當遣之回家，計六月旬可以抵湘。如體氣日旺，七月中旬赴省鄉試可也。

New words/expressions

1. 致 *zhì*: a letter written to ... (formula used in envelopes/superscriptions written to rank-equals); to send a letter; to convey

2. 夫人 *fūrén*: Madam, Lady (term of address used towards high-ranking ladies); here this term of address implies that the recipient is the author's legal (first) wife

3. 午刻 *wǔkè*: 11 a.m.–1 p.m. (according to the system of the so-called Horary Characters, or 十二地支 Shí'èr-dìzhī)

4. 亢旱 *kànghàn*: severe draught

5. 甘雨 *gānyǔ*: seasonal rain

6. 栽插 *zāichā*: to plant (rice seedlings)

7. 出痘 *chūdòu*: to have smallpox

8. 庇佑 *bìyòu*: to protect, to bless

9. 全癒/痊癒/痊瘉 *quányù*: to recover from illness

10. 發體 (发体) *fātǐ*: to regain one's weight

11. 結實 (结实) *jiēshí*: strong; solid

12. 抵 *dǐ*: to arrive at; to support; to resist; to compensate for; to be equal to

Proper names

1. 歐陽夫人 (欧阳夫人) Ōuyáng-fūrén: 'Lady Ōuyáng' (1806–1871), the wife of Zēng Guófān

2. 金陵 Jīnlíng: an archaic name for Nanking

3. 科一 Kēyī: a nickname for Zēng Jìhóng (cf. the previous letter)

4. 湘 Xiāng: abbreviated name of Húnán Province

Translation

To Lady Ōuyáng   On the 5th Day of the 5th Month, [written during the] *wǔkè* period

Revered Lady Ōuyáng:

Since I came back to Jīnlíng everything has gone smoothly. Only, the weather has been extremely dry and although on the 24th Day of the Fourth Month and the 3rd Day of the Fifth Month we had some seasonal rain, but rice seedlings could not be planted in the fields and this is very worrying. Kēyī had smallpox, which was extremely dangerous; fortunately, the spirits of our ancestors protected him, and he has already recovered and put on weight, and regained his former appearance. On the 15th Day when exactly two months will have passed [since his illness] I shall send him home, and I estimate that during the first tenday of the Sixth Month he will arrive at [our home in] Húnán. If his health will further strengthen with the passing days, in the second tenday of the Seventh Month it will be possible for him to proceed to the provincial capital and take the triennial examination.

Section 2

余精力日衰，總難多見人客。算命者常言
十一月交「癸運」，即不吉利，余亦不願久居此
官，不欲再接家眷東來。夫人率兒婦輩在家，須
事事立個一定章程。居官不過偶然之事，居家乃
是長久之計。能從勤儉耕讀上做出好規模，雖一
旦罷官，尚不失為興旺氣象。若貪圖衙門之熱
鬧，不立家鄉之基業，則罷官之後，便覺氣象蕭
索。凡有盛，必有衰，不可不預為之計。望夫人
教訓兒孫婦女，常常作家中無官之想，時時有謙
恭省儉之意，則福澤悠久，余心大慰矣。

New words/expressions

1. 算命者 *suànmìngzhě*: fortune-teller

2. 癸運 (癸运) *guǐyùn*: technical term for an unlucky period, calculated on the basis of one's so-called 'eight characters of birth' (八字 *bāzì*)

3. 久居 *jiǔjū*: to occupy a position for a long time; to occupy a low position (often used by officials to humbly refer to their actual posts)

4. 家眷 *jiājuàn*: family members; wife and children; wife

5. 章程 *zhāngchéng*: rules

6. 貪圖 (贪图) *tāntú*: to seek

7. 蕭索 (萧索) *xiāosuǒ*: desolate; bleak and chilly

8. 省儉 (省俭) *shěngjiǎn*: frugal

9. 福澤 (福泽) *fúzé*: good fortune

Translation

My vigour weakens day by day, and I always [find it] difficult to receive visitors. The fortune-teller often says that in the Eleventh Month I will enter the *guǐyùn* period, that is it will be an unfortunate [time]. Also, I do not wish to hold this post for long, and therefore I do not want you to come hither to the East again. My revered wife should govern the children and their wives at home by setting strict regulations in every matter. Holding a government office is an uncertain situation, while living at home is a long-term issue. If one is able to form a good pattern [of life] from being hard-working and frugal, as well as studying and working at the same time, even if he is dismissed from office some day, he may nevertheless consider [his home town] a prosperous place. If one [merely] seeks the excitement of official life and does not establish his foundations, then after being dismissed he will feel that [his home town] is desolate. Aught that flourishes shall surely weaken [with time], and one can but prepare for this in advance. I hope that my revered wife will teach the sons, grandsons and women [in such a way that they] will often consider [living alone] without officials in the family, and realize [that they need to be] deferential [when interacting with others] and frugal [in their lifestyle]; in this way our fortune shall be long-lasting and my heart will be greatly comforted.

Section 3

余身體安好如常。惟眼矇日甚，說話多則舌頭蹇澀。左牙疼甚，而不甚動搖，不至遽脫，堪以告慰。

New words/expressions

1. 眼矇 *yǎnméng*: the weakening of one's eyesight

2. 蹇澀 (蹇涩) *jiǎnsè*: difficult, hard

Translation

My health is as usual. Only, my eyesight is weakening as the days pass and also when I talk a lot I find it difficult to speak. My tooth on the left side pains me greatly but it does not move much, and it will not fall out in the near future. These things I can relate to comfort you.

Section 4

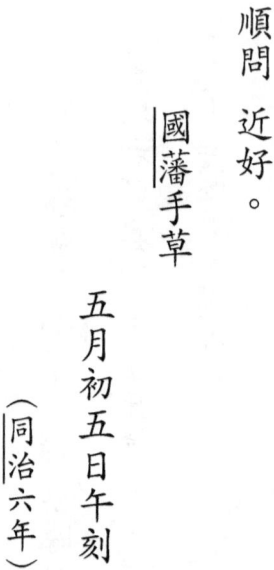

New words/expressions

手草 *shǒucǎo*: lit. 'to write by hand in haste', respectfully write some words in haste (honorific epistolary closing expression, used towards one's inferior within the same generation)

Translation

Hereby I wish you blessing.

Guófān respectfully sends this letter in haste on the 5th Day of the Fifth Month, [written during the] *wǔkè* period (the Sixth Year of Tóngzhì [i.e. 1867])

Brief overview

Similar to the previous work the present letter, addressed to Zēng's wife Lady Ōuyáng, belongs in the category of instructive family letters. In this letter, written from his post in Nanking where he served as viceroy, Zēng discusses the way in which his wife should educate the younger generations. Zēng believed the education of the younger members of the family to be of fundamental importance; it is therefore not surprising that he gave practical instructions to his wife on this issue: as the most senior woman in the family Lady Ōuyáng controlled the younger generations. It is more surprising that the letter touches upon theoretical issues such as the importance of the attachment to the home town; usually, theories and philosophical ideas were discussed between males. However, Lady Ōuyáng was a talented person, a worthy companion for Zēng who admired her intelligence, hence the present letter's involvement in theoretical issues (Zēng's appreciation of Lady Ōuyáng also manifested itself in that he never officially married anyone else unlike most of the high-officials in his time).

Rhetorical, pragmatic and sociocultural features

1. The author's chain of thought is as follows:

Section 1: Description of the situation of the author in Nanking → Description of Zēng Jìhóng's state of health → Mentioning the good news that most probably Jìhóng will be able to take part in the examinations.

Section 2: Description of the author's declining state of health and the approaching unlucky period → Mentioning the author's decision to abandon his post (in fact, he retired a few years later), due to which his family members should not move to Nanking → Instructions to his wife as regards how to educate the younger generations: they should become hardworking, frugal and diligent and create their own life ideals, so if they will be relieved from office they will not be isolated in their hometown → This is necessary because finally returning to one's hometown is unavoidable → In order to provide a successful future for the family, the recipient should encourage younger family members to support themselves, without relying on the influence of the elders.

Section 3: Description of the author's state of health.

Section 4: Formal closing.

Perhaps the most difficult part of this letter is the relationship between Sections 1 and 2: in Section 1 the author updates the recipient on daily personal matters, while in Section 2 first he seemingly continues this description and then 'suddenly' switches to the discussion of educational principles. In fact, this switch is logical. Section 1 is an informative part where the author first discusses the situation in the city and then describes the state of Jìhóng's health; he connects Section 1 with Section 2 when he describes his own state of health: by pointing to his own decline due to which he will return home he opens the discussion on the need to have a solid base in one's hometown; finally, the switch of theme is a logical continuation of this chain of thought. The fact that in Section 3 the author discusses again his own state of health in more detail demonstrates that in Section 2 the reference to his own decline functions as a link to the main topic of the letter.

2. In Section 1 it may seem to be unusual for the reader that the author first discusses the situation in Nanking and only then describes the state of Jìhóng's health, despite the fact that this must have been a vital issue to him and the recipient (even though at the time of this letter Jìhóng had already recovered). However, the discussion of the situation in Nanking is not a simple 'report of events': the author was the viceroy of the city, and so here he describes the difficulties he had to cope with and that might have resulted in political unrest in the area, hence the priority of this topic.

3. When analysing the previous letter it was already mentioned that envelope texts, superscriptions and subscriptions usually contain honorific and other formulaic expressions that signal the relationship between the author and the recipient. The present letter demonstrates that it can be quite illuminating not only to study such vocabulary but also its *lack* in certain texts. In contrast with the previous work, here the relationship between the author and the recipient is a relatively equal one: although in historical Chinese families husbands were higher-ranking than wives, they were members of the same generation and so rank hierarchy between them was much less apparent than between members of older and younger generations. Furthermore, in the case of the present letter the rank difference between the recipient and the author was even less: not only was the recipient the author's first and only legal wife, but also their interpersonal relationship was a particularly close one (this is not a self-evident fact in the historical Chinese context where marriages were arranged by parents and young people could not meet before the wedding). On the one hand this relatively equal relationship manifests itself in that the author

(i) uses the honorific form 手草 *shǒucǎo* ('to write by hand in haste') – which is used towards one's younger relatives in the same generation – in the subscription of the letter;

(ii) refers to himself by using his personal name, which implies closeness in Chinese communication (the use of the author's literary name in the previous letter implied a larger interpersonal distance).

On the other hand, unlike in the previous and following letters, the author also *omits* formulaic expressions that would 'frame' the recipient as his inferior or superior (see, for example, 諭 *yù* in the previous letter). This 'neutrality', caused by the lack of such formulae, aids the author to maintain his basically rank-equal relationship with the recipient.

Exercise 5

1. **Task:** Reread and punctuate the text below.

凡有盛必有衰不可不預為之
計望夫人教訓兒孫婦女常常
作家中無官之想時時有謙恭
省儉之意則福澤悠久余心大
慰矣余身體安好如常惟眼蒙
日甚說話多則舌頭塞澀左牙
疼甚而不甚動搖不至遽脫堪
以告慰順問近好

2. **Task**: Interpret the text below, which unlike the 'main' text above contains several 'missing' characters, and define the 'missing' characters (denoted with squares):

歐陽夫人左右：

自余□金陵後，諸事順遂。

惟□□亢旱，雖四月二十四、五

月□三日兩此甘雨，稻田尚不能

□插，深以□慮。科一出痘，非

□危□，幸祖□□靈庇佑，現已

全癒發體，變一結實模□。十五

日滿兩□月後，即當遣之回家，

計六月旬可以抵湘。如體氣日

旺，七月中□赴省鄉試可也。

Question

1. When discussing the ways in which his wife should teach members of the younger generation, the author refers to them as either 兒婦輩 *érfùbèi* ('the children and their wives') or 兒孫婦女 *érsūn-fùnǚ* ('the sons, the grandsons and the women'), that is "wives" and "women" are included in the group of youths who should be properly educated. Yet, the author's main topics are (i) preparation for the time when one must retire from his office, and (ii) the self-sufficiency of younger family members. That is, these topics must have been relevant to males who were allowed to enter official life and earn money, and so the author's request that his wife should instruct female family members on these issues may seem to be unusual. What could be the author's reason for involving female relatives, as well?

Answer

1. Despite the fact that women themselves were not allowed to have an official career in historical China, their role in a family's success was regarded as an important one. That is, through properly educating their children and wisely advising their husband women were also responsible for a family's future.

Illustration 1 Zēng Guófān's portrait

Letter 6

Section 1

稟父母　七月初四日

男國藩跪稟父母親大人萬福金安：

六月二十八日接到家書，係三月十四日所發。知十九日四弟生子，男等合室相慶。四妹生產雖難，然血暈亦是常事。且此次既能保全，則下次較爲容易。男未得信時，常以爲慮，既得此信，如釋重負。

New words/expressions

1. 稟 (禀) *bǐng*: lit. 'to report to a superior', to send a letter to a higher ranking person (honorific addressee-elevating verbal form); petition

2. 跪稟 (跪禀) *guìbǐng*: lit. 'to report in a kneeling position', to humbly report (honorific verbal form)

3. 萬福金安 (万福金安) *wànfú-jīn'ān*: lit. 'ten thousand luck and golden peace', to wish wealth and happiness (honorific epistolary formula)

4. 血暈 (血晕) *xuèyùn*: weakness after childbirth due to excessive loss of blood

5. 如釋重負 (如释重负) *rúshì-zhòngfù*: to feel relieved (formulaic epistolary expression)

Proper names

1. 四弟 Sìdì: 'Fourth Younger Brother', familiar reference to Zēng Guófān's eldest younger brother Zēng Guóhuáng 曾國潢/曾国潢 (1820–1886)

2. 四妹 Sìmèi: 'Fourth Younger Sister', familiar reference to Zēng Guóhuáng's wife (her exact dates are unknown)

Translation

With due respect to Father and Mother   On the 4th Day of the Seventh Lunar Month

The son Guófān humbly sends this letter [and hereby wishes] wealth and happiness for his revered father and mother:

On the 28th Day of the Sixth Month I received the letter from my family: it was sent on the 24th Day of the Third Month. Upon learning that on the 19th Day my Fourth Brother's son was born, the whole family of this son [of yours] rejoiced. Although Fourth Younger Sister had a difficult childbirth, weakness after childbirth due to excessive loss of blood is a common phenomenon. If she will make it [through this] safely, then her next [childbirth] shall be considerably easier. Before this son received your letter he was often worried, but after receiving it he was relieved.

Section 2

六月底，我縣有人來京捐官王道窿。渠在寧鄉界住，言四月縣考時，渠在城内并在彭興岐雲門寺、丁信風兩處面晤四弟、六弟。知案首是吳定五。男十三年在陳氏宗祠讀書，定五纔發蒙作起講，在楊畏齋處受業。去年聞吳春岡說定五甚爲發奮，今果得志，可謂成就甚速。其餘前十名及每場題目，渠已忘記。後有信來，乞四弟寫出。

New words/expressions

1. 捐官 *juānguān*: to purchase an official rank (by paying a larger sum to the state treasury; such a rank was nominal only)

2. 案首 *ànshǒu*: the first person on the list of graduates of a district examination

3. 發蒙 (发蒙) *fāmēng*: to learn the basics

4. 起講 (起讲) *qǐjiǎng*: the introductory passage of an examination dissertation

5. 發奮 (发奋) *fāfèn*: to work energetically; to make a determined effort

Proper names

1. 王道隆 Wáng Dàolóng: the exact details of his life are unknown

2. 寧 (宁) Nìng: a county next to 湘 Xiāng County, the home of the Zēng Clan

3. 彭興岐 (彭兴岐) Péng Xìngqí: the exact details of his life are unknown

4. 雲門寺 (云门寺) Yúnmén-sì: name of a temple and district in 湘 Xiāng County

5. 丁信風 (丁信风) Dīng Xìnfēng: the exact details of his life are unknown

6. 六弟 Liùdì: 'Sixth Younger Brother', a familiar reference to Zēng's younger brother 曾國華/曾国华 Zēng Guóhuá (1822–1858)

7. 吳定五 (吴定五) Wú Dìngwǔ: the exact details of his life are unknown

8. 楊畏齋 (杨畏斋) Yáng Wèizhāi: the exact details of his life are unknown

9. 吳春岡 (吴春冈) Wú Chūngāng: the exact details of his life are unknown, an older relative of Wú Dìngwǔ

Translation

At the end of the Sixth Month a man ([called] Wáng Dàolóng) from our county came to the capital in order to purchase an official title. He lives on the boundary of Nìng County and our own, and he told me that when he participated in the county examination in the Fourth Month, he met Fourth Brother and Sixth Brother in the city, at the homes of Péng Xìngqí ([from] Yúnmén-sì) and Dīng Xìnfēng. I was informed that the first graduate was Wú Dìngwǔ. When this son of yours studied at the Ancestral Temple of the Chén Clan in the Thirtieth Year [of 道光 Dàoguāng; that is 1833], Dìngwǔ had just started to study how to write the introductory section of examination papers, and was being taught by Yáng Wèizhāi. Last year I heard Wú Chūngāng saying that Dìngwǔ studies with great energy, and his [subsequent] success can be hailed as an extremely swift achievement. The names of the others among the ten candidates after him, as well as all the examination topics I have already forgotten. When my family next writes, I pray my Fourth Brother will inform me of these [details].

Section 3

四弟、六弟考運不好，不必掛懷。俗語云：「不怕進得遲，只要中得快。」從前邵丹畦前輩甲名 四十三歲入學，五十二歲作學政，現任廣西藩臺。汪朗渠鳴相 於道光十二年入學，十三年點狀元。阮芸臺元 前輩於乾隆五十三年縣、府試皆未取頭場，即於其年入學、中舉，五十四年點翰林，五十五年留館，五十六年大考第一，比放浙江學政，五十九年升浙江巡撫。些小得失，不足患，特患業之不精耳。兩弟場中文若得意，可將原卷領出寄京。若不得意，不寄可也。

New words/expressions

1. 考運 (考运) *kǎoyùn*: luck in an examination
2. 中得 *zhōngdé*: to develop (one's morality)

3. 前輩 (前辈) *qiánbèi*: one's senior; member of an older generation; here it functions as a deferential suffix, referring to the fact that the indicated person is a senior of the author in the 翰林 Hànlín Academy

4. 入學 (入学) *rùxué*: lit. 'to enter learning', to start one's studies; here: a synonym for 生員/生员 *shēngyuán*, that is successful candidate at a local (lowest) examination

5. 學政 (学政) *xuézhèng*: provincial educational commissioner

6. 藩臺 (藩台) *fāntái*: vice-governor of a province

7. 點 (点) *diǎn*: to be selected

8. 狀元 (状元) *zhuàngyuán*: the best graduate at the highest imperial examination

9. 府試 (府试) *fǔshì*: prefectural examination

10. 頭場 (头场) *tóuchǎng*: place among the successful candidates

11. 中舉 (中举) *zhòngjǔ*: to pass the provincial examination

12. 留館 (留馆) *liúguǎn*: title for Hànlín scholars who passed the internal examinations with the best results and so received internal positions within the Academy

13. 大考 *dàkǎo*: special examination held for scholars who previously graduated at the Hànlín Academy

14. 特 *tè*: special; here: synonym for 只 *zhǐ* ('only')

15. 精 *jīng*: perfect

16. 領 (领) *lǐng*: lit. 'to lead'; here: to obtain (the original copy of the examination dissertation)

Proper names

1. 邵丹畦 Shào Dānqí: a renowned Qīng Dynasty official (his exact dates are unknown)

2. 汪朗渠 Wāng Lǎngqú: a renowned Qīng Dynasty official (1794–1840)

3. 阮芸臺 Ruǎn Yúntái: a renowned Qīng Dynasty official (1764–1849)

Translation

The luck of Fourth and Sixth Brothers in the examination was not good, but there is no need to worry about this. As the saying goes: "One should not fear

Historical Chinese Letter Writing

if his career is slow, he should only develop swiftly inside". In the past my senior Shào Dānqí ([his name] Jiǎmíng) was forty three years old when he successfully passed the local examination, he was fifty two when he became a provincial educational commissioner, and now he holds the post of vice-governor in Guǎngxī Province. Wāng Lǎngqú ([his name] Míngxiāng) passed the local examination in the Twelfth Year of the Dàoguāng [Era], and in the Thirteenth Year he was selected as the best graduate in the highest imperial examination. My senior Ruǎn Yúntái ([his name] Yuán) in the Fifty Third Year of the Qiánlóng [Era] failed in both the county and the provincial examination, but in the same year passed the county and the provincial examinations, in the Fifty Fourth Year became a member of the Hànlín Academy, in the Fifty Fifth Year successfully passed the internal examination [of the Academy], in the Fifty Sixth Year became first in the examination held for Hànlín graduates, and then was promoted [to the rank of] provincial educational commissioner, and [finally] in the Fifty Ninth Year he rose to the rank of Governor of Zhèjiāng Province. [These examples demonstrate that] tiny success and failure are not worth one's anxiety – one should worry only if their learning is imperfect. If my two younger brothers feel that their examination essays were satisfactory, they should obtain the original documents and send them to [me in] the capital. If they are dissatisfied [with the works] they should not send them.

Section 4

男等在京平安。紀澤兄妹

二人體甚結實，皮色亦黑。

逆夷在江蘇滋擾，於六月

十一日攻陷鎮江，有大船數十

只在大江游弋。江寧、揚州二

府頗可危慮。然而天下降災，

聖人在上，故京師人心鎮定。

New words/expressions

1. 逆夷 *nìyí*: disobedient barbarians (a contemptuous reference to the English)

2. 滋擾 (滋扰) *zīrǎo*: to cause trouble

3. 攻陷 *gōngxiàn*: to storm and capture (a city)

4. 游弋 *yóuyì*: to patrol (for naval vessels)

5. 京師人 *jīngshīrén*: the people of Peking

6. 鎮定 (镇定) *zhèndìng*: calm

Proper names

1. 鎮江 (镇江) Zhènjiāng: prefecture in Jiāngsū Province

2. 江寧 (江宁) Jiāngníng: literary name for 南京 Nanking

3. 揚州 (扬州) Yángzhōu: a famous city and prefecture in Jiāngsū Province

Translation

This son and his family are well in the capital. Jìzé and his younger sister are in good health and the colour of their skin is dark.

 The disobedient barbarians [i.e. the English] cause trouble in Jiāngsū Province, in the 11th Day of the Sixth Month they stormed and captured Zhènjiāng, and around ten of their large warships patrolled on the Yangtze River. [The prefects of] Jiāngníng and Yángzhōu must be very worried at this dangerous [situation]. But even if disaster has fallen upon the world, a sage person [i.e. the emperor] resides above us and so the hearts of the people in Peking are calm.

Section 5

同鄉王翰城繼賢，黔陽人告假出京。男與陳岱雲亦擬送家眷南旋，與鄭莘田、王翰城四家同隊出京鄭名世任，給事中，現放貴州貴西道。

男與陳家本於六月

底定計，後於七月

初一請人乩另紙錄出大

仙示語，似可不必輕

舉妄動，是以中

止。現在男與陳家

仍不送家眷回南

也。

New words/expressions

1. 同鄉 (同乡) *tóngxiāng*: fellow villager, fellow townsman

2. 告假 *gàojià*: to ask for leave

3. 給事中 (给事中) *gěi-shì-zhōng*: official title, roughly: 'supervisory official'

4. 道 *dào*: abbreviated form of 道臺 *dàotái* ('magistrate')

5. 扶乩 *fújī*: planchette writing

6. 輕舉妄動 (轻举妄动) *qīngjǔ-wàngdòng*: to act recklessly (formulaic expression)

Proper names

1. 王翰城 Wáng Hànchéng: a renowned Qīng Dynasty official (1792–1850)

2. 黔陽 (黔阳) Qiányáng: a county in Húnán Province

3. 陳岱雲 (陈岱云) Chén Dàiyún: a distant relative of Zēng Guófān (his exact dates are unknown); he is often referred to as 陳源充 Chén Yuánchōng (his personal name)

4. 鄭莘田 (郑莘田) Zhèng Shēntián: a renowned Qīng Dynasty scholar (1787–?)

5. 貴西 (贵西) Guìxī: a county in Guìzhōu Province

Translation

With my fellow villager Wáng Hànchéng ([name] Jìxián, from Qiányáng) [we] asked for leave from the capital. This son of yours and Chén Dàiyún already planned to send their wives and children to the South, and with Zhèng Shēntián and Wáng Hànchéng the four of us to leave the capital (Zhèng's name is Shìrèn, a supervisory official, he has now been promoted to the post of the magistrate of Guìxī in Guìzhōu). This son of yours and the Chén family made this plan at the end of the Sixth Month, but on the first day of the Seventh Month we asked a man [to tell our fortune by] planchette writing (I copy the words manifested by the great immortals on a different sheet). [The oracle promised bad fortune for the journey] and it seemed to us that we had better not act recklessly, and therefore abandoned [the plan to travel].

Section 6

同縣謝果堂先生興嶢來，京，爲其次子捐鹽大使。男已請至寓陪席。其世兄與王道薶尚未請，擬得便亦須請一次。

New words/expressions

1. 同縣 (同县) *tóngxiàn*: fellow county-man

2. 鹽大使 (盐大使) *yán-dàshǐ*: rank of officials in charge of collecting and storing salt

3. 世兄 *shìxiōng*: deferential form of address, referring to the son of the recipient or a third person

Proper names

1. 謝果堂 (谢果堂) Xiè Guǒtáng: a Qīng Dynasty official (his exact dates are unknown)

Translation

My fellow county-man Mr. Xiè Guŏtáng ([name] Xìngyáo) came to the capital, in order to purchase the [rank of] salt official for his second son. This son of yours has already invited him to his residence to [be his] company for a banquet. His respected son and [my fellow villager] Wáng Dàolóng I have not yet invited, and I wait for a convenient [occasion] when I can invite them together.

Section 7

正月間俞岱青先生出京，男寄有鹿
脯一方，託找彭山屺轉寄。俞後託謝吉
人轉寄，不知到否？又四月託李昌岡榮燦
寄銀寄筆，託曹西垣寄參，並交陳季牧
處，不知到否？

New words/expressions

1. 鹿脯 *lùpú*: dried deer meat

2. 託 (讬)/托 *tuō*: to entrust

3. 轉寄 (转寄) *zhuănjì*: to forward a letter/parcel

4. 參 (参) *shēn*: Ginseng

Proper names

1. 俞岱青 Yú Dàiqīng: the exact details of his life are unknown

2. 彭山屺 Péng Shānqǐ: the exact details of his life are unknown

3. 謝吉人 (谢吉人) Xiè Jírén: a Qīng Dynasty official (his exact dates are unknown)

4. 李昺岡 (李昺冈) Lǐ Bǐnggāng: the exact details of his life are unknown

5. 曹西垣 Cáo Xīyuán: the exact details of his life are unknown

6. 陳季牧 (陈季牧) Chén Jìmù: the exact details of his life are unknown

Translation

During the First Month Mr. Yú Dàiqīng left the capital, and this son of yours entrusted a box of dried deer meat to him and asked him to contact Péng Shānqǐ to forward it [to my parents]. Later Yú entrusted Xiè Jírén to bring it back [to you], and I wonder whether it has reached you? Furthermore, in the Fourth Month I entrusted Lǐ Bǐnggāng ([name] Róngcàn) to bring back silver and writing brushes, and Cáo Xīyuán to bring back Ginseng [to my parents], both of them to convey [the goods] to Chén Jìmù, and I wonder whether these have reached you?

Section 8

前父親教男養鬚之法，男僅留上唇鬚，不能用水浸透。色黃者多，黑者少。下唇擬待三十六歲始留。

New words/expressions

1.   浸透 *jìntòu*: to soak

Translation

Previously my father taught this son how to [properly] cultivate his beard, and this son of yours has only kept his moustache and may not soak it with water. Many of [the whiskers in my moustache] are blond and only a few are black. I plan to wait until I reach my thirtieth year and then I will start to grow a beard.

Section 9

男每接家信，嫌其不詳，嗣後更願詳示。

男謹稟

七月初四日（道光二十二年）

New words/expressions

1.   嗣後 (嗣后) *sìhòu*: hereafter

2.   謹稟 (谨禀) *jǐnbǐng*: to respectfully send (honorific letter closing formula)

Translation

Whenever this son of yours receives letters from his family, he is angry at himself for not being clear [in his own letters], and hereafter he will be even more determined to write clearly.

Your son respectfully sends [this letter]

On the 4th Day at the beginning of the Seventh Month (the Twenty Second Year of Dàoguāng [1842])

Brief overview

This letter, written in 1842, is addressed to Zēng Guófān's parents from the capital. This work represents historical Chinese family letters written to one's seniors in the sense that unlike the previous two epistles it does not only discuss issues related to the family but also *reports on* the life of Zēng in detail. Furthermore, the author applies several honorific forms and deferential strategies in the letter in order to acknowledge the status of his parents (see 3. below).

Rhetorical, pragmatic and sociocultural features

1. The present letter is arguably the most difficult one among the six family letters studied in this book, partly due to its long chain of thought, which is as follows:

Section 1: Formal opening → Reference to the recipients' letter → Expression of joy at the birth of Fourth Brother's son → Encouragement: Fourth Brother's wife will recover from the weakness after childbirth in due time.

Section 2: Report on Wáng Dàolóng, the neighbour of the author's family, who previously met Fourth and Sixth Brothers when he participated at the county examination → Report on Wú Dìngwǔ and his success in the examination → Indirect request to Fourth Brother to send the names of the other successful candidates and the examination tasks to the author.

Section 3: Mentioning the failure of Fourth and Sixth Brothers in the examination and encouraging them to not worry about this → Introduction of some acquaintances of the author who failed at the examinations first, in a similar way to his brothers, and then went on to have outstanding careers → Encouragement of Fourth and Sixth Brothers to not worry about such a minor failure and to concentrate on their development → Offering to read their works if they feel that they were turned down unjustly.

Section 4: Report on the good health of the author and his children in the capital → Report on the unsuccessful war against the English (the letter is written during the First Opium War) and on the mood of the people in the capital.

Section 5: Report on the author's original plan to go on leave and first send his family back to the South and then follow them in the company of some intellectuals → Introduction of the reason for the cancellation of the journey → Intertextual reference to the result of the planchette writing recorded on another sheet.

Section 6: Report on the author's keeping contact with some fellow county-men in the capital by means of a banquet.

Section 7: Detailed description of different items sent back by the author to his parents and introduction of the persons entrusted with the delivery → Enquiry as to whether the parents received the goods in order.

Section 8: Description of the author's treatment of his beard in accordance with the advice of his father.

Section 9: Polite self-critical promise that the author will later write to his parents in a clearer style → Deferential formal closing.

This long chain of thought makes it difficult for the reader to find the 'main' message of the letter. To some extent, this letter has a less clearly identifiable main message than the previous ones, due to the fact that the author discusses different topics. Also, the ideas raised in the work do not constitute a strictly coherent chain simply because in Sections 4–7 the author *reports on* different issues. Yet, the letter has a primary message, namely, the indirect encouragement of the author's younger brothers. This becomes evident if one considers the time of the present letter's writing and compares the length of the paragraphs: the author wrote this letter soon after the unsuccessful examination of his brothers, and also he wrote about the examination issue in more detail than about any other topic (this topic is raised already in Section 2, which functions as an introduction for Section 3).

2. Another difficult aspect of this letter is that the author refers to a large number of different persons by using their literary names, including (i) his fellow county-men, most of whom must have been familiar to his parents; (ii) his seniors in the Hànlín Academy (at the time of writing this letter the author was a member of the Academy); and (iii) colleagues in the capital. It is possible for the reader to identify some of these persons, while many others are non-famous persons who do not occur in other historical sources and so it is difficult or even impossible to identify them. When reading Chinese letters one unavoidably meets this phenomenon: letter writing – unlike, for example, historical writing – is a 'situated' activity in that the authors refer to persons with whom he and/or his recipients are familiar, and it often happens that such persons do

not occur in other sources; in fact, it may even occur that a letter is addressed to a recipient who is not known from any other historical source. Insofar as the reader does not approach a letter with a strictly philological goal, it is usually not needed to devote much time and energy to identify such persons.

3. Unlike in the previous works, in the present letter the author uses different honorific forms and deferential strategies in order to maintain his deferential relationship with the recipients. These honorifics, in a similar way to the 'sub-ordinative' epistolary expressions in Letter 4 and the lack of formulae in Letter 5 serve to reinforce the author's relationship with the recipients. Along with honorific forms, the author also applies politeness strategies; the most obvious example of this is that he refers to himself in the third person, by using the form of address 男 *nán* ('this son of yours') and the third person pronoun 其 *qí*. These strategies fulfil the same function as honorific forms.

4. The family letters of Zēng received relatively few editorial changes compared with many other edited epistolary collections. Due to this fact they not only include different formal parts, such as superscriptions, but also the author's original explanatory comments. Such comments play a particularly important role in letters written to his parents, or other senior clan members, where Zēng makes detailed reports on certain matters and persons. These commentary parts are preserved in modern editions in an identical form to that in the original letter, that is they are written using smaller characters than the main text in order to signal their subordinate (explanatory) role.

Exercise 6

1. **Task:** Reread and punctuate the text below.

男等在京平安紀澤兄
妹二人體甚結實皮色
亦黑逆夷在江蘇滋擾
於六月十一日攻陷鎮
江有大船數十只在大
江游弋江寧揚州二府
頗可危慮然而天下降
突聖人在上故京師
人心鎮定同鄉王翰
城維賢黔陽人告假出京

男與陳岱雲亦擬送家
眷南旋與鄭莘田王翰
城四家同隊出京 鄭名世任
給事中現放貴州貴西道 男與陳
家本於六月底定計後
於七月初一請人扶乩 另
紙錄出大仙示語 似可不必輕
舉妄動是以中止現在
男與陳家仍不送家眷
回南也

2. **Task:** Interpret the text below, which unlike the 'main' text above contains several 'missing' characters, and define the 'missing' characters (denoted with squares):

同鄉王翰城 繼賢，黔陽 □告假□京。
男與陳岱雲亦擬送家□南旋，與鄭莘
田、王翰城四□同隊□京 鄭名世任，給事中，
現放貴州貴西道。男與陳家本於六月底□
計，後於七月初一請人扶乩 另紙錄□ 大仙示
語，似可不必輕舉妄動，是以中□。現
男與陳家仍不送家眷□南也。
同縣謝果堂先生 興嶢 來京，爲其次
子捐鹽□使。男已□至寓陪席。其世兄
與王道隆尚□請，擬得便亦須請□次。

Questions

1. In Section 7 the author mentions that he asked Yú Dàiqīng to contact Péng Shānqǐ. What does this mean?

2. In Section 3 the author refers to the failure of his Fourth and Sixth Brothers in the examination as 考運不好 *kǎoyùn bù hǎo* (lit. 'examination luck no good'). What could be his reason for applying such an indirect description?

Answers

1. The author must have asked Yú Dàiqīng to contact Péng Shānqǐ because Yú would not pass through the author's home in his journey back to his home town, and so he gave the meat to another person (Péng) who was a resident of the same area as the author.

2. This is a euphemistic description, and the author probably applied it in order to avoid offending his parents. Furthermore, as previously mentioned, such letters were designed to be read by a wider audience and the author could rightly suppose that the letter would be read by his younger brothers (this is also demonstrated by the fact that in Section 2 the author makes an indirect request to Fourth Brother).

Further Reading

For readers with interest in reading Zēng Guófān's letter in Chinese, the most reliable source is the collection 曾文正公家書全集 *Zēng Wénzhèng-gōng jiāshū quánjí* (*The Collected Family Letters of Zēng Wénzhèng-gōng*, 2001, Taipei, 三民書局 Sanmin shuju). This collection does not only contain reliable typography but also detailed commentaries and reliable modern Chinese translations of the original texts. Another reliable edition is 曾國藩家書 *Zēng Guófān jiāshū*, by 唐浩明 Táng Hàomíng a renowned expert of Zēng Guófān-research (2003, Taipei, 麥田出版 Maitian chuban). The edition 曾國藩手札 *Zēng Guófān shǒuzhá* (2007, Shanghai, 上海書畫出版社 Shanghai shuhua chubanshe) contains some photographed letters of Zēng, and it may be a relevant source to those who intend to learn to read Chinese letters in their original calligraphic form.

A brief literary historical analysis of Zēng Guófān's epistolary activity can be found in 趙樹功 Zhào Shùgōng's 中國尺牘文學史 *Zhōngguó chǐdú wénxuéshǐ*

(*History of Chinese Epistolary Literature*, 1999, Shijiazhuang, 河北人民出版社 Hebei renmin chubanshe, 624–626).

Readers with interest in Zēng's life and political career may consult Jonathan Porter's book *Tseng Kuo-Fan's Private Bureaucracy* (Berkeley, University of California Press, 1972).

Part II

'Specialized' Epistolary Discourse

Chapter 3

'Specialized' Epistolary Discourse I:
Literary Letters of Jīn Shèngtàn 金聖嘆

In this chapter we examine 'specialized' epistolary discourse. This label describes letters that discuss the authors' ideas on certain abstract topics. They differ from 'regular' letter writing, which serves a certain social function: 'specialized' letters have more abstract literary, scholarly, philosophical, etc. goals, and the relationship between the correspondents is usually not too important. The label 'specialized' does not mean that such letters do not have social goals – in fact the border between 'specialized' and 'non-specialized' letters is vague – rather, it could be said that in 'specialized' letters abstract discussion has a more prominent role.

In the present chapter we study the genre of 'literary letters', that is letters that discuss abstract literary ideas, such as aesthetics. The author of the letters studied in this chapter, 金聖嘆 Jīn Shèngtàn (c.1610–1661), was one of the most outstanding literary theoreticians of the Qīng Dynasty, and in fact Chinese literary history in general. Jīn was a highly talented person who came in conflict with the ruling literary theories and theorists of his time due to the fact that he studied and evaluated literary works, including both Classical and the then-despised vernacular novels, on the basis of their literary merit. Since, according to the ruling Confucian view, literary works should be evaluated based on their morality, Jīn was widely criticized due to his progressive ideas. Jīn did not have any official career, and he died at a relatively young age, in 1661, when he joined a protest against the appointment of a corrupt official and along with other protesters was sentenced to public decapitation.

Jīn gained fame as a letter writer due to his refined style and the innovative and often humorous content of his letters. In fact, one of the most well-known anecdotes about him is also connected to letter writing. When waiting to be beheaded in prison Jīn wrote this brief letter to his son:

字付大兒看：鹹菜與黃豆同吃，大有胡桃滋味。此法一傳，我無遺憾矣。

I write the following words to my Eldest Son: When you eat salted vegetables and soybeans together they will have a walnut flavour. Having passed this knowledge to you, I now have nothing to fear.

This short letter is an example of Jīn's black humour and eccentric negligence of worldly things in accordance with 禪/禅 Chán Buddhism (Jīn was a follower of this school).

The correspondence of Jīn Shèngtàn has been published in different collections; in this chapter the letters studied are cited from the collection 金聖嘆尺牘/金圣叹尺牍 *Jīn Shèngtàn chǐdú* (*Letters of Jīn Shèngtàn*). This brief collection, published in 1935 in Shànghǎi (中西書局/中西书局 Zhongxi shuju), contains only Jīn's most representative 'specialized' correspondence relating to his literary criticism. The three letters in this chapter are among Jīn's most renowned epistolary works; they display Jīn's ideas on the famous Míng Dynasty novel 水滸傳/水浒传 *Shuǐhǔ zhuàn* (*Water Margin Story*), which he was the first to annotate (he completed this work in 1641). These letters are not only noteworthy because they introduce rather innovative ideas on the novel – Jīn was called the 'Champion' of vernacular Chinese literature – but also due to their style. Since Jīn tried to promote the study of vernacular literature, in his 'specialized' letters he adopted a style that drew on vernacular language; for example, he typically preferred the application of polysyllabic words and spoken grammatical structures. Thus, these letters not only introduce the reader to 'specialized' epistolary discourse, but they also present a unique 'vernacular' aspect of historical Chinese letter writing.

Letter 7

Section 1

與張原田

予昔曾謂，水滸勝似史記。人都嗤爲妄，即如足下，平日于弟一切深信者，亦竟疑之。然予作此説，並非狂妄不稽，亦自是從讀書中領悟出來。其實史記是以文運事，水滸是因文生事。以文運事，是先有事。生成如此如此，卻要算計出一篇文字來。雖是史公高才也，畢竟是喫苦事。因文生事即不然，只是順著筆性去，削高補低都由我。史記不限于文，水滸不礙于事，即是水滸勝似史記處。

New words/expressions

1. 嗤 *chī*: to sneer

2. 狂妄不稽/羈 (羁) *kuángwàng-bù-jī*: arrogant and obstinate (formulaic expression)

3. 以文運事 (以文运事) *yǐwén-yùnshì*: to use words to animate events

4. 因文生事 *yīnwén-shēngshì*: to use words to create events

5. 如此如此 *rúcǐ-rúcǐ*: lit. 'like this and this', here this expression describes a fictional story

6. 喫苦事/吃苦事 *chīkǔ-shì*: lit. 'hardship-bearing-duty', here: a synonym for prosaic and monotonous task

7. 筆性 (笔性) *bǐxìng*: lit. 'the nature of one's writing brush', a literary description of one's writing mood

8. 削高補低 (削高补低) *xuēgāo-bǔdī*: lit. 'to cut what is high and to mend what is low', a formulaic expression for one's free literary creation

9. 由我 *yóu-wǒ*: lit. 'from me', synonym for personal free decision

Proper names

1. 張原田 (张原田) Zhāng Yuántián: the exact details of his life are unknown

2. 史公 Shǐ-gōng: lit. 'Lord Historian', deferential title for 司馬遷/司马迁 Sīmǎ Qiān (*c*.145–86 BC) author of the famous *Historical Records* (史記/史记 *Shǐjì*)

Translation

To Zhāng Yuántián

I have said that the *Water Margin Story* surpasses the *Historical Records*. Others [upon hearing this] sneered and regarded [my words] as absurd, and it seems as if you, sir, who at other times have firmly believed this humble younger brother of yours, were also sceptical. However, when stating these words [about the novel] I truly am not being arrogant and obstinate, but I have reached this [conclusion] in the course of my studies. In fact, the *Historical Records* uses words to animate [past] events and the *Water Margin Story* uses words to give life to [imaginary] events. Using words to animate events means that [these] events occurred. To create a story requires one to construct a text. Although the Historian had great talent, he nevertheless had to struggle with an unpleasant [prosaic] task. This is not the case if one creates events through a text: he can follow his writing mood and freely create the events as he likes. The *Historical Records* is not only a text [i.e. based on real events], whereas the *Water Margin Story* is unrestricted by [real] events, and this is where the *Water Margin Story* surpasses the *Historical Records*.

Section 2

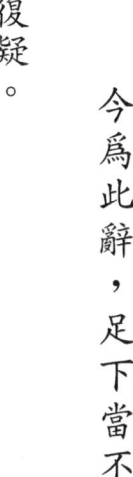

Translation

Having phrased this, you, sir, should no longer doubt [my words].

Brief summary

This letter of unknown date is one of the most important pieces in Jīn Shèng-tàn's epistolary discourse on the *Water Margin Story*, as in it he favourably compares the novel with the *Historical Records* (it should be noted that Jīn was an expert and admirer of the *Historical Records* and in fact he did not have a negative opinion of that work). Considering that at the time of writing this letter historiography was one of the most respected genres, and this was particularly relevant to the *Historical Records* the 'ancestor' of the Chinese dynastical historical writing, discussing Jīn's literary view must have required courage. Furthermore, the notion that the free creation of events is more valuable than the proper recording of historical facts, which was a kind of *ars poetica* of Jīn, was different from the official literary thinking. Therefore, the present letter can rightly be considered to be an important literary discussion, which was ahead of its time.

Rhetorical, pragmatic and sociocultural features

1. This letter has a relatively simple chain of thought:

Section 1: Introduction of the author's literary view → Reference to the fact that even the recipient does not agree with this → Mentioning that the author's belief is based on deduction rather than being an unfounded and arrogant claim of an extravagant scholar → Introduction of the deduction upon which the author has formed this literary view.

Section 2: Expression of the hope that this chain of thought will convince the recipient.

Generically, the present letter (along with the others in this chapter) belongs to the category of literary epistles, that is it makes discourse on a literary notion. Nevertheless, in a similar way to 'ordinary' epistles the present letter has a practical communicational goal as well, namely the attempt to convince the recipient that the author's literary notion is correct. Furthermore, the argument indirectly serves the strengthening of the interpersonal relationship between author and recipient because by justifying his view the author aims to demonstrate to the recipient that he is not 'arrogant and careless'.

When reading 'specialized' Chinese epistolary discourse of this kind, it is worth looking into both the theoretical discussion and the communicational goal of the given work.

2. As mentioned in the introduction, the letters in this chapter contain some 'vernacularisms'. This is a result of the author's situated discursive activity: as Jīn Shèngtàn's goal was to promote the study of vernacular literature, he adopted vernacular elements in his letters. In fact, many Qīng Dynasty private letter writers adhered to a relatively 'loose' Classical style in order to make their works easily accessible to readers; for example, polysyllabic expressions quite often occur within the Qīng corpora. Nevertheless, Jīn's letters contain some explicitly *spoken* elements, which must be intentionally applied vernacularisms. The most typical examples of these vernacularisms are (i) grammatical structures common in spoken Chinese, such as resultative verbal complements, and (ii) colloquial vocabulary items. For example, the sentence

生成 如此如此 ，卻要 算計出 一篇文字 來 。

To create a story requires one to construct a text.

contains the resultative verbal complementary structure 算計出 ... 來 *suànjì-chū ... lái* and the colloquial expression 如此如此 *rúcǐ-rúcǐ* (lit. 'like this-and-this').

3. In the present letter the author makes use of both non-familiar and familiar honorifics, that is, when referring to the addressee he uses the non-familiar

form 足下 *zúxià* ('sir') and when referring to himself he uses the deferential form 弟 *dì* ('younger brother'). Such a mixing of non-familiar and familiar forms is absolutely typical to non-familiar Chinese letters written to friends, and we will continuously meet this phenomenon in the letters in this and the following chapters. As we have already seen in Zhèng Bǎnqiáo's letters to Cousin Hǎo, in family letters to distant relatives authors frequently mix non-familiar and familiar honorific forms of address. This, however, is much more regular a phenomenon in non-familiar letters written to rank equals, in which the authors mix familiar and non-familiar forms in order to maintain emotional closeness with the recipient.

Exercise 7

1. **Task:** Read the text again and find words and expressions that can be recognized from modern Chinese studies.

2. **Task:** Reread and punctuate the text below:

予昔曾謂水滸勝似史記人都嗤為妄即如
足下平日于弟一切深信者亦竟疑之然予
作此說並非狂妄不稽亦自是從讀書中領
悟出來其實史記是以文運事水滸是因文
生事以文運事是先有事生成如此如此卻
要算計出一篇文字來雖是史公高才也畢
竟是契苦事因文生事即不然只是順著筆
性去削高補低都由我史記不限于文水滸
不礙于事即是水滸勝似史記處

3. **Task:** Interpret the text below, which unlike the 'main' text above contains several 'missing' characters, and define the 'missing' characters (denoted with squares):

予昔曾謂，水□勝似史記。□都嗤爲妄，即如□
下，平□于弟一切深信□，亦竟疑之。然予□此
說，並非狂□不稽，亦自是從讀□□悟□□。
其實□記是以文運事，□□因文生事。以□運
事，是先有事。生成如□□□，卻要算計出一篇
文□來。雖是史公高□也，畢□是喫苦事。因文
生事即不□，只是順著筆性去，削高補低都□
我。史記不限□□，水滸不礙于事，即□水滸勝
似史記處。

Questions

1. Although the superscription and the subscription of this letter have been lost, it is possible to deduce that the relationship between the author and the recipient was a friendly one, due to the fact that familiar and non-familiar honorific forms of address are mixed in the text (see above). Can you find a communicational strategy in the text that reinforces this claim?

2. Besides demonstrating to the recipient that he is not "arrogant and careless", is there any discursive strategy in this letter by means of which the author tries to strengthen the ties between the recipient and himself?

Answers

1. In the closing sentence the author directly 'commands' the recipient to not doubt him anymore, by using 當 *dāng* ('should'), which expresses imperative. Such an imperative form would sound impolite in hierarchical contexts but when used towards friends it serves the reinforcement of friendship, and thus it demonstrates that there was a friendly relationship between the author and the recipient.

2. There are several such strategies used in the letter. Not only does the author mix honorifics of different style as mentioned above, but also for example in the beginning of the text he differentiates the recipient from less worthy people. That is, while he describes the behaviour of "others" in negative terms, about the recipient he mentions only that the recipient "doubted" him, and also he refers to the emotive relationship between the recipient and himself ("you, sir, who at other times have firmly believed this humble younger brother of yours"). Such strategies also serve the strengthening of the ties between the correspondents.

Letter 8

Section 1

與
王
㠖
山

先生昔嘗爲予言：

「不登泰山不知天下之
高；登泰山不登日觀，
不知泰山之高也；不觀
黃河不知天下之深；觀
黃河不觀龍門，不知黃
河之深也。不見聖人，
不知天下之至；見聖人
不見仲尼，不知聖人之

至也。」斯言耿耿，未嘗一刻忘之。今批水滸至設祭一篇，不覺拍案狂叫：「讀書不讀水滸不知天下之奇；讀水滸而不讀設祭，是不知水滸之奇也。」嗚呼！耐庵之才，固不可以斗石量也。

New words/expressions

1. 耿耿 *gěnggěng*: bright and shining, that is illuminating

2. 批 *pī*: to write annotations for a work; to criticize

3. 設祭 (设祭) *shèjì*: to make a sacrifice

4. 斗石 *dǒu-dàn*: measures for grains, *dǒu* describes a quantity of grain equals 1 dekalitre and *dàn* describes that of 1 hectolitre, thus the compound *dǒu-dàn* can be translated as 'minor and major measures'; here it is used as a synonym for 'common norms'

Proper names

1. 王斲山 Wáng Zhuóshān: the author's best friend (his exact dates are unknown)

2. 日觀 (日观) Rìguān: that is 日觀峰 Rìguān-fēng (lit. 'Sun-view Peak'), a famous peak of the Mountain Tài (泰山 Tàishān)

3. 龍門 (龙门) Lóngmén: a gorge of the Yellow River which is famous for its temple grottos

4. 仲尼 Zhòngní: the courtesy name of Confucius (551 BC–479 BC)

5. 耐庵 Nài'ān: that is 施耐庵 Shī Nài'ān (*c*.1296–1372), the author of the *Water Margin Story*

Translation

To Wáng Zhuóshān

You, sir, previously told me that if one does not climb the Mountain Tài he will not know how high the world is; if one climbs the Mountain Tài but does not climb the Sun-view Peak he will not know how high Mountain Tài is. If one does not see the Yellow River he will not know how deep the world is; if one sees the Yellow River but not the Lóngmén Gorge, he will not know how deep the Yellow River is. If one does not meet the wise he will not know [the highest virtue and accomplishments] reached in the world; if one meets the wise but does not meet [i.e. read the words of] Confucius, he will not know [the highest virtue and accomplishments] reached by the wise. Your words are illuminating, and I have never forgotten them even for a moment. Now, writing commentaries for the *Water Margin Story* I reached the chapter where the sacrifice is made, and I unconsciously struck the table in amazement, saying: "If one reads books but does not read the *Water Margin Story* he will not know the miraculous [nature] of the world; if one reads the *Water Margin Story* but does not read the [chapter of] the sacrifice, he will not know the miraculous [nature] of the *Water Margin Story*." Ah! Nài'ān's talent cannot be measured by common norms.

Section 2

前奉呈之六卷，不知已
讀竟否？亦有不愜意處否？
須知我批此書，全是替古人
做一件公事，並非聖嘆自己
私事。儘管直直言之，彼中
于客氣而說摸稜兩可話者，
是生平所大惡。先生幸毋蹈
此惡轍。

New words/expressions

1. 奉呈 *fēngchéng*: to respectfully submit something to the recipient (deferential epistolary verbal form)

2. 愜意 (惬意) *qièyì*: to be satisfied with ...

3. 須知 *xūzhī*: it must be noted; point for attention

4. 摸稜兩可 *mōléng-liǎngkě*: vague opinion or behaviour (idiomatic expression)

5. 轍 (辙) *zhé*: way, rhyme

Translation

Previously, I respectfully submitted six chapters [of the novel with my comments], and I know not whether you were able to finish reading them and whether there were any parts that you found displeasing? I must state that in making commentaries for this book I undertake a public service on the behalf of the men of old, and this is by no means a personal affair of Shèngtàn. Thus, you should tell me bluntly [what you think]: If you were to speak vaguely out of politeness, I would loathe this above else in life. Prithee, sir, do not tread this evil path!

Brief summary

This letter of unknown date is the first in an exchange between Jīn Shèngtàn and his best friend Wáng Zhuóshān on the *Water Margin Story*. In a similar way to the previous work the author describes the novel in glowing terms that would have been rather unusual for his contemporaries. Furthermore, a special feature of this letter is that the author overviews his motivation for his groundbreaking annotation of the novel (i.e. to complete a long-awaited task in the interest of the public).

Rhetorical, pragmatic and sociocultural features

1. The chain of thought of the present letter is as follows:

Section 1: Reference to the recipient's previous words that in order to see the extremes of the world it is not sufficient to visit certain places and meet the wise, but it is also necessary to visit their most superb spots and meet the wisest of the wise (Confucius) → In accordance with this view the author believes that in order to read the most miraculous novel one has to read the *Water Margin Story*, but in order to understand the miraculous nature of the novel one also has to read the chapter in which the sacrifice occurs (see more below) → Appraisal of Shī Nài'ān's talent.

Section 2: Reference to the author's request to the recipient to review the annotations he made for six chapters of the novel and enquiry about the review's state of readiness → Description of the author's motivation for this work → Request that the recipient should be strict when commenting on the author's work: due to the fact that this work is a "public affair" the recipient should be particularly critical.

As was already discussed in the case of the previous letter, 'specialized' literary letters of this kind often have some practical discursive function(s), as well. The present letter is a letter of request, as it becomes evident from Section 2.

2. A difficult aspect of this letter is that it contains some information that can be interpreted in the wider context only. The section

今批水滸至設祭一篇...

Now, writing commentaries for the *Water Margin Story* I reached the chapter where the sacrifice is made ...

can only be interpreted if the reader is (i) aware of the fact that Jīn Shèngtàn was the annotator of the novel, and (ii) familiar with the novel. Regarding the latter of these points, Jīn here refers to the 26th chapter of the novel, in which the hero 武松 Wǔ Sōng makes a sacrifice for his deceased elder brother and kills his murderess.

The best way to interpret such points is to carry out some background reading on the author. An alternative approach to translate sections, such as 設祭一篇 *shèjì yī-piān* above that does not make sense in the given text unless one is familiar with their origin, is to search for them on the internet.

3. This letter ends with a prohibition, which in a formal context would sound even ruder than the imperative 當 *dāng* in the previous letter. Furthermore, the author applies several expressions of negative meaning, such as 惡轍 *è-zhé* ('evil path'), which would be quite rude in other contexts. Again, due to the fact that this letter is written to a close friend such directness is acceptable and in fact fulfils an important pragmatic function, that is it emphasizes the author's request for the recipient to be blunt.

Exercise 8

1. **Task:** Make some search on the life and literary work of Jīn Shèngtàn and then read the following section cited from one of his letters:

究何者爲古之才子？究何書爲古之才子之書？
曰惟莊周、屈原、史遷、杜甫、施耐庵、王實
甫，實古之才，而莊子、離騷、史記、杜詩、
水滸、西廂記，乃爲古之才子之書。

Compare your translation with the translation and explanation below:

What persons should we study as the talented men of old? What books should we study as books written by the talented men of old? I say that only Zhuāng Zhōu, Qū Yuán, the Historian Qiān, Dù Fǔ, Shī Nài'ān and Wáng Shífǔ are real talents of old times, and the *Zhuāngzǐ*, the *Encountering Sorrow*, the *Record of the Grand Historian*, the poetry of Dù, the *Water Margin Story* and the *Romance of the Western Chamber* are the books written by the talented men of old.

Here Jīn lists six authors and works that he studied thoroughly; he labelled these books 六才之書 *Liùcái-zhī-shū* (*The Books of the Six Talented Scholars*). The authors of *The Books of the Six Talented Men* include the Taoist philosopher 莊周/庄周 Zhuāng Zhōu (*c.*4 BC), the poet 屈原 Qū Yuán (*c.*340 BC–278 BC), Sīmǎ Qiān (here referred to as 史遷 Shǐ-Qiān, that is 'the Historian Qiān'), the poet 杜甫 Dù Fǔ (712–770), Shī Nài'ān, and 王實甫/王实甫 Wáng Shífǔ (1250–*c.*1307); the six works include the following titles: the Taoist 'Classic' 莊子 *Zhuāngzǐ*, the poem 離騷/离骚 *Lí Sāo* (*Encountering Sorrow*), the *Records of the Grand Historians*, the poetry of Dù Fǔ, the *Water Margin Story*, and the drama 西廂記/西厢记 *Xīxiāng-jì* (*Romance of the Western Chamber*).

2. **Task:** Reread and punctuate the text below:

之高也不　不知泰山　不登日觀　高登泰山　知天下之　登泰山不　爲予言不　先生昔嘗

觀黃河不知天下之深觀黃河不觀龍
門不知黃河之深也不見聖人不知天
下之至見聖人不見仲尼不知聖人之
至也斯言耿耿未嘗一刻忘之今批水
滸至設祭一篇不覺拍案狂叫讀書不
讀水滸不知天下之奇讀水滸而不讀
設祭是不知水滸之奇也嗚呼耐庵之
才固不可以斗石量也

3. **Task:** Interpret the text below, which unlike the 'main' text above contains several 'missing' characters, and define the 'missing' characters (denoted with squares):

斯言□耿，未嘗一刻忘□。

今批水滸至設祭一篇，不覺

拍□狂□：「□□不讀水滸而□

不知天□之□；讀水滸而□

讀設祭，是不知□□之奇

也。」嗚□！耐庵□才，固

不可□斗□量也。

所大惡。先□幸□蹈此惡轍。

□而說摸稜兩可話者，是生□

事。□管□直言之，彼中于客

一□公事，並非□嘆自己私

□我批□書，全是□□人□

□竟否？亦□不愜意處否？須

前奉呈□六卷，不知已

Questions

1. How does the author mitigate the 'face-threatening' closing sentence?
2. The author refers to famous historical persons (Confucius and Shī Nài'ān) by using their courtesy/personal names, without using family names, which implies some intimacy. What is the author's reason for this?

Answers

1. The author mitigates this sentence by using an honorific expression 先生 *xiānshēng* ('sir') and also by putting the prohibition in the form of a request.

2. This means of reference is in fact part of the ongoing intellectual discourse: in order to acknowledge the importance of these renowned persons the author refers to them in a familiarizing way, that is he emphasizes the fact that they belong to the same 'school' of intellectuals. Yet, it should be noted that historical Chinese authors are usually not too consistent in the use of such references. For example, in other letters (see, for example, the next letter) Jīn refers to Shī Nài'ān by using his whole name.

Letter 9

Section 1

與王斲山

前雲衢聞予批點水滸傳，以爲不足浪
費筆墨而批稗史，其見恰左。聖嘆不問其書
之爲正史稗史，只問其書之文章，做得好不
好。文章好，即稗史亦不必不批。文章不
好，即正史亦不必批。水滸一書，眞是天下
古今奇絕妙絕之文，奈何可以不批？吾非必
願批是書，吾但覺不批是書，中心殊不能自
寬也。

New words/expressions

1. 批點 (批点) *pīdiǎn*: to punctuate and annotate

2. 稗史 *bàishǐ*: unofficial history

3. 左 *zuǒ*: wrong; here: disagree

4. 奇絕 (奇绝) *qíjué*: unsurpassably wonderful

5. 妙絕 (妙绝) *miàojué*: uniquely fine

6. 自寬 (自宽) *zìkuān*: to find comfort

Proper names

雲衢 (云衢) Yúnqú: literary name of a common acquaintance of the author and the recipient

Translation

To Wáng Zhuóshān

When Yúnqú learnt that I am punctuating and annotating the *Water Margin Story*, he claimed that it is not worth wasting one's brush and ink to annotate an unofficial history [like this work]. However, I entirely disagree with his view. Shèngtàn never inquires whether a book is an authorized history or an unauthorized history, he only examines whether the book is well-written or not. If it is well-written then it is not certain [i.e. self-evident] that an unauthorized history should not be annotated. If its text is not good then it is not certain that an authorized history should be annotated. The *Water Margin Story* is an unsurpassably wonderful and uniquely fine text of the old and new times of the world, and how would it be possible to not annotate it? It is not [merely] my fond wish to annotate this book: I simply felt that if I do not annotate it my heart will surely be unable to find comfort.

Section 2

足下書來，言曾一見
此書，不見其佳處，特爲俗
相蒙耳。夫水滸所敘，敘一
百八人之事。而此一百八人
者，人有其性情，人有其氣
質，人有其形狀，人有其聲
口。夫以一手而畫數面，則
將有兄弟之形；一口而吹
數聲，斯不免再映。施耐庵

以一心之所運，而一百八
人，各自入妙，此豈迂儒腐
士所能為，庸夫俗子所能領
略者乎？予故謂水滸傳乃天
下古今之一部奇書，施耐庵
乃天下古今一個才子。所批
前六卷，已呈嶯山先生，不
妨往索閱，定能如願，且證
予言不虛也。

New words/expressions

1. 蒙 *méng*: licentious

2. 兄弟之形 *xiōng-dì-zhī-xíng*: equivalent of 'pictures of similar shape'

3. 映 *yāng*: to echo

4. 迂儒腐士 *yūrú-fǔshì*: impractical and decadent scholar (formulaic expression)

5. 庸夫俗子 *yōngfū-súzǐ*: ordinary persons and laymen, that is worthless persons (formulaic expression)

6. 領略 (领略) *lǐnglüè*: to carry out a great work; to appreciate

7. 不妨 *bùfáng*: might as well

8. 索閱 (索阅) *suǒyuè*: to seek reference

Translation

In your letter you wrote, sir, that when you previously read this book you did not find any beauty in it, and that it was particularly vulgar and licentious. Now, the *Water Margin Story* describes the deeds of one hundred and eight persons. However, every one of these one hundred and eight men has his own temperament, his own disposition, his own appearance, and his own manner of speech. If one draws several pictures single-handedly, then they will be of similar shape; if one whistles alone it cannot be avoided that the melodies will echo each other. Shī Nài'ān used his mind only and each of these one hundred and eight men has become wonderful. Could an impractical and decadent scholar do this, or a worthless person achieve such as this? This is why I say that the *Water Margin Story* is a remarkable book of the old and modern times of the world, and Shī Nài'ān is a great scholar of the old and modern times. The six chapters I previously annotated and submitted to you, my lord Zhuóshān, may as well serve as reference: they will surely fulfil my wish and shall demonstrate that my words are not void.

Brief overview

This letter of unknown date is the second in an exchange between Jīn Shèng-tàn and his best friend on the *Water Margin Story*. This is perhaps the most important letter in Jīn's epistolary discourse on the novel because it includes both his innovative concept as to the value of the novel (Section 1), and a discussion on the way in which the literary value of the novel should be understood (Section 2). That is, in this letter Jīn does not only challenge the accepted literary norms of his time, which could be observed in his previous letters, but also challenges the main criticism against the *Water Margin Story*, that is its vulgarity, and provides a sophisticated literary view that the reader should seek the novel's worth in its true-to-life style.

Rhetorical, pragmatic and sociocultural features

1. The chain of thought of the present letter is as follows:

Section 1: Reference to a common acquaintance of the author and the recipient who evaluated the annotation of the novel as a worthless activity → Analysis of the problem whether one should annotate an 'unofficial' (i.e. fantastic) historical work, such as this novel, and the description of the author's view on this issue → Description of the author's motivation to annotate the novel.

Section 2: Intertextual reference to the recipient's letter and negative comment on the novel → Description of the author's view on the real value of the work → Request to the recipient to reconsider his negative opinion on the novel by means of the six annotated chapters sent by the author (indirect repeated request to the recipient to read the author's annotation for these chapters).

2. While this letter is relatively easy to read due its vernacular style, it contains some elements that might be confusing. For example, in Section 1 the author makes use of the auxiliary verb 不必 *bùbì* ('need not') in the following way:

文章好，即稗史亦 不必不批 。文章不好，即正
史亦 不必批 。

*If its text is well-written then an unauthorized history need not be not
annotated. If its text is not good then an authorized history need not to be
annotated.* (this translation differs from the 'main' text)

Although the use of *bùbì* seemingly makes this section unnecessarily verbose
and fuzzy, in fact this negative form has an important rhetorical role, that is it
underlines the author's argument (in historical Chinese rhetoric double nega-
tion and negative forms are often stronger than assertions).

Another difficult stylistic feature of this letter is that the author uses different
typically colloquial vernacular forms. An example of this is 左 *zuǒ*, which means
'to disagree' and 'incorrect' in colloquial Chinese. When one meets such elements, which cannot be interpreted according to their 'ordinary' Classical Chinese meaning, the best way is to look into their colloquial meaning(s) by means
of vernacular/modern Chinese dictionaries.

Finally, the present text contains a form, 兄弟之形 *xiōng-dì-zhī-xíng* (lit.
'elder and young brother form', that is 'pictures of similar shape'), which does
not occur in any other Classical Chinese texts (as far as the author of this book is
aware), and it is supposedly a literary 'invention' of the author. This inventive
activity is typical to Jīn Shèngtàn, and the reader unavoidably meets such forms
in his letters. Most of these expressions, such as *xiōng-dì-zhī-xíng*, can easily be
interpreted in the context in which they occur, and they cause some difficulty to
one only if (s)he tries to find them in dictionaries.

3. This letter, like the previous ones, contains information that can be interpreted only if the reader enquires into the *Water Margin Story* and Jīn Shèngtàn's discourse on the work. For example, the author's reference to the "one
hundred and eight persons" can only be understood if one is familiar with the
fact that the novel has one hundred and eight heroes and heroines. While this
is a relatively simple example, a much more complex reference is made in
this letter to Jīn's literary theory on the work, which in fact allows a twofold
interpretation of a section. The term 才子 *cáizǐ* ('gifted scholar') in the section

施耐庵乃天下古今一個才子

Shī Nài'ān is a great scholar of the old and modern times of the world has a literary-theoretical implication. As already mentioned in this chapter, Jīn created the group of so-called 六才 Liù-cái ('Six Talented [Scholars]'), which includes the authors of the six works that Jīn believed to be the best ones in the history of Chinese literature. Thus, while 一個才子 *yī-ge cáizǐ* above has the primary meaning that Shī Nài'ān was *a* most talented scholar, and the sentence was translated to English in this way, it has a secondary discursive meaning, that is, that Shī Nài'ān belongs to *the* group of *cáizǐ*, that is the Liù-cái. Considering the recipient was the author's best friend, one can rightly assume that he was familiar with the concept of Liù-cái, and so the sentence was intentionally designed to convey this secondary meaning.

This section demonstrates that before reading 'specialized' letters of this kind, it is advisable to examine the author's main ideas, in order to be able to find implicit references to such ideas.

Exercise 9

1. It is a regular phenomenon that certain theories and ideas repeatedly occur in the epistolary discourse of the authors. This can be observed, for example, in Zēng Guófān's discourse in the previous chapter and, as the following example illustrates, in Jīn Shèngtàn's letters, too.

Task: Read the following section from a letter of Jīn, and identify a general literary concept of Jīn that occurs in this text, as well:

今閒評水滸，不覺拍案狂呼曰：「此眞窮奇盡變，出妙入神之文章也，孰爲稗官無才子筆也？

Compare your translation with the translation and explanation below:

> Now in my free time I annotate the Water Margin Story and I cannot refrain from striking the table in amazement and crying in bewilderment: "[This work] is truly miraculous, its text goes from wonder to wonder – who would say that a common storyteller [such as Shī Nài'ān] cannot have a gifted pen [lit. 'pen of a gifted scholar']?"

Again, *cáizǐ* has a secondary interpretation, that is along with its concrete meaning it also refers to the category of Liù-cái.

2. **Task:** Reread and punctuate the text below:

前雲衢聞予批黜水滸傳以為不足浪費筆墨

而批稗史其見恰左聖嘆不問其書之為正史

稗史只問其書之文章做得好不好文章好即

稗史亦不必不批文章不好即正史亦不必批

水滸一書真是天下古今奇絕妙絕之文奈何

可以不批吾非必願批是書吾但覺不批是書

中心殊不能自寬也足下書來言曾一見此書

不見其佳處特為俗相蒙耳夫水滸所敘敘一

百八人之事而此一百八人者人有其性情人

有其氣質人有其形狀人有其聲口

3. **Task:** Interpret the text below, which unlike the 'main' text above contains several 'missing' characters, and define the 'missing' characters (denoted with squares):

足□書來，言曾一

見此書，不見其佳處，

特爲俗□蒙耳。夫水滸

所敘，敘一百八人之

事。而此一□□人□，

人□其性□，人有□氣

質，人□形狀，□□□

聲口。夫以□手而畫數

面，則將□兄弟之形；

一口而吹□聲，斯□免

願　□　批　乃　古　□　爲　妙　運　再
，　，　前　天　□　？　，　，　，　映
且　不　六　下　之　予　庸　此　而　。
證　妨　卷　古　一　故　夫　豈　一　施
□　往　，　今　部　□　俗　迂　百　耐
言　索　已　□　奇　水　子　儒　□　庵
不　閱　呈　□　書　滸　□　腐　□　以
虛　，　斷　才　，　傳　能　士　，　一
也　定　山　子　施　乃　領　所　各　心
。　能　先　。　耐　天　略　□　自　之
　　如　　　□　庵　下　者　　　入　所

Questions

1. Is there any linguistic evidence in this letter that the recipient was the author's friend?

2. In this letter the author refers to his motivation for annotating the *Water Margin Story*. Is there any similarity between this and the way in which he discussed his motivation in the previous letter?

Answers

1. In the section 呈斷山先生 *chéng* Zhuóshān *xiānshēng* ('submitted to you, my lord Zhuóshān') the author uses honorific forms along with the recipient's literary name (without family name), in order to simultaneously express closeness and deference. As in historical China only close friends could address each other without using family names, this section proves that the relationship between the author and the recipient was a close one. Along with this section, in the beginning of the letter the author refers to himself by using his personal name, which again conveys intimacy.

2. In Letter 8 the author mentions that this "by no means is a personal affair of Shèngtàn", and in Letter 9 he notes that "It is not my fond wish to annotate this book." That is, in both letters the author emphasizes that this work is more important to him than a passionate personal activity.

Further Reading

In the Western sinological literature there has not been any work published on the letters of Jīn Shèngtàn. In Chinese, a brief discussion on Jīn's letters is available in 趙樹功 Zhào Shùgōng's 中國尺牘文學史 *Zhōngguó chǐdú wén-xuéshǐ* (*History of Chinese Epistolary Literature*, 1999, Shijiazhuang, 河北人民出版社 Hebei renmin chubanshe, 518–520).

For those who are interested in reading Jīn's letters in Chinese, perhaps the most reliable edition is 金聖嘆尺牘 *Jīn Shèngtàn chǐdú* (*The Letters of Jīn Shèngtà*) (1989, Taipei, 廣文書局 Guangwen shuju). This is a reprint of the original 1935 edition (see the introductory section of the chapter).

Readers with an interest in the life and principal ideas of Jīn may consult John Ching-yu Wang's essential work *Chin Sheng-t'an: His Life and Literary Criticism* (1972, New York, Twayne).

Chapter 4

'Specialized' Epistolary Discourse II:
Scholarly Letters of Gù Yánwǔ 顧炎武

In this chapter we continue the examination of 'specialized' epistles, by studying three scholarly letters written by the renowned philologist and geographer Gù Yánwǔ 顧炎武/顾炎武 (1613–1682). Gù was born in the time of the late Míng Dynasty and he spent his youth in anti-Manchu activities (he participated in military resistance). After the Míng Dynasty was overthrown, Gù decided that he would not serve the Manchus and devoted himself completely to his studies, and also travelled around the country with the goal of learning. He was one of the finest scholars in the history of China, who among others contributed to phonological studies by demonstrating that the Old Chinese language had its own phonological system. Gù recorded his scholarly ideas in several works, such as the 音學五書/音学五书 *Yīnxué-wǔ-shū* (*The Five Books of Phonology*), which have become the seminal works of the philological tradition of the early Qīng Dynasty. Among his works, arguably the most famous is the 日知錄/日知录 *Rì-zhī-lù* (*Record of Daily Progressive Knowledge*), which is a lexicon-like book.

The three letters of this chapter represent Gù's 'specialized' scholarly epistolary discourse: they discuss a central topic, namely 學/学 *xué* or 'learning', this 'specialized' discussion (rather than obtaining any social goal) being their fundamental objective. The concept of *xué* was a basic notion in Confucian scholarship, but it had a prominent role in Gù Yánwǔ's letters. This is because Gù, in a similar way to some other early Qīng Dynasty intellectuals, opposed the then-dominant Neo-Confucian school, and argued that in fact the Míng Dynasty's destruction was a result of following this philosophical school. That is, Gù was a traditionalist thinker who argued that scholars must correctly learn the 'pure' morality and truth of the Classics, and in his epistolary discourse *xué* occurs as an (often abstract) collective term for his ideas on proper learning.

Along with their content, the letters studied here are also interesting because they inform the reader on several details of Gù Yánwǔ's scholarly work, which make these works 'scholarly' in the strict sense of the word. For example, Letters 10 and 12 record the criteria according to which he wrote the *Record of Daily Progressive*

Historical Chinese Letter Writing

Knowledge, and Letter 11 contains an important reference to his interest in empirical exploration through travelling.

It should be noted that the letters in this chapter have been selected in a way that they should represent the two often-contrasted types of historical Chinese letter writing, that is short and long letters (it should be noted that in reality there is no clear-cut border between these types, and hence this categorization is not discussed elsewhere in this book). The first two letters, taken from a series of intellectual discursive letter-notes written to an anonymous friend or maybe group of friends represents the 'category' of brief letters; the last letter represents long ones.

Letter 10

Section 1

與人書十

嘗謂今人纂輯之書。正如今人之鑄錢。古人采銅於山。今人則買舊錢。名之曰廢銅。以充鑄而已。所鑄之錢。既已粗惡。而又將古人傳世之寶。春剉碎散。不存於後。豈不兩失之乎。

New words/expressions

1. 纂輯 (纂辑) *zuǎnjí*: to compile

2. 鑄錢 (铸钱) *zhùqián*: to mint money

3. 廢銅/废铜 *fèitóng*: lit. 'waste copper', scrap copper

4. 鑄 (铸) *zhù*: mould, casting

5. 舂剉碎散 *chōng-cuò-suìsăn*: to pound, cut and smash to pieces, that is destroy

Translation

10th letter to my friend[1]

I always said that the way books are compiled by the men of our time is similar to [the way in which] our contemporaries mint money. The men of old gathered copper in the mountains; the men of our time buy antique money, call it scrap and use it to fill the mould. The money they cast is coarse and of poor quality and they also destroy the treasures handed down by the men of old from ancient times, which will thus cease to exist thereinafter. Is this not a double loss?

Section 2

承問日知錄又成幾卷。蓋期之以廢銅。而某自別來一載。早夜誦讀。反復尋究。僅得十餘條。然庶幾采山之銅也。

New words/expressions

1. 承問 (承问) *chéngwèn*: to respectfully receive one's enquiry (honorific epistolary verbal form)

2. 庶幾 (庶几) *shùjī*: to hope that; maybe; almost

Translation

[In your respected letter] you kindly enquired how many new chapters of the *Record of Daily Progressive Knowledge* have been completed. [This sounds to me as if you were] expecting my work to be akin to scrap. In fact, during the year that passed since our parting I read from day to night, I repeatedly carried out thorough investigations, and [so far] have completed just over ten entries. But in this way I can hope that [my work] will be [similar to] the bronze collected in the mountains.

Brief overview

This letter is one of the so-called 與人書/与人书 *Yǔ-rén-shū* (*Letter to My Friend*) group, a series of 25 intellectual letters, written by Gù Yánwǔ. This series of brief letters represent Gù's scholarly epistolary discourse: these works primarily serve the conveyance of strictly scholarly views on certain topics. Thus, as these epistles unlike 'regular' letters have not much to do with the relationship between author and recipient, it is supposedly not a coincidence that the recipient is anonymous.

The letter studied here is an important source of evidence regarding Gù's scholarly approach to the authoring of his main work, the *Rì-zhī-lù*.

Rhetorical, pragmatic and sociocultural features

1. The present letter has a relatively simple chain of thought:

Section 1: Opening analogy: editing a book is similar to casting money → Description of the ways in which modern men cast money, in contrast with the ancient and proper way → Negative evaluation of the practice of modern times.

Section 2: Intertextual reference to the recipient's letter and his enquiry on the state of the *Record of Daily Progressive Knowledge*'s readiness, supposing that the author has already completed a significant part of the work → This enquiry was incorrect, supposedly because the recipient expected the author to follow the shallow modern scholarly attitude → Expression of the author's wish that he will be able to accumulate real and well-founded knowledge in his book, similar to the way in which the men of old cast money.

The only potentially difficult communicational feature of this letter is that the author approaches the point of discussion in a circumspective way, that is the anecdotic description on casting money in Section 1 is in fact considerably longer that the main discussion in Section 2. Such an indirect symbolic approach is often used in historical Chinese letter writing, and it has an important role in epistolary rhetoric because it aids the author in creating a 'frame story' to start and end an argument. For example, in the case of the present letter the opening anecdote returns in the end of Section 2, that is it serves as a 'frame' for the letter.

2. In the present work an indirect reference is made in the text to the *Record of Daily Progressive Knowledge*, which can be interpreted only if one is familiar with the structure of the work. That is, the word 條 (条) *tiáo* (lit. 'strip', 'item') in the following section seems to be rather vague:

僅得十餘條

I only completed a few more than ten strips [i.e. entries] (literal translation)

In fact, *tiáo* is the basic unit of the *Record of Daily Progressive Knowledge*: as the *Rì-zhī-lù* is an encyclopaedia-like work in which every *tiáo* studies an issue centred on a keyword, *tiáo* should be translated as 'entry'.

Exercise 10

As the present letter illustrates, the symbolic description of certain thoughts is important in historical Chinese intellectual letters. Such symbolic discussions can be carried out utilizing analogies, as in the case of the present letter, and also by means of more indirect rhetorical tools.

1. **Task:** Read the following brief letter of Gù (use a dictionary if required), taken from the same *Yǔ-rén-shū* (*Letter to My Friend*) group, and try to interpret the way in which the message is conveyed, from a rhetorical perspective.

與人書十九

彈琵琶佑酒，此倡女之所爲，其識則然也。苟欲請良家女子出而爲之，則艴然而怒矣。何以異於是？

Compare your translation with the translation and explanation below:

19th letter to my friend

Playing guitar and serving wine [to guests], this is the engagement of a courtesan, and it is proper for her to know such things. If one wants to ask a
woman from a respectable family to do these [things], she will give an angry
look and will be furious. What might be the difference between them?

This is an allegory: the author, through comparing the behaviour of a courtesan
and that of a woman from a respectable family, implicitly describes the difference between the ways in which the author and most of his contemporaries approach scholarly activities, most of the author's contemporaries being corrupted
by trifling. Such indirect rhetorical tools can be interpreted only if one knows the
context in which they were written.

2. **Task:** Read the following brief letter, also taken from the *Yǔ-rén-shū* group,
    and try to identify the rhetorical technique used in it:

與人書二十

某君欲刻其文集，以求名於世，此如人之失足
而墜井也。若更爲之序，豈不猶之下石乎？惟
其未墜之時，猶可及止。止之而不聽，彼且以
入井爲安宅也，吾已矣夫。

Compare your translation with the translation and explanation below:

20th letter to my friend

If a certain gentleman wishes to publish his own collected works in order to
gain a reputation in the world, he can be likened to someone who has lost his
footing and fallen into a well. If one then agrees to write a preface for him, is
it not as if he was to throw a stone down at him [in the well]? Before falling
into the well I would rather halt him. If I halt him but he nevertheless jumps
into the well, believing this to be the ideal place for him, I will then ignore
him in disappointment.

This letter, describing the author's reason for not writing prefaces for pushy scholars who publish their collected works themselves, starts with an analogy (publishing one's own work is like falling in a well), in a similar way to Letter 10.

3. **Task:** Reread and punctuate the text below, printed with more archaic characters than the main text above:

嘗謂今人纂輯之書正如今人
之鑄錢古人采銅於山今人則
買舊錢名之曰廢銅以充鑄而
已所鑄之錢既已粗惡而又將
古人傳世之寶春剉碎散不存
於後豈不兩失之乎承問日知
錄又成幾卷蓋期之以廢銅而
某自別來一載早夜誦讀反復
尋究僅得十余條然庶幾采山
之銅也

4. **Task:** Interpret the text below, which unlike the 'main' text above contains several 'missing' characters, and define the 'missing' characters (denoted with squares):

嘗謂今人□輯□書。正
□今□之鑄錢。古□采
銅於山。今人則買舊
□。名之□廢銅。以充
鑄而□。□鑄之錢。既
已粗惡。而又將□人傳
世之寶。春□碎散。不
存□後。□□不兩失之
□。

承□□□錄又□幾。蓋期□以廢銅。而某□別來一載。早□誦□。反復尋究。僅□十□條。然庶幾采山□銅也。

Questions

1. Did the author mean to 'teach a lesson' to the recipient by mentioning that "[This sounds to me as if you were] expecting my work to be akin to scrap."?

2. Apart from presenting Gù Yánwǔ's concept on proper scholarly work this letter is also valuable as a description of a concrete phenomenon. What phenomenon might this be and how is it related to Gù's research?

Answers

1. This is a description of the author's writing concept, and it is not aimed at teaching the recipient a lesson. The author, in fact, presupposes the recipient's opinion in order to describe his view on proper scholarly writing. And he mitigates this 'face-threatening' utterance by using the honorific verb 承問 *chéngwèn* ('[In your respected letter] you kindly enquired'), and also by making this section *indirect*, that is, by implicitly presupposing that the recipient possesses the author's own principles of writing and enquired in this way only because he did not expect the work to be serious.

2. The letter documents the money-minting customs of the author's time; it is an interesting document because in this letter Gù Yánwǔ expresses a scholarly worry for the destruction of relics. Money-

minting and numismatics belonged to Gù Yánwǔ's topics of research: in the 15th chapter of the *Record of Daily Progressive Knowledge* he devoted several entries to numismatic studies.

Letter 11

與人書一

人之爲學。不日進則日退。獨學無友。則孤陋而難成。久處一方。則習染而不自覺。不幸而在窮僻之域。無車馬之資。猶當博學審問。古人與稽。以求其是非之所在。庶幾可得十之五六。若既不出戶。又不讀書。則是面牆之士。雖子羔原憲之賢。終無濟於天下。子曰。十室之邑。必有忠信如丘者焉。不如丘之好學也。夫以孔子之聖。猶須好學。今人可不勉乎。

New words/expressions

1. 孤陋 *gūlòu*: to be ignorant

2. 習染 (习染) *xírǎn*: to contract bad habits

3. 窮僻之域 (穷僻之域) *qióngpì-zhī-yù*: a distant place

4. 車馬之資 (车马之资) *chēmǎ-zhī-zī*: lit. 'the help of chariot and horses', that is money to make study through travel (formulaic expression)

5. 十之五六 *shí-zhī-wǔ-liù*: lit. 'five or six from ten', that is some success

6. 面牆之士 (面墙之士) *miànqiáng-zhī-shì*: unlearned scholar

Proper names

1. 子羔 Zǐgāo: disciple of Confucius who was dwarfish and ugly but of great worth and ability; he is often referred to as 高柴 Gāo Chái (his personal name)

2. 原憲 (原宪) Yuánxiàn: a disciple of Confucius noted for his purity and modesty

3. 丘 Qiū: the personal name of Confucius

Translation

1st letter to my friend

When one is engaged in learning and is unable to continuously develop he shall gradually fall behind [in his studies]. If one learns alone, without [discussing his findings] with friends, he will have little knowledge and it will be difficult for him to succeed. If one dwells in one place for too long, he will contract bad habits and will lack self-awareness. If one is unlucky, lives in a faraway place, and lacks funds to study through travel, he should nevertheless "make extensive studies and in-depth enquiries", and [always] check whether [his thoughts] are correct or not [by means of] comparing [them with that] of the men of old; [acting in such a way] he should be able to achieve some result. If one does not leave his household and does not learn, he will become an ignorant scholar, and even if he were to possess the wisdom of Zǐgāo and Yuánxiàn he would in the end not be of much aid to the world. The Master said: "In every hamlet of ten families, there should be someone who is as faithful and honest as I, Qiū, am; however, he may not be so fond of learning." If even a Sage such as Confucius needs to be fond of learning is it possible for the men of our time to not strive [to learn]?

Brief overview

This letter of unknown date is the first and most renowned piece in a series of 25 brief epistles written by Gù Yánwǔ (see Letter 10). This work is a brief summary of Gù's view on 'learning' 學 *xué*, which is a central theme in his epistolary discourse.

Rhetorical, pragmatic and sociocultural features

1. Although this work, in a similar way to the previous one, could be defined as a brief letter, it has a fairly complex chain of thought due to the author's complex argumentation:

The central theme: engagement in learning → If one is unable to develop himself daily he will gradually fall back in his studies → Such a lack of development may have two reasons: (i) the lack of study partners, and (ii) living at home without actively learning → As regards (ii) it is argued that although some students may lack the necessary financial sources to travel, they should make use of the Classics and thus widen their knowledge → If one does not leave his house or does not learn the Classics, he will become an ignorant scholar → Reference to Confucius and his concept of 好學 (好学) *hàoxué* ('to be fond of learning') → Everyone needs to follow his example.

The most difficult part of this letter is that after discussing the potential reasons (i) and (ii) for the lack of one's development, the author starts a lengthy argumentation, which may seem to be a sudden switch of topic. However, this argumentation is in fact related to (ii), that is, here the author surveys the means to avoid (ii).

2. In letters written by and to Chinese intellectuals it is a regular phenomenon that the authors make reference to Classical sources; as previously mentioned, in Chinese culture reference to the sages of old is an important rhetorical tool due to the revered status of the sages and the Classical literature. The present letter illustrates the twofold way in which literary references are made in Chinese letters, that is the author makes an *explicit* and an *implicit* citation from the Confucian Classics. The explicit citation is the following:

子曰：「十室之邑，必有忠信如丘者焉，不如丘之好學也。」

The Master said: "In a hamlet of ten families, there should be someone who is as faithful and honest as I, Qiū, am; however, he may not be so fond of learning."

When meeting explicit citations the reader has simply to translate them and interpret their relevance to the context in which they occur. Should a difficult citation occur, the easiest way to proceed is to trace its origin and read it in its original context. For example, the above citation originates in the *Analects* (論語/论语 *Lúnyǔ*; section 28 of the 5th chapter), the basic book of Confucianism.

One has to make considerably more effort with implicit citations. The present letter contains the following implicit citation:

猶當 博學審問

He should nevertheless make extensive studies and in-depth enquiries.

The words 博學 *bóxué* ('to make extensive studies') and 審問 *shěnwèn* ('to make in-depth enquiries') are cited from *The Doctrine of the Mean* (中庸 *Zhōngyōng*, section 19 of the 20th chapter), one of the Four Books of the Confucian Canon, which contains the following words:

博學之，審問之，慎思之，明辨之，篤行之。

To this attainment there are requisite the extensive study of what is good, accurate inquiry about it, careful reflection on it, the clear discrimination of it, and the earnest practice of it. (James Legge's translation)

Usually, authors make such implicit references for an intellectual reason, that is they 'hide' these translations within the text and invite the reader into the 'game' of identifying them. Also authors such as Gù Yánwǔ, who had a thorough knowledge of the Classics, might have had a practical reason for using a large number of implicit citations: relying on the succinct wording of the Classics was a simple way to put certain thoughts into words.

Usually, there is no reason for the Western reader to identify such citations because many of them can be contextually interpreted. Yet, as the last letter in this chapter illustrates, in some cases it is necessary for the reader to track citations and read them in their original context, in order to understand their proper meaning.

If one is somewhat unfamiliar with the Classics, the best practical alternative to find the origin of a citation is to try the major internet search engines; most of the reliable translations of the Confucian Classics, such as that of the renowned sinologist James Legge, can be found online and by means of search engines one can find the part in question within the translations. A reliable website that contains translations is that of *Association Francaise des Professeurs de Chinois*: http://afpc.asso.fr/wengu/.

There is no general methodology for identifying implicit citations in a text; after reading a larger number of Chinese letters one will gradually obtain the skill of 'catching' parts that seem to be citations. For newcomers the best course is to pursue this issue if a section in a letter seemingly does not make any sense in the given context.

Exercise 11

1. The expression 動心忍性 *dòngxīn-rěnxìng* ('aroused be able to endure') is used in Chinese letters as a synonym for the author's ability to restrain his temper. This is an indirect reference to a Classical source.

Task: Find the origin of this indirect reference and compare the result with what is written below:

This is a reference to the Classic *Mencius* (孟子 *Mèngzǐ*, 告子下 *Gàozǐ-xià* [*Master Gào,* part 2] chapter, section 2), which contains the following section:

所以動心忍性，增益其所不能。

By all these methods his [a high-ranking person's] ability to restrain his temper when aroused is developed and his incompetencies are eroded.

2. In Chinese letters the authors often use the expression 屋梁落月 *wūliáng-luòyuè* (lit. 'roof beam and setting moon', that is '[the glimmer of] the descending moon at the roof beam') in order to express their longing for the recipient. This is an indirect literary reference.

Task: Find the origin of this reference and compare the result with what is written below:

This expression is a reference to the Táng Dynasty poet 杜甫 Dù Fǔ's (712–770) poem 夢李白之一 *Mèng Lǐ Bó zhī-yī* (*Seeing Lǐ Bó in My Dream, First Version*), which contains the following couplet:

落月滿屋梁，猶疑照顏色...

[I woke and] in the descending moon's glimmer a rafter seemed to be your face . . .

This poem can be found in the famous collection 唐詩三百首 *Tángshī sānbǎi-shǒu* (*Three Hundred Táng Dynasty Poems*, I.1.11).

3.   **Task:** Reread and punctuate the text below:

人之爲學不日進則日退獨學無友
則孤陋而難成久處一方則習染而
不自覺不幸而在窮僻之域無車馬
之資猶當博學審問古人與稽以求
其是非之所在庶幾可得十之五六
若既不出戶又不讀書則是面牆之
士雖子羔原憲之賢終無濟於天下
予曰十室之邑必有忠信如丘者焉
不如丘之好學也夫以孔子之聖猶
須好學今人可不勉乎

4. **Task:** Interpret the text below, which unlike the 'main' text above contains several 'missing' characters, and define the 'missing' characters (denoted with squares):

人□爲學。不□進□日退。
獨學無友。則孤陋而難成。久□
一方。則□染而不自覺。不幸□
在窮□之□。無車□之資。猶當
博學審問。古□與稽。以求其是
非之所在。□幾□得十□五六。

若既□出戶。又不□書。則是□牆之士。雖子羔原憲之賢。終無濟□天下。子□。十室之邑。必□忠□如丘□焉。不□丘□好學也。夫以孔□之聖。猶須□□。今人可不勉□。

Questions

1. What may be the author's reason for ending this letter with a rhetorical question?

2. What could be the author's personal reason to encourage the youth to leave their homes and travel?

Answers

1. In historical Chinese epistolary discourse rhetorical questions, being weightier than assertions, had an important argumentative role, and so the argumentation of letters is often concluded by rhetorical questions.

2. Not only did Gù devote much attention to 'learning through travel', which he claimed to be a pivotal activity in widening one's knowledge, but he also made extensive travels in China himself (see the introductory section).

Letter 12

Section 1

與友人論門人書

伏承來教。勤勤懇懇。閔其年之衰暮。而
悼其學之無傳。其爲意甚盛。然欲使之效曩者二
三先生。招門徒。立名譽。以光顯於世。則私心
有所不願也。若乃西漢之傳經。弟子常千餘人。
而位富者至公卿。下者亦爲博士。以名其學。可
不謂榮歟。而班史乃斷之曰。蓋祿利之路然也。
故以夫子之門人。且學干祿。子曰。三年學。不
至於穀。不易得也。而況於今日乎。

New words/expressions

1. 伏承 *fúchéng*: lit. 'to respectfully receive with prostration', that is to respectfully receive (honorific epistolary verbal form)

2. 來教 (来教) *láijiào*: lit. 'coming teaching', that is honourable letter (honorific addressee-elevating form)

3. 勤勤懇懇 (勤勤恳恳) *qínqín-kěnkěn*: conscientious and careful (formulaic expression)

4. 衰暮 *shuāimù*: old and weak

5. 悼 *dào*: to grieve

6. 效 *xiào*: to imitate; effect, result

7. 曩者 *nǎngzhě*: of old, in the past

8. 傳經 (传经) *chuánjīng*: teachers of the Confucian Classics; to hand down sacred documents

9. 祿利 (禄利) *lùlì*: obtaining official rank and gaining profit

10. 干祿 (干禄) *gānlù*: scheme for a lucrative official position

11. 穀 (谷) *gǔ*: grain; here: official position

Proper names

1. 班史 Bān-shǐ: lit. 'the Historian Bān', that is 班固 Bān Gù (32–92), a famous historian who completed the 漢書/汉书 *Hànshū* (*The Book of the [Western] Hàn Dynasty*)

Translation

A letter [in which I] discuss [the matter of] principles with my friend

I respectfully received your honourable letter: it was conscientious and careful, expressing sympathy for my old age and sincere regret for [the fact] that I do not pass on my learning [to disciples]. These thoughts [i.e. kind feelings] of yours are profound. But [the passing on of my art] would require me to imitate some gentlemen of old who became revered in the world through recruiting disciples who [later] gained reputation. This is what I would not do of my own will. For example, the teachers of Confucian Classics in the Western Hàn Dynasty often had more than a thousand disciples, and those among them who attained high ranks became high officials, and [even] those behind became court academicians, thus they brought fame to their learning – can one not call this glory? But Bān Gù criticized this [practice], saying: 'This [kind of teaching] is surely the path to obtaining official rank and thus gaining profit.' This is why Confucius, [when seeing] that his disciples studied with the goal of gaining official posts, said: "It is not easy to find a man who can study for three years without thinking of earning a salary." Is this not even more the reality in our day?

116 — Historical Chinese Letter Writing

Section 2

今之爲祿利者。其無藉於經術也審矣。窮年所習不過應試之
文。而問以本經。猶茫然不知爲何語。蓋舉唐以來帖括之淺。而
又廢之。其無意於學也。傳之非一世矣。矧納貲之例行。而目不
識字者可爲郡邑博士。惟貧而不能徙業者。百人之中尚有一二。
讀書而又皆躁竟之徒。欲速成以名於世。語之以五經則不願學。
語之以白沙陽明之語錄。則欣然矣。以其襲而取之易也。其中小
有才華者。頗好爲詩。而今日之詩。亦可以不學而作。吾行天下
見詩與語錄之刻。堆幾積案。殆於瓦釜雷鳴。而叩之以二南雅頌
之義。不能說也。於此時而將行吾之道。其誰從之。

New words/expressions

1. 藉/借 *jiè*: to gain profit from, to take advantage of

2. 審 (审) *shěn*: indeed, certain, to know for sure; to interrogate

3. 窮年 (穷年) *qióngnián*: (during) the whole year

4. 茫然不知 *mángrán-bùzhī*: to be completely in the dark (formulaic expression)

5. 帖括 *tiěkuò*: formal writing compulsory for candidates

6. 矧 *shěn*: moreover, also (epistolary form)

7. 納貲 (纳赀) *nàzī*: to obtain a post for money

8. 徙業 (徙业) *xǐyè*: to change profession

9. 躁竟 *zàojìng*: to be eager to finish (one's studies)

10. 襲 (袭)-取 *xí-qǔ*: to learn (a historical work)

11. 堆幾積案 (堆几积案) *duī-jǐ-jī'àn*: 'a large pile of [the documents of] several long-pending cases', that is documents that fill one's table

12. 瓦釜雷鳴 (瓦釜雷鸣) *wǎ-fǔ-léi-míng*: lit. 'the sound of thunder that comes from a cooking utensil', that is mediocre works masquerading as something more (idiomatic expression)

Proper names

1. 白沙 Báishā: that is 陳白沙/陈白沙 Chén Báishā/Bóshā (1482–1500; often referred to as 獻章/献章 Xiànzhāng, his personal name), a Míng Dynasty philosopher

2. 陽明 (阳明) Yángmíng: that is 王陽明/王阳明 Wáng Yángmíng (1472–1529), a famous Neo-Confucian philosopher of the Míng Dynasty

3. 二南雅頌 (二南雅颂) *Èr-nán Yǎ Sòng*: names of several groups of poems in the 詩經/诗经 *Shī Jīng* (*Book of Odes*); *Èr-nán* refers to the groups of 周南 Zhōunán (*Odes of Zhōu and South*) and 召南 Zhàonán (*Odes of Zhào and South*), 雅 *Yǎ* (lit. 'elegant') refers to a larger group (or subgenre) of 105 ceremonial poems, and 頌 *Sòng* (lit. 'Odes') refers to another larger group or subgenre of 40 hymns; in the English translation, for the sake of clarity, *Èr-nán Yǎ Sòng* occurs simply as '*Book of Odes*'

Translation

It is apparent that those in our days who wish to obtain official rank and thus gain profit cannot gain advantage from studying the Classics [anymore]. During the whole year they study nothing but examination essays, and if they meet the texts of the Classics they will be completely in the dark as regards what sort of words these are. This shows that [the memorization of] formal examination texts, which began in the time of the Táng Dynasty, is not only shallow but also a waste [of work]. This lack of interest in [real] learning has been passed on for [much] longer [time] than a generation. And due to the practice of obtaining a post through payment now even an illiterate man can become a prefectural instructor! The number of those who are poor and thus are unable to quit the trade [of scholars] should be one or two among a hundred persons, but when engaged in learning they also [prove to be] disciples who are anxious to complete [their studies], they want to be educated swiftly and then gain reputation. If you want to explain the Five Classics to them, they will not be eager to learn, but if you teach them the discourses of Chén Bóshā and Wáng Yángmíng they will be glad because it is easy to understand [the content of] these [works]. Those among them who have a little literary talent are rather fond of writing poems, but the poems of our day can be written without [prior] learning. While wandering around the world I read so many block-printed editions of poetry and discourses that they [would fill my table] like piled up long-pending official documents, but almost all of them are mediocre works masquerading as something more, and if one wants to ask [i.e. learn] the [ancient] justice of the Book of Odes from them they will not be able to give an answer [i.e. will not be of use]. If I wanted to implement my principles in this time, who would follow me?

Section 3

大匠不爲拙
工改廢繩墨。羿
不爲拙射變其彀
率。若徇眾人之好
而自貶其學。以來
天下之人。而廣其
名譽。則是枉道以
從人。而我亦將有
所不假。惟是斯道
之在天下。必有時

而興。而君子之教人有
私淑艾者。雖去之百世
而猶若同堂也。所著日
知錄三十餘卷。平生之
志與業皆在其中。惟多
寫數本以貽之同好。庶
不為惡其害己者之所
去。而有王者起。得以
酌取焉。亦可以畢區區
之願矣。

New words/expressions

1. 繩墨 (绳墨) *shéngmò*: marking line

2. 彀率 *gòulǜ*: lit. 'the proportion to which one draws his bow', that is one's rule for drawing his bow

3. 徇 *xùn*: to yield to

4. 枉道 *wǎngdào*: to violate the proper way

5. 假 *jià*: here: free (variant of 暇 *xiá*)

6. 私淑艾 *sī-shū-yì*: to privately cultivate and correct oneself (by learning from the works of an ancient master)

7. 貽 (贻) *yí*: to bequeath, to hand down

8. 王者 *wángzhě*: true sovereign, here: a real sage

9. 酌 *zhuó*: to consider

10. 區區 (区区) *qūqū*: this trivial person (honorific self-denigrating form of address)

Proper names

1. 羿 Yì: a legendary archer and great hero

Translation

[As Mencius said:] "A great artisan does not alter or abandon the marking-line due to an inferior workman, [the legendary archer] Yì did not change his rule for drawing the bow due to an inferior archer." If I yield to the preference of the people and deprecate what I teach to them, in order to [attract] people to come to me, thus making my reputation spread, I would violate the proper way so as to follow others, and I would be deprived of my free time, as well. Now, the learning that exists in the world should prosper from time to time, and there always [exist] persons who "privately cultivate and correct themselves" [by means of] the teachings of the wise, and [even though] they [i.e. the wise of former times and those who wish to learn] are separated by hundred generations, they are [in fact as close] as if they were living under the same roof. The *Record of Daily Progressive Knowledge* has more than thirty chapters, the ideas and learning of my life are included in it. I only need to make more copies and bequeath them to my friends, [and thus the copies will be] enough so as to not be destroyed by those who "dislike the [book] as injurious to themselves". Therefore [the work may be preserved until] "a real sage will arise" who will be able to consider [its contents] and select [some of its parts]. This would accomplish my personal humble wish.

Section 4

先生者如此。高明何以教之。

自勉。鄙哉硜硜所以異於今之

若爲己而不求名。則無不可以

夫道之污隆。各以其時。

New words/expressions

1. 爲己 (为己) *wèijǐ*: to cultivate self

2. 鄙哉硜硜 *bǐ-zāi kēngkēng*: lit. 'vulgar!, obstinate', roughly: to be shallow and obstinate (formulaic expression, see more below)

3. 高明 *gāoming*: lit. 'high brilliant', brilliant person, honorific addressee-elevating form of address; brilliant

4. 教 *jiào*: lit. 'to teach', here: honorific verbal form, which refers to the recipient's comment on the author's behaviour or his advice for the author

Translation

Both the decline and prosperity of learning have its own time. If someone develops himself and does not set his mind on obtaining fame there will be naught in which he cannot apply himself. [I am] "shallow and obstinate" in order to differentiate myself from the gentlemen of our days. What advice would your brilliant self give me?

Brief summary

The present letter of unknown date, addressed to an anonymous acquaintance, is the most important epistolary work of Gù Yánwǔ. This writing is a summary of Gù's scholarly motivations, that is his traditionalism and opposition to the then-influential Neo-Confucian ideas, his rigorous approach to 'learning', and the aim of producing the *Record of Daily Progressive Knowledge* that will record his ideas. The importance of this letter is well illustrated by the fact that it is the opening piece in Gù Yánwǔ's collected letters (see more on this collection in 'Further Reading').

Rhetorical, pragmatic and sociocultural features

1. This is a long letter with a complex chain of thought:

Section 1: Intertextual reference to the recipient's letter through ritual opening → Polite reference to the recipient's enquiry as to why the author does not take disciples, which is the central theme of the letter → Introduction of the author's reason for not taking disciples: this would require him to follow the example of some persons who became famous as educators; historical reference to the Confucian teachers of the Western Hàn Dynasty → Although being a renowned teacher is glorious a position, it is unavoidably problematic because most of the

students learn with the hope of gaining profit: this was Bān Gù's reason for criticizing the Western Hàn Dynasty teachers → Even a great sage such as Confucius
complained about his students.

Section 2: In the author's time the situation is even worse than at the time of the
Western Hàn Dynasty: the students do not learn the Classics anymore but instead
they are required to study specialized examination writing, and thus are unable to
understand Classical texts → This results in a continuing lack of interest in
'learning' → This negligence is further encouraged by the government that sells
official posts to anyone → Even those who are 'forced' to become scholars due
to their strained circumstances, and who would probably be appropriate students,
are merely interested in success, as well → Teaching such students does not
make sense because they only have interest in 'light' literature, including Neo-
Confucian literature and 'new' poetry → However, these works are shallow and
they cannot substitute learning the Classics → In sum, there are no students who
would follow the traditionalist ideas of the author.

Section 3: The author is also unwilling to change his own concepts in order to
find students: this would have several negative consequences → Real learning
survives through generations, and so instead of taking students the author prefers
to produce a work, the *Record of Daily Progressive Knowledge*, which will preserve his ideas for later generations → In order to prevent members of the domi-
nant Neo-Confucian scholarship from 'destroying' (either practically or in a
symbolic way) his work, the author makes several copies and hopes that a capa-
ble person will someday come who will use the work and thus become his student.

Section 4: Conclusion: learning is rising and declining, and one should always
focus on his own development instead of seeking fame → Thus, the author will
not follow the example of others (either in scholarly approach or by taking disciples) → Deferential closing request to the recipient to give the author his opinion
on this view.

   Perhaps the most difficult part of this letter is Section 2, which touches various
topics, including the incapability of students, the corrupt practices of the author's
time and the author's negative view of Neo-Confucian ideas. Yet, this is in fact a
coherent discussion: all the ideas in this section are centred on the reasoning that
it is not useful for contemporary students to follow the author, who is traditionalist. The discussion of this theme has an important role in the argumentation of the
letter: after Section 1 that raised the general topic of the letter, Section 2 discusses first the rationale for students not following the author, and then in Section 3 the author introduces his own reason for not taking students.

When reading this letter one should be aware of the relationship between the main topic, that is the author's reason for not taking students, and the theoretical view on 'learning'. The concept of 'learning' continuously enters into the discussion of the main theme because the author's traditionalist view on 'learning' is the core reason for not taking disciples.

2. Section 3 of the present letter contains different implicit citations from the Classical Work *Mencius* (孟子 *Mèngzǐ*). Some of them make sense without tracking their original contextual meaning. For example, the section

> 大匠不爲拙工改廢繩墨，羿不爲拙射變其彀率。

> A great artisan does not alter or abandon the marking-line due to an inferior workman, [the legendary archer] Yì did not change his rule for drawing the bow due to an inferior archer.

makes sense without reading it in its original context (section 41 of chapter 盡心 *Jìnxīn* [*With all One's Heart*], part 1). This is because when reading this implicit citation it becomes evident for the reader that this is a symbolic reference to the author's situation. However, there is, for example, another citation that makes sense only if one knows its original contextual meaning. That is, the section

> 有王者起

> to have ruling one arise (literal translation)

can be translated in different ways, and it does not seem to make sense in the present context. Therefore, in order to properly interpret it one needs to read section 3 of the 滕文公 *Téng-Wén-gōng* (*Duke Wén of Téng*) chapter (part 1) of the *Mencius*, which contains these words:

> 有王者起，必來取法，是爲王者師也。

> Should a real sovereign arise, he will certainly come and take an example from you; and thus you will be the teacher of this true sovereign.

If one compares this section with the contents of the letter it becomes evident that 王者 *wángzhě*, which means a 'true sovereign' in *Mencius*, must mean 'a real sage' in the present context, hence the translation in the main text. In brief, this is a more complex implicit citation than those previously studied in this chapter.

Exercise 12

1. The present text contains different explicit and implicit citations, denoted by citation marks in the English translation.

Task: Find the origin of the following citations with the aid of the internet:

(i) 三年學，不至於穀，不易得也。

(ii) 蓋祿利之路然也。

(iii) 有私淑艾者

(iv) 惡其害己

(v) 鄙哉硜硜

Compare your findings with the answers below:

(i) Cited from the *Analects* (VIII.12)

(ii) Cited from the 88th chapter of the 漢書/汉书 *Hànshū* (*The Book of the [Western] Hàn Dynasty*)

(iii) Cited from section 40 of the *Jìnxīn* chapter of *Mencius* (see above)

(iv) Cited from section 11 of the 萬章/万章 *Wàn Zhāng* (*Wàn Zhāng*) chapter (part 2) of *Mencius*

(v) Cited from the *Analects* (XIV.39)

2. In this chapter we have practised reading the 'specialized' scholarly epistolary discourse of Gù Yánwǔ.

Task: With Gù's scholarly concepts in mind, translate the following brief letter cited from the *Yǔ-rén-shū* group, and draw similarities to the arguments of Letter 12:

與人書二十三

能文不爲文人，能講不爲講師。吾見近日之爲文人，爲講師者，其意皆欲以文名以講名者也。子不云乎：「是聞也，非達也。」、「默而識之。」愚雖不敏，請事斯語矣。

Compare your translation with the translation and explanation below:

23rd letter to my friend

A person who can write is not a man of letters [yet], and one who can talk is not yet a teacher. What I see is that recently all of those who act as men of letters and teachers want to attain a reputation in literature and fame in teaching. Did not the Master say: "This is notoriety, not distinction" and that "One should silently treasure knowledge"? Although this foolish person is not clever, he seeks guidance in these words.

This letter, like Letter 12, criticizes the contemporaries of Gù for seeking fame instead of being interested in learning.

4. **Task:** Reread and punctuate the text below:

今之為祿利者其無藉於經術也審矣窮年所習不過應試之文而問以本經猶茫然不知為何語蓋舉唐以來帖括之淺而又廢之其無意於學也傳之非一世矣矧納貲之例行而目不識字者可為郡邑博士惟貧而不能逃業者百人之中尚有一二讀書而又皆躁竟之徒欲速成以名於世語之以五經則不願學語之以白

沙陽明之語錄則欣然矣以其襲
而取之易也其中小有才華者頗
好爲詩而今日之詩亦可以不學
而作吾行天下見詩與語錄之刻
堆幾積案殆於瓦釜雷鳴而叩之
以二南雅頌之義不飴說也於此
時而將行吾之道其誰從之

5. **Task:** Interpret the text below, which unlike the 'main' text above contains several 'missing' characters, and define the 'missing' characters (denoted with squares):

大匠不□拙工改廢□墨。羿
□拙射變其彀率。若徇眾
□好□自貶其學。以來□
下□人。而□其名譽。□是
枉道□從人。而我亦將有□
不假。惟是斯道之在□下。
必有時□興。而君□之教人
有私淑艾者。雖去之□世而

猶□同堂也。所著□□

錄三十餘□。平生之志

與業皆在□中。惟多寫

數□以貽之同好。庶不

□惡其害己者之□去。

□有王者起。得以酌取

焉。亦可以畢區□之願

矣。

Questions

1. What might have been the author's reason for criticizing the memorization of examination texts?

2. It becomes evident from the author's letter that although he did not believe that the students of former times were better than those in his own time, he was nevertheless more dissatisfied with contemporary learning practices. What could be his reason for this?

Answers

1. The reason for this traditionalist critique of modern methods is that the examinees were required to learn the writing of 'eight-part essays' (八股文 *bāgǔwén*) and to memorize certain texts selected for the purpose of the examinations, instead of focusing on the Classics.

2. Gù as a leading traditionalist intellectual of his time believed, in a similar way to some others, that the then-dominant Neo-Confucian school caused the gradual weakening of the Míng Dynasty, and so he was particularly disappointed by the fact that Neo-Confucian works were quite popular among young intellectuals.

Further Reading

There has been not any study published on the letters of Gù Yánwǔ in English. In Chinese a discussion on Gù Yánwǔ's letters can be found in 趙樹功 Zhào Shùgōng's 中國尺牘文學史 *Zhōngguó chǐdú wénxuéshǐ* (*History of Chinese Epistolary Literature*, 1999, Shijiazhuang, 河北人民出版社 Hebei renmin chu-banshe, 480–484).

For readers with interest in Gù's letters in Chinese the best source is 顧亭林尺牘/顾亭林尺牍 *Gù Tínglín chǐdú* (*Letters of Gù Tínglín*, that is Gù Yánwǔ, 1989, Taipei, 廣文書局 Guangwen shuju).

Readers with interest in Gù's life may consult the research paper 'The life of Ku Yen-wu', published by Willard J. Peterson in the *Harvard Journal of Asiatic Studies* (1968, Vol. 28,114–156).

Part III

Non-family 'Social' Letter Writing

Chapter 5

Non-family 'Social' Letter Writing I:
Letters of Xǔ Jiācūn 許葭村

In this chapter we study the genre of non-family 'social' letters by analyzing three works of the renowned epistolary expert 許葭村/许葭村 Xǔ Jiācūn (his exact dates are unknown; his personal name was 思湄 Sīméi). As it was already mentioned in the Preface, the label 'social' describes letters that were written with some social purpose, such as forming a certain interpersonal relationship between the writer and the recipient or conveying a discursive act, such as request, apology or invitation. That is, the 'social' group involves the large corpus of 'ordinary' letters that are not 'specialized', unlike the letters studied in the previous two chapters (but it should be emphasized again that there is not any clear border between these 'categories'). From two perspectives this considerably larger group of letters is more difficult to read than the smaller group of 'specialized' letters studied previously. First, a social letter necessitates the application of a large inventory of honorific forms and politeness strategies, which make the reading of these letters fairly difficult for the Western reader. Secondly, this genre presupposes the application of difficult complex tools: while in 'specialized' epistolary genres the authors employ a relatively clear and technical way of discussing things, a social letter presupposes formality and utilizes complex rhetoric on the part of the author.

The genre of 'social' letters was important to officials and office clerks, due to the fact that such letters enforce interpersonal relationships. As in historical (and modern) China maintaining personal connections (關係/关系 guānxi) was (and is) a pivotal means by which to attain social success, such letters are of the perhaps largest quantity in the historical Chinese epistolary corpus.

The author of the letters studied in this chapter is not a renowned historical figure. Xǔ Jiācūn was a clerk from 紹興/绍兴 Shàoxīng (Zhèjiāng Province), a city famed for its literary tradition. Xǔ was a member of the so-called 紹興師爺/绍兴师爷 Shàoxīng-shīye or 'Shàoxīng Clerks' circle, which was a group of office clerks and minor officials working in Peking and other Northern areas.[1] Some of these men of letters became renowned for their skill in letter writing: as office clerks the Shàoxīng literati practised letter writing on a professional basis, and they are often referred to as 'expert letter writers'. Furthermore, for the

Shàoxíng clerks the 'social' genre was particularly important: the members of this group lived in the capital and relied on each other in order to gain success in their alien surroundings. Within the Shàoxīng-circle, the two most renowned letter writers were Xǔ Jiācūn and his older friend 龔未齋/龚未斋 Gōng Wèizhāi (read more on him in the following chapter). The works of Xǔ and Gōng had a great influence on Qīng Dynasty letter writing, which is illustrated by the fact that their collected letters – 秋水軒尺牘/秋水轩尺牍 *Qiūshuǐ-xuān chǐdú* (*Letters from Autumn Water Retreat*, the collected letters of Xǔ) and 雪鴻軒尺牘/雪鸿轩尺牍 *Xuěhóng-xuān chǐdú* (*Letters from Snow Swan Retreat*, Gōng's work) – became the most popular models for letter writing until the 20th Century. Between these two collections, the one written by Gōng Wèizhāi is the more difficult to read, and thus the letters of Xǔ are studied first in this book despite the fact that he was born later than Gōng.[2] This difference is rooted in these two authors' styles: while Xǔ was an expert of the art of letter writing and made use of all the complex requirements of this genre, Gōng was a real master of the art who often went beyond mere generic requirements (see more in the following chapter).

In order to represent the genre of social letters, in Chapters 5 and 6 we study the correspondence between Xǔ and Gōng. As both of them were epistolary experts who appreciated each other's skill, in their correspondence they intentionally made use of many generic features of 'social' letter writing, hence the representative nature of these works.

Letter 13

Section 1

與冀未齋

客冬抱牘而來既費錦心
并飲珍饌別後馬首東指承歡匝
月即又束裝正擬探訪游蹤適秦
含章有札致弟道足下依紅仍舊
高山流水入耳同傾既非彈之不
調何必碎之遽去耶

New words/expressions

1. 費 (费) *fèi*: lit. 'cost'; here: to resort to the recipient's aid (deferential expression)

2. 錦心 (锦心) *jǐnxīn*: skilful thinking/advice (deferential epistolary form)

3. 珍饌 (珍馔) *zhēnzhuàn*: lit. 'treasure delicacy', that is wonderful delicacies (honorific epistolary form)

4. 馬首東指 (马首东指) *mǎshǒu-dōngzhǐ*: lit. 'the head of one's horse points East', that is to return home (idiomatic expression, see more below)

5. 承歡 (承欢) *chénghuān*: to do everything to please the parents; here: to stay with one's parents (deferential expression; here it refers to the author's mother due to the fact that at the time of this letter's writing the author's father was already deceased)

6. 匝月 *zāyuè*: a full month

7. 束裝 (束装) *shùzhuāng*: to pack up

8. 游蹤 (游踪) *yóuzōng*: the whereabouts of a traveller

9. 紅 (红) *gōng*: to labour

10. 仍舊 (仍旧) *réngjiù*: as before; here: the recipient's previous post

11. 高山流水 *gāoshān-liúshuǐ*: lit. 'high-mountain and flowing-water', that is to be close friends (idiomatic expression, see more below)

12. 入耳 *rù'ěr*: pleasant to listen to; here: to listen to one's advice

Proper names

1. 秦含章 Qín Hánzhāng: the details of his life are unknown

Translation

To Gōng Wèizhāi

This person in the winter [of the last year] took his official documents and visited you, and not only did I trouble you by asking your precious advice but also consumed your wonderful delicacies. When we parted I returned home and stayed with my mother for a month, and then I took my luggage [and returned to my post]. I was about to enquire as to your whereabouts when Qín Hánzhāng's letter came to this younger brother of yours, saying that you, sir, still work in your old [post]. As you have an excellent relationship [with your master], you listen to and admire each other and there is no disharmony between you, you have no reason to destroy [this joyous situation] by suddenly leaving your post.

Section 2

津鹽帶水驛使，時逢折柳贈梅勿虛，所望。

New words/expressions

1. 驛使 (驿使) *yìshǐ*: courier

2. 折柳 *zhéliǔ*: lit. 'to break [a branch of] willow', to send off a friend; here: to present the author with a letter (honorific epistolary form, see more below)

3. 贈梅 (赠梅) *zèngméi*: lit. 'to present [a branch of] plum', that is revered letter (honorific epistolary form, see more below)

Proper names

1. 津 Jīn: that is 天津 Tiānjīn

2. 鹽 (盐) Yán: that is 鹽山/盐山 Yánshān, a county in Héběi Province

Translation

[Our posts in] [Tiān]jīn and Yán[shān] [are only] belted [i.e. separated] by a river, official couriers [who go from one place to the other] frequently come, [and so I ask you to often] present me with your revered letters: do not make me wait in vain.

Brief overview

This brief work of Xǔ Jiācūn is a typical example for 'social letters', that is its primary goal is the enforcement of the relationship between the author and the recipient.

Rhetorical, pragmatic and sociocultural features

1. This letter has a simple chain of thought:

Section 1: Reference to the previous meeting of the author and the recipient → Description of the events that have taken place since the author and the recipient separated → Reference to Qín Hánzhāng's letter, which not only provided information about the recipient's whereabouts but also about his pleasant situation → Expression of the author's pleasure at this news.

Section 2: Description of the fact that the author and the recipient now work in bordering districts (due to the fact that the author was transferred to a new post, although this fact is not explicitly mentioned) → Request to the recipient to revive a frequent exchange of letters.

In spite of its simple chain of thought this letter is not easy to read. Although it does not include special concepts like the 'specialized' letters, the correct interpretation of this work requires some research into the circumstances of the author and recipient. For example, when describing the author's pleasant work situation, which was a pivotal issue for the group of Shàoxīng clerks, the author uses the idiomatic expression 高山流水 *gāoshān-liúshuǐ* (lit. 'high-mountain and flowing-water', that is to be close friends), without specifying the relationship itself; this expression can be interpreted only if one is aware that it refers to the recipient's service. A similar example can be found in the following section:

正擬探訪游蹤...

I was about to enquire as to your whereabouts . . .

If one reads this section without understanding the background (s)he may reach the conclusion that the recipient is on a long journey. However, this is not the case: in fact, the members of the Shàoxīng group often referred to themselves as 'travellers' in order to emphasize that they worked in distant posts, that is this is a group-specific terminology, and so 游蹤 *yóuzōng* (lit. 'the whereabouts of a *traveller*') refers simply to the whereabouts of the recipient without implying that he is on a real journey (this phenomenon also manifests itself in the author's self-reference as 客 *kè*, that is 'guest').

2. We have already seen that in Chinese letter writers often made use of idiomatic expressions; these expressions are particularly frequent in the works of expert letter writers, such as Xǔ Jiācūn and Gōng Wèizhāi, and so they are discussed in the present chapter. Idioms function in a similar way to historical references in that (i) they make analogy between an event in the past and a situation discussed in the letter, and (ii) their application presupposes a strong command of Classical Chinese literature. Yet, a unique feature of idiomatic expression is that they are lexicalized in a four-character unit form, and so it is relatively easy to identify them. On the other hand, idioms are more difficult than other references in that it is often impossible to interpret them without knowing their lexicalized meaning. If one comes across such expressions, the best option is to look them up in an idiom dictionary (成語辭典/成语词典 *chéngyǔ cídiǎn* in Chinese).

For example, the following two idioms, which occur in the present letter, do not make a sense in a word-by-word way:

(i) 馬首東指/马首东指 *mǎshǒu-dōngzhǐ* (lit. 'the head of horse points to East')

(ii) 高山流水 *gāoshān-liúshuǐ* (lit. 'high-mountain and flowing-water')

By means of specialized dictionaries it can be found that *mǎshǒu-dōngzhǐ* originates in the *Chronicle of Zuǒ* (左傳 *Zuǒ Zhuàn*; 襄公十四年 *Xiāng-gōng shísìnián, The 14th Year of Lord Xiāng* section), which contains the following section:

欒黶曰：「[…] 余馬首欲東。」乃歸。

Luán Yǎn said: "… The head of my horse wants [to go to] East." Then he returned home.

In later times, the idiom *mǎshǒu-dōngzhǐ* was derived from this section, and it became a synonym for 'returning home'.

Gāoshān-liúshuǐ (or *liúshuǐ-gāoshān*) originates in the Confucian philosophical work 列子 *Lièzǐ* (湯問/汤问 *Tāng-wèn*, *The Questions of Tāng*), which contains the following section:

伯牙鼓琴，志在登高山 [⋯] 志在流水

When Bó Yá plays on the zither he thinks of high mountains […] he thinks of flowing water.

In later texts the expression *gāoshān-liúshuǐ*, derived from this section, first meant 'beautiful musical composition', which is similar to 'high mountains and flowing water' and later it became a synonym for 'intimate friendship', which is similar to a 'beautiful musical composition'.

It should be noted that usually it is unnecessary to trace the background story of an idiomatic expression, that is it is enough only to check its lexical meaning in a dictionary.

3. Although in the previous chapters we have practiced reading unpunctuated texts, in the present chapter the main text occurs itself in unpunctuated form, for the first time, in order to aid the reader to develop the skill of reading non-edited letters. Therefore, it is necessary to address the method of working with unpunctuated texts. In fact, there is no perfect method to doing this: the best way is simply to translate as many unpunctuated letters as possible. Nevertheless, there are two literary principles that may aid the interpretation of such texts, even though they are not rules and they are not relevant to every text. The first principle is related to the *rhythm* of Classical Chinese prose: when writing letters (especially non-family 'social' ones that had a more formal style) the authors usually preferred using sentences of either four characters or characters of even number. The second principle is that historical Chinese authors preferred a *parallel prose style*, that is they often made subsequent sentences have equal length and to some extent related content (in many cases the parallel sentences even apply identical syntactic structures, as well as either resembling or intentionally contrasting lexical items). These principles make it somewhat easier to read unpunctuated texts; let us analyze, for example, the opening section of the present letter by means of this approach:

客冬抱牘而來既費錦心并飲珍饌別後馬首東指承歡
匝月即又束裝

Both of the above-mentioned principles manifest themselves in this section, in the following way:

客冬抱牘而來，既費錦心，并飲珍饌。
　　(6)　　　　　　(4)　　　　　　(4)

別後馬首東指，承歡匝月，即又束裝。
　　(4)　　　　　　(4)　　　　　　(6)

This person in the winter [of the last year] took his official documents and visited you, and not only did I trouble you by asking your precious advice but also consumed your wonderful delicacies.

When we parted I returned home and stayed with my mother for a month, and then I took my luggage [and returned to my post].

These two 'lines' (they are not distinct lines in the real text) narrate two temporally related events. Furthermore, these lines share an identical 'internal' symmetry, that is an introductory section of six characters narrate the main event, and the next two sections of four characters describe the event in detail.

4. Historical Chinese letters often make use of abbreviated toponyms, as in the case of 津鹽 Jīn-Yán (天津 Tiānjīn and 鹽山/盐山 Yánshān) in the present text. Abbreviations are particularly frequent when two toponyms occur together. Usually, it is easy to interpret such abbreviations by checking on the internet, as many of them exist in Modern Chinese.

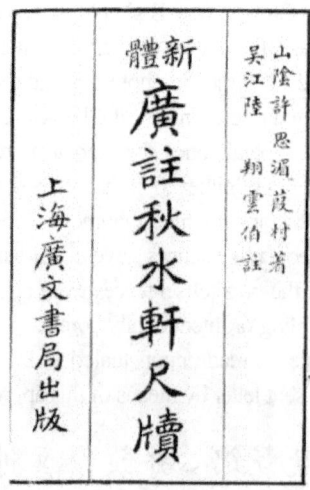

Illustration 2 Cover of a Republican Era edition of the *Qiūshuǐ-xuān chǐdú*

Letter 14

Section 1

與冀未齋（譽其待人之厚）

吾黨傾心丰采幾如士仰荊州平時嚮往

有心而天緣不假奉教無從今春因藹堂而得

見先生即荷忘年投分垂愛逾常頻飫郇氏之

廚屢醉公瑾之醴銘心若篆留齒猶芬兼以藹

堂之將入省也而假以一塵安其片席綢繆委

曲無微不至先生之愛人以德更於此想見一

斑矣

New words/expressions

1. 丰采/風采 (风采) *fēngcǎi*: elegant demeanour (elevating expression)

2. 嚮往/向往 *xiàngwǎng*: to long for

3. 有心 *yǒuxīn*: to be careful, to have a mind for; here: to gain the recipient's attention

4. 假 *jiǎ*: to provide (a chance)

5. 奉教 *fèngjiào*: to respectfully receive the recipient's instructions (honorific elevating form)

6. 無從 (无从) *wúcóng*: to be unable to obtain something

7. 荷 *hè*: to respectfully receive something (honorific epistolary expression)

8. 忘年投分 *wàngnián-tóufèn*: a great friendship that ignores age and difference in rank (formulaic expression)

9. 垂愛 (垂爱) *chuí'ài*: lit. 'condescending love', that is tender care (honorific recipient-elevating form)

10. 逾常 *yúcháng*: unusual

11. 屢 (屡) *lǚ*: repeatedly

12. 醴 *lǐ*: sweet wine (archaic expression)

13. 銘心若篆 *míngxīn-ruò-zhuàn*: (the gratitude for the kindness of the recipient has been) inscribed in the author's heart as if it were sealed there (formulaic epistolary expression)

14. 廛 *chán*: lodging (archaic expression)

15. 片席 *piàn-xí*: a piece of mat; here: sleeping mat

16. 綢繆 (绸缪) *chóumóu*: to be sentimentally attached, here: to take care of someone

17. 委曲 *wěiqū*: lit. 'in every minute detail', with the greatest attention

18. 無微不至 (无微不至) *wúwēi-bùzhì*: meticulous, here: to meticulously take care of someone (idiomatic expression)

19. 想見一斑 (想见一斑) *xiǎngjiàn-yī-bān*: lit. 'to visualize [the leopard] from one spot', that is to understand a phenomenon from a sign (idiomatic expression, see more below)

Proper names

1. 荊州 Jīngzhōu: name of a district in Húběi Province; here: a historical reference to the renowned Táng Dynasty statesman and man of letters 韓愈/韩愈 Hán Yù (768–824); Hán was the magistrate of the Jīngzhōu District, hence this reference to him

2. 藹堂 (蔼堂) Ǎitáng: the details of his life are unknown

3. 郇氏 Xún-shì: Lord Xún, that is 韋陟封 (韦陟封) Wéi Zhìfēng (his exact dates are unknown), a renowned person of the Táng Dynasty who became famous for the delicious cuisine of his residence; Wéi was promoted to the rank of the Lord of Xún (郇公 Xún-gōng), and thus he is often referred to as Xún-shì (see more below)

4. 公瑾 Gōngjǐn: that is 周公瑾 Zhōu Gōngjǐn (175–210), or 周瑜 Zhōu Yú in his personal name, a famous military strategist; in historical Chinese texts Zhōu is often associated with drinking pleasant wine (see more below)

Translation

To Gōng Wèizhāi (eulogy of the magnanimous manner in which he treats others)

The way in which our circle admires your elegant demeanour seems to be akin to [the way in which] the scholars [of the Táng Dynasty] admired Hán Yù. Although I always dreamed of gaining your attention, destiny did not provide [a chance for us to meet], and thus I was unable to follow your instruction. But in the summer of this year Ăitáng introduced us [to each other], and I was favoured with your great friendship that ignores age and difference in rank, and also I was granted your extraordinarily tender care. Several times you invited me to eat myself full in your excellent kitchen and to get myself drunk in your venerable home, and the gratitude for your kindness has been inscribed into my heart as if it were sealed there and the fragrance [of those delicacies remains on] my teeth. Furthermore, when Ăitáng [and I] ventured into the provincial capital you even borrowed a lodging where we could lay out our mats: you treated us with the greatest attention and meticulously took care of us. The way in which you, sir, love others with virtue can be observed in these deeds [of yours].

Section 2

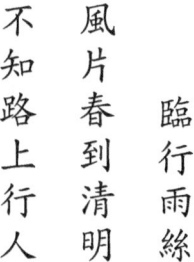

不　風
知　片
路　春
上　到　臨
行　清　行
人　明　雨
　　　　絲

殘梅雅興當復不淺也
琴裝已卸坐東閣而對
幾問杏花村酒想此日

New words/expressions

1. 雨絲風片 (雨丝风片) *yǔsī-fēngpiàn*: drizzling rain and light breeze (formulaic expression)

2. 杏花村 *xìnghuā-cūn*: lit. 'apricot-flower village', that is rustic tavern (see more below)

3. 琴裝 (琴裝) *qínzhuāng*: lit. 'zither dress', literary reference to one's travel garments

4. 卸 *xiè*: to remove (a cloth); to discharge; to unload

5. 東閣 (东阁) *dōnggé*: lit. 'eastern cabinet', that is guestroom

6. 殘梅 (残梅) *cánméi*: the falling petals of plum trees

7. 雅興 (雅兴) *yǎxìng*: enthusiasm in refined pursuits, aesthetic mood

Translation

When we parted the rain was drizzling and a light wind blew; now the spring came and the Tomb Sweeping Festival [was upon us], and I know not whether you, my ever-wandering friend have already been able to taste wine in rustic taverns? I imagine that today you have already changed your travel garments and are now sitting in your guestroom, looking on at the falling petals of plum trees, with deep and refined interest.

Section 3

弟以鳩心之拙謬作螳臂之當橐筆
素餐正與南郭先生齊門溷食應不免爲
當道所嗤惟望玉律之頒藉獲金針之度
則此感豈有既耶

New words/expressions

1. 鳩心 (鳩心) *jiūxīn*: lit. 'the mind of the turtledove', that is stupidity (the turtledove is associated with stupidity in traditional Chinese culture)

2. 螳臂之當 (螳臂之当) *tángbì-zhī-dāng*: lit. 'mantis arm task', a task that surpasses one's skill (see more below)

3. 橐筆 (橐笔) *tuóbǐ*: to make one's living as a clerk

4. 素餐 (素餐) *sùcān*: lit. 'vegetarian meal', here: 'undeserved meal' (deferential expression)

5. 當道 (当道) *dāngdào*: the authorities

6. 玉律 *yùlǜ*: lit. 'jade regulation', honourable letter (honorific elevating expression)

7. 頒 (颁) *bān*: lit. 'to issue a document' (by an authority), that is to send a letter (honorific addressee-elevating verbal form)

8. 金針之度 (金针之度) *jīnzhēn-zhī-dù*: 'the transmission of golden needle', to teach one the tricks of the trade (see more below)

9. 有既 *yǒujì*: to have limitations (here *jì* is a synonym for 盡/尽 *jìn*)

Proper names

1. 南郭先生 Nán'guō-xiānshēng: lit. 'South-wall-gentleman', that is the reclusive scholar of the Southern City wall (see more below)

Translation

This younger brother of yours has the clumsiness of a turtledove, and he erroneously undertakes his task that surpasses his ability, wielding the brush [the whole day] in order to earn his undeserved meal. I am indeed akin to the reclusive scholar of the Southern City wall who mingled [with the crowd of musicians] in the gate of Qí [Kingdom in order to] earn a living, and who could finally not avoid becoming a laughing stock of the authorities. I only hope that you will condescend to send me your honourable letter, and thus I will be able to obtain your teaching [as regards how to improve myself]; my gratitude for this will be boundless.

Section 4

阮昔侯於廿一日赴磁州破題兒第一夜鍾情如先生當亦爲之黯然也

New words/expressions

1. 破題兒 (破題儿) *pòtí'er*: lit. 'the opening sentence of an examination essay', that is the first ... (epistolary expression)

2. 鍾情 (钟情) *zhōngqíng*: affectionate; to fall in love

3. 黯然 *ànrán*: dejection, dejected

Proper names

1. 阮昔侯 Ruǎn Xīhóu: (his exact dates are unknown) a younger protégé of the author and Gōng Wèizhāi who also worked as an office assistant

2. 磁州 Cízhōu: name of a county in Héběi Province

Translation

On the 21st day Ruǎn Xīhóu left for [his post at] Cízhōu. He spent the first night [faraway from his wife], and his deep affection should be akin to that of yours, sir – I feel dejection for him.

Brief overview

This is one of the first letters within the correspondence of Xǔ Jiācūn and Gōng Wèizhāi. In a similar way to the previous letter, the present work, written during the early phase of the friendship between Xǔ and Gōng, is a 'social letter'. It is a rather long work that addresses different topics, and from the perspective of the student of letter writing it is noteworthy because it represents quite a few special literary and rhetorical elements typical to historical Chinese non-family private letters (see more below).

Rhetorical, pragmatic and sociocultural features

1. This long letter has a relatively complex chain of thought:

Section 1: Praising the recipient's character → Reference to the first meeting of the author and the recipient → Description of the recipient's kindness towards the author and his friend.

Section 2: Reference to the author's parting from the recipient and the long period that has passed since then (indirect expression of the author's longing for the recipient) → Literary enquiry about the recipient's well-being → Imaginary positive description of the way in which the recipient spends his time while the author is writing the present letter.

Section 3: Complaint for and description of the author's lack of ability → This inability will unavoidably make him subject of the disdain of his principal(s) → The only way to escape from this unfortunate situation is to initiate an active correspondence with the recipient and thus obtain his advice (indirect symbolic request to the recipient).

Section 4: Reference to Ruǎn Xīhóu, the protégé of the author and the recipient → Description of Ruǎn's affection that seems to be equally deep as that of the recipient → Expression of the author's empathy for Ruǎn's situation (indirect enforcement of his friendship towards the recipient).

The perhaps most difficult aspect of this chain of thought is the relationship between (i) Sections 1–2 and Section 3, and (ii) Section 3 and 4. In fact, Sections 1–2 and Section 3 are closely linked: Sections 1 and 2 reinforce the existing friendship between the author and the recipient by first emphasizing the recipient's kind behaviour towards the author and then praising the recipient, and Section 3 calls for the further strengthening of this friendship though an active exchange of letters and the recipient's teaching of the author. Section 4 is more loosely linked to the previous sections, and seemingly it discusses a different issue: the situation of a protégé of the author and the recipient. However, this section has its own important role in this 'social letter' because it further strengthens the ties between the author and the recipient.

2. As mentioned above, the present letter represents some literary and rhetorical tools that are particularly frequent in the 'social' letters of epistolary experts such as Xǔ. In what follows, let us briefly introduce these tools:

(i) *Altered idiomatic expressions*: As the previous texts of this book might already have suggested, idiomatic expressions are frequently applied tools in Chinese letters: by using such expressions the author has an opportunity to demonstrate his skill in Classical Chinese literacy and he can also 'invite' the recipient to join him in a literary exchange, that is to use such forms in his letter of response. Further, such forms are pivotal rhetorical tools, due to the fact that they connect a certain situation in the past and another in the present; considering the Chinese's respect for old persons and deeds, the frequency of these expressions in epistolary rhetoric – in particular as forms of expression deferential elevation/denigration – is quite understandable. However, as a matter of fact, in Chinese letters idioms also occur in altered forms, that is some authors made changes to their generally accepted lexicalized forms. Although these new forms differed from the 'normal' ones, for well-educated readers, they must have been recognizable. Supposedly, the main reason for creating such forms was that they provided a better opportunity to authors to involve the recipients in the above-mentioned literary 'game'.

In the present letter, the following altered idiomatic expressions can be found:

(a) 想見一斑 *xiǎngjiàn-yī-bān* (lit. 'to visualize [the leopard] from one spot', that is to understand a phenomenon from a sign) in Section 1: this is a slightly altered version of the idiom 略見一斑 *lüèjiàn-yī-bān*;

(b) 螳臂之當 *tángbì-zhī-dāng* (lit. 'mantis arm task', a task that surpasses one's skill) in Section 3: this has been derived from 螳臂當車 *tángbì-dāng-chē* ('to overrate oneself as a mantis who tries to stop a chariot');

(c) 金針之度 *jīnzhēn-zhī-dù* ('the transmission of golden needle', to teach one the tricks of the trade) in Section 3: the original version of this expression is 金針度人 *jīnzhēn-dù-rén* ('the golden needle is transmitted to someone').

(ii) *Conventional references*: As previously discussed in this book, historical Chinese authors often make references to historical and legendary persons and stories in order to draw some kind of analogy between historical men and events and current ones. While many such analogies were drawn by the authors individually, in non-family letter writing there is a core group of analogies, which frequently occur in Chinese letters. Thus, such conventional references function in a similar way to idiomatic expressions that express the elevation of the recipient and the denigration of the author, even though they are not lexicalized.

In the present letter the following 'conventional references' occur:

(a) In Section 1 the author refers to the renowned statesman 韓愈 Hán Yù as 荆州 Jīngzhōu, which is the name of the district where he served. The comparison of the recipient with Hán Yù (and other literati of the Táng and Sòng Dynasties such as 杜甫 Dù Fǔ) is a common way to elevate the recipient;

(b) In Section 1 the author refers to 韋陟封 Wéi Zhìfēng, in order to deferentially describe the recipient's hospitality; 郇氏之廚 (厨) Xún-shì-*zhī-chú* ('the kitchen of Lord Xún') is a conventional deferential elevating reference in Chinese letters (it elevates the recipient's hospitality);

(c) A little bit more complex, but still rather conventional, historical reference is 醉公瑾之醴 *zuì* Gōngjǐn-*zhī-lǐ* (lit. 'to get drunk on the sweet wine of Gōngjǐn', that is 'to get drunk in your venerable home'). This section refers to the following historical event: 周瑜 Zhōu Yú was an outstanding strategist and everyone respected him except 程普 Chéng Pǔ (his exact dates are unknown) who was irritated, at first, at having to serve under such a young commander. However, Chéng was soon amazed by Zhōu's talent and said the following words:

與周公瑾交，如飲醇醪，不覺自醉。

Being a friend of Zhōu Gōngjǐn is like drinking strong wine, you will unknowingly become drunk.

In later texts, Zhōu is associated with 'good/strong wine', and in the present text the author conventionally describes his drinking with the recipient by referring to this story, in order to draw an analogy between the recipient and Zhōu and thus convey deference;

(d) In Section 3 the author applies the conventional reference 南郭先生 Nán'guō-xiānshēng (lit. 'South-wall-gentleman', that is the reclusive scholar of the Southern City wall) in order to denigrate himself. This reference originates in the Legalist philosopher 韓非 Hán Fēi's (280–233 BC) work 韓非子 *Hán Fēizi* (內儲說上 *Nèichǔ-shuō-shàng, Inner Congeries, 1st part*). According to this story, King Xuān (宣王 Xuān wáng, r. 319–301 BC) of the ancient 齊 Qí State loved the music of the flute (竽 yú), and so kept 300 hundred musicians in his court. One of them, 'the reclusive scholar of the Southern City Wall', could not play the flute but managed to get himself mingled in the crowd and nobody noticed his lack of talent, while he enjoyed all the benefits that the king gave to the musicians. After the death of the king his son who followed him on the throne tested the ability of the court musicians one by one. Fearful that his lack of talent would be exposed by the new king he escaped from the capital. Due to this background story, Nán'guō-xiānshēng is often used to denigrate one's own ability.

It should be noted that it is quite difficult to translate some of these conventional references, such as (c) above, to other languages, and when meeting such a diffi-cult-to-translate expression it is a reasonable approach to describe its content instead of translating it in a word-by-word manner.

(iii) *Emotive-imaginary descriptions*: Historical Chinese 'social' letters often make use of emotive descriptions of imaginary scenes, in order to reinforce the friendship between the author and the recipient by praising the latter. In the present letter, such emotive-imaginary descriptions occur in the following places:

(a) In Section 2 the author imagines the recipient "looking on at the falling petals of plum trees, with deep and refined interest";

(b) In Section 4 he makes an imagined comparison between the "deep affection" of the recipient and that of Ruǎn Xīhóu.

(iv) *Literary frame*: The label 'literary frame' means that expert letter writers, such as Xǔ, often made use of a certain literary work, such as a piece of poetry, in order to 'frame' a section of a letter or a whole text. That is, the author associates the theme of a letter with a certain literary work and applies several citations from, and references to, that work in the course of the discussion.

In order to illustrate this relatively complex method, let us have a look at Section 2 where Xǔ Jiācūn applies a 'literary frame' in relation to his parting from Gōng Wèizhāi. The central theme of this section is that a long time has passed since the author and the recipient have been parted, and now the celebration of the Qīngmíng Festival has arrived. Here Xǔ makes use of a renowned poem, 杏花村 *Xìnghuā-cūn* (*Apricot Flower Village*), written by 杜牧 Dù Mù (803–852), which reads as follows:

清明時節雨紛紛，
路上行人欲斷魂。
借問酒家何處有？
牧童遙指杏花村。

A drizzling rain falls like tears on the Qīngmíng Day;
The traveller's heart is breaking on his way.
Where can a wine house be found to drown my sadness?
A cowherd points to Apricot Flower Village in the distance.

Section 2 contains citations from, and references to, this poem. The author refers to Gōng as 路上行人 *lùshàng-xíng-rén* (lit. 'traveller on the road', that is you, my ever-wandering friend); this is a skilful citation because it also connects the recipient's person with the Shàoxīng-circle (cf. the previous letter). Furthermore, the author uses 杏花村 *xìnghuā-cūn*, the title of the poem, as a literary synonym for 'rustic tavern'. Along with citations, a reference is also made to the poem in the opening sentence

臨行雨絲風片。

When we parted the rain was drizzling and a light wind blew.

As this sentence is somewhat different from the first line of the poem, it is a reference to and not a citation from the poem.

It should be noted that although such 'literary frames' might be rather complex, usually it is unnecessary to find and analyze them. Nevertheless, in some cases, such as the expression 杏花村 *xìnghuā-cūn* that otherwise would not make a sense, it is necessary to analyze the 'literary frame' applied in the given letter.

Letter 15

Section 1

挚

時而不憐然憐於跡究不若憐於心者爲尤

也弟謂同志者或有時而不求同病者則無

同志則相求同病則相憐此人之情

慰龔未齋喪妾并答遲慰

New words/expressions

1.　挚 (摯) *zhì*: sincere; true

Translation

Consoling Gōng Wèizhāi for the loss of his concubine and explaining my delay in writing correspondence

[Those who have] the same aspirations [should] help each other; [others who suffer from] the same illness [should] feel compassion for each other: this is a [basic] rationale for humans. This younger brother of yours believes that those who have the same aspirations in fact often do not help one another, but those who are [grieved by] the same illness unavoidably feel mutual pity. Yet, the outward demonstration of compassion is not akin to the compassion from one's heart, which is more sincere.

Section 2

弟自去秋失恃踉蹌而來冬杪於冰
天雪地中捧檄赴都途次為風寒所感歸而
病竟不止履端後三日仍腹藥閱今一載日
與倉公扁鵲為友又不能舍此毛錐靜加攝
養每念疾苦竊自憐之

New words/expressions

1. 失恃 *shīshì*: to be bereaved of one's mother

2. 踉蹌 *liàngqiàng*: to stagger

3. 杪 *miǎo*: the end of a season or a month; tip of a twig

4. 冰天雪地 *bīngtiān-xuědì*: lit. 'icy sky and snowy earth', ice and snow as far as the eye can see (idiomatic expression)

5. 捧檄 *pěngxí*: to receive orders and take up one's post

6. 履端 *lǚduān*: the 1st Day of the First Lunar Month

7. 舍/捨 *shě*: to abandon

8. 毛錐 (毛锥) *máozhuī*: writing brush

9. 攝養 (摄养) *shèyăng*: to conserve one's health

Proper names

1. 倉公 (仓公) Cāng-gōng: 'Lord Cāng', that is 倉淳于 Cāng Chúnyú (*c*.205 BC–*c*.140 BC), a renowned physician; here his name functions as a literary reference to 'physicians'

2. 扁鵲 (扁鹊) Biăn Què: the respect-name of the famous physician 秦越人 Qín Yuèrén (*c*. the 5 BC); a literary reference to 'physicians'

Translation

This younger brother of yours was bereaved of his mother in the last autumn and came [hither to the North] staggering [from the pain]. [That was] the end of the winter when the air was ice cold and the ground was covered with snow, but I received an official order to proceed to the capital and take up my post, and during the journey I suffered from the wind and cold and when I finally returned I fell into an illness, which did not cease. When three days passed after the New Year I was still taking medicine, and although thus far one year has passed, I still visit the physicians daily. However, I cannot abandon my writing brush [as I must earn my living], and I silently try to keep fit, and whenever I remember my hardships I secretly feel pity for myself.

Section 3

春間足下病繼又聞

失寵得耗之下爲足下憐

更有甚於爲己憐者蓋足下

年居賜鳩非人不適何意好

花易落好月難圓傷桃葉之

遽摧感朝雲之長逝情之所

至其何能堪況值衰病相侵衾裯半冷噓

寒問燠誰與爲懽此尤足下所悲從中來

不堪回首者每欲致書慰問恐足下當頤

養之時處煩惱之境一紙相投徒亂心曲

故未致尺書於左右此正弟之略於跡而

憐於心也

New words/expressions

1. 耗 *hào*: bad news

2. 賜鳩 (赐鸠) *cìjiū*: lit. 'to grant turtledove', epistolary synonym for one's seventieth year

3. 非人 *fēi-rén*: here: to lack anyone who would look after the recipient

4. 花易落 *huā-yìluò*: lit. 'the flowers easily fall', emotive reference to one's declining years

5. 月難圓 (月难圆) *yuè-nányuán*: lit. 'the moon cannot become round', its meaning is identical with that of the previous expression

6. 遽摧 *jùcuī*: sudden death

7. 衾裯 *qīnchóu*: coverlets and sheets

8. 噓寒問燠 (嘘寒问燠) *xūhán-wènyù*: a slightly altered version of the idiom 嘘寒問暖 *xūhán-wènnuǎn*, that is to enquire after someone's well-being

9. 懽 *huān*: a variant of 歡/欢 *huān* ('to like something')

10. 悲從中來 (悲从中来) *bēi-cóng-zhōng-lái*: to be overcome by grief (formulaic expression)

11. 頤養 (颐养) *yíyǎng*: to keep fit

12. 心曲 *xīnqǔ*: one's mind

Proper names

1. 桃葉 (桃叶) Táoyè: 'Peach Leaf' (her exact dates are unknown), the beautiful and charming concubine of the famous calligrapher 王獻之/王献之 (344–386)

2. 朝雲 (朝云) Cháoyún: 'Morning Cloud', that is 王子霞 Wáng Zǐxiá (?–1096), the beautiful concubine of the poet 蘇東坡/苏东坡 Sū Dōngpō (1031–1101)

Translation

I heard that during the spring you, sir, fell ill, and then lost your concubine. Although upon hearing this terrible news I felt compassion for you, sir, even more I grieved for myself. You, sir, already passed your seventieth year, with no one looking after you and feeling unhealthy – why would you like [old age, which is similar to] flowers that are about to fall and a moon that cannot become full? Furthermore, you were injured and grieved by the sudden death [of your concubine who was as graceful as] Táoyè and Cháoyún [of old]. You suffered from illness and old age at the same time, your coverlets and sheets were cold [after the demise of your concubine], and [many people came] to inquire after your health: who would be happy after this? Such [inquiries] must have made you, sir, all the more overcome with grief, so much so that you may not be able to bear to recall them. Therefore, whenever I thought to send you a letter in order to convey my sympathy, I was afraid that if my letter should arrive at a time when you, sir, should take care of keeping fit and are in a vexed state, it would cause confusion in your heart. Thus, I did not send you a letter, sir, as I [may appear] negligent on the surface but feel compassion for you in my heart.

Section 4

來書以弟無一函致慰謂是愛之乎怒之乎
弟竊以爲子言過矣夫君子有自反之道無求人
之理愛之怒之雖在人而所致愛致怒則在我我
而可愛人必愛之我而可怒人必怒之弟與足下
相印以心相要以久愛之不暇怒於何來禮曰君
子之交淡以成弟之所以落落者竊有味乎淡交
之義而欲自附於君子之未也

New words/expressions

1. 相印 *xiāngyìn*: to fit each other

2. 相要 *xiāngyào*: to be engaged in friendship

3. 落落 *luòluò*: aloof

4. 竊 (窃) *qiè*: in my humble opinion … (deferential form used before expressing one's opinion)

Translation

In your letter you asked this younger brother of yours whether he chose not to send a letter of consolation out of love for, or anger at, yourself. This younger brother of yours

Historical Chinese Letter Writing

privately suspects that your words, Master, are erroneous [this time]. A gentleman should possess the ability of self-examination, and he should not ask explanation from others. Love and anger reside in others, but that which makes others love or hate us resides in ourselves: if I am to be loved others will love me, but if I am to be hated others will hate me. This younger brother of yours and yourself, sir, possess hearts that match completely; we have been friends for many years, and have loved each other continuously – from whence should anger arise? The *Book of Rites* says that "friendship between noble men succeeds by being exempt from sweetness." This younger brother of yours humbly believes that his aloof [behaviour] is noble, [it is] the cornerstone of relationships that are free of over-sentimentality, thus he tries to humbly follow [the ideal of being a] noble-man.

Section 5

尺牘心折已久付之梨棗定當
紙貴一時以弟譾陋無文亦蒙採入
恐因魚目而減夜光之價削而去之
則為我藏拙多矣

New words/expressions

1. 尺牘 (尺牍) *chǐdú*: letter (usually describes edited letters)

2. 心折 *xīnzhé*: to greatly admire

3. 付 *fù*: to give/pay something; here: to submit a manuscript for printing

4. 梨棗 (梨枣) *lízǎo*: lit. 'pear and date', that is printing blocks (traditionally made of pear and date), a synonym for 'printing'

5. 紙貴 (纸贵) *zhǐguì*: a work being widely popular

6. 譾陋 (谫陋) *jiǎnlòu*: shallow and ignorant (honorific self-denigrating form)

7. 無文 (无文) *wúwén*: to lack literary talent (often expresses self-denigration)

8. 魚目 (鱼目) *yúmù*: lit. 'fish eye', fake pearl

9. 夜光 *yèguāng*: a type of real pearl

10. 藏拙 *cángzhuō*: to hide one's inadequacy (honorific self-denigrating verbal form)

Translation

I have sincerely admired your epistles for a long time. Now you have submitted them for publication, and the time will come when they will be appreciated far and wide. But you also want to include the shallow, ignorant and artless [letters] of this younger brother of yours in [the volume], and I am afraid that they will be like fake pearls that decrease the value of real ones. You [should] cut them out and get rid of them, [acting] thus [you would aid me] greatly by hiding my inadequacy.

Brief overview

The present letter was written when Gōng Wèizhāi lost his concubine. As becomes evident from the correspondence between Xŭ and Gōng, as well as some other letters of Gōng, this was a great loss for Gōng, not only because he loved his concubine but also because he married her quite late with the hope that she would give birth to an heir (Gōng's marriage was childless). The present letter is interesting because it represents a case when a non-family 'social' letter has different themes: (i) to console the recipient, (ii) to explain the author's delay in writing, and (iii) to politely decline the recipient's invitation to publish the author's letters (such a refusal was required according to the norms of historical Chinese politeness even if the author was about to accept the offer).

Rhetorical, pragmatic and sociocultural features

1. The present letter has the following complex chain of thought:

Section 1: Opening concept: people with same aspiration should help each other, and those who have the same problem should feel compassion for each other →

Although the former does not usually happen, the latter is a basic characteristic of humankind → Yet, superficial and real compassion are two different things.

Section 2: The author previously experienced great problems (the loss of his mother and a serious illness) → He is still suffering from the illness, which makes it difficult for him to continue his life as an office clerk, but he must work hard in order to earn his living (stereotypical complaint of the Shàoxīng circle) → The author feels pity for himself.

Section 3: Reference to the recipient's problems → The author feels strong compassion for the recipient, but he grieves for himself even more → The recipient suffered a great loss in the death of his concubine and also he suffers from illness in unpleasant circumstances → The recipient's situation is all the more unpleasant because many people disturb him by expressing their sympathy → The author did not want to join this group because he feels real compassion for the recipient, hence his delay in writing a letter of condolence.

Section 4: Intertextual reference to the recipient's letter in which he enquired about the author's delay in writing → Ritual-symbolic reprimanding of the recipient and a brief philosophical discussion on the way in which the recipient should regard such a behaviour → Confirmation of the author's friendship for the recipient → Explanation of the author's unique behaviour by arguing that such a seemingly standoffish and unusual behaviour is the manifestation of real friendship, and by acting thus the author only tries to follow the morale of the ancients.

Section 5: Implicit intertextual reference to a previous letter in which Gōng asked for Xǔ's letters (see Letter 16 in the following chapter), in order to include them in his collected letters → Polite claim that the author's letters are not worth printing.

A rhetorical feature of this letter that may be unusual for the reader is the way in which the author consoles the recipient in Section 3. The author not only states that although he feels compassion for the recipient he grieves for himself even more, but also he (over-)emphasizes the recipient's difficult situation. Obviously, in a modern Western context such rhetoric would not be the best way to console someone. However, in the author's rhetoric, and in the historical Chinese cultural context, making both of these points is important and effective for the following reasons:

(i)   By ritually claiming that he feels pity for himself the author reinforces that he and the recipient suffer from the same problems and thus his compassion is real rather than superficial;

(ii) By describing the recipient's problems in detail the author implicitly emphasizes that he completely understands and feels compassion for the recipient's problem, and also this description serves as an introduction to the argument regarding the author's delay in writing a letter of condolence.

2. In the present letter a phenomenon can be observed that could be defined as 'incorrect citation', which is rather frequent in historical Chinese 'social' letters. In Section 4 when describing his reason for behaving in a seemingly standoffish and cool manner, at odds with the norm, the author makes the following citation from the *Book of Rites* (禮記 *Lǐjì*), in order to demonstrate that his behaviour is proper:

禮曰：「君子之交淡以成。」

The *Book of Rites* says that "friendship between noble men succeeds by being exempt from sweetness."

However, this citation is incorrect, and the 表記 *Biǎojì* (*Record on Example*) chapter of the *Book of Rites* in fact contains the following section:

故君子之接如水，小人之接如醴。君子淡以成，小人甘以壞。

Therefore the connection between noble men is [tasteless, that is aloof] like water, while that between worthless men is [sweet] like sweet liquor. [The friendship between] noble men will succeed through its aloofness and [that of] the worthless men will fail due to its sweetness.

The 'cited' text differs from the original source, and in fact it shows more resemblance with the following section of the Taoist Classic 莊子/庄子 *Zhuāngzǐ* (山木 *Shānmù* [*Mountains and Trees*] chapter):

且君子之交淡若水，小人之交甘若醴。君子淡以親，小人甘以絕。

The relationship between gentlemen is insipid as water; the relationship between worthless men is sweet as sweet wine. The noble men become friends due to being tasteless [i.e. aloof] and the worthless men spoil [their friendship] due to being sweet.

It is difficult to define the authors' reason for making such 'incorrect' citations, but they are probably products of literary freedom. In fact, one usually does not have to devote much attention to this issue, but it is important to be aware of the existence of this phenomenon as such 'citations' can cause problems if one wants to read them in their original context.

Further Reading

There has been no study published on the letters of Xǔ Jiācūn in English, although they are briefly discussed in the 'Introduction' of the work *Model Letters in Late Imperial China: 60 Selected Epistles from 'Letters from Snow Swan Retreat'* (2009, München/Newcastle, Lincom), written by the author of this book. In Chinese, a discussion on Xǔ's letters can be found in 趙樹功 Zhào Shùgōng's 中國尺牘文學史 *Zhōngguó chǐdú wénxuéshǐ* (*History of Chinese Epistolary Literature*, 1999, Shijiazhuang, 河北人民出版社 Hebei renmin chubanshe, 575–578), although this is a rather ideologized description as was mentioned in the 'Preface'.

For those who have interest in reading Xǔ's letters in Chinese the most reliable source is the 1985 edition of the work by 上海書店 Shanghai shudian (this is a joint edition of the works of Xǔ and Gōng). Another reliable source is 廣文書局 Guangwen shuju's (Taipei) 1994 edition.

More information on the Shàoxīng-circle is available in the monograph of Zhìyǒng Zhū 朱志勇 and Yǒngxīn Lǐ 李永鑫, 紹興師爺與中國幕府文化 *Shàoxīng shīye yǔ Zhōngguó mùfǔ wénhuà*, that is *The Shàoxīng Masters and the Chinese Office Assistant Culture* (1999, Beijing, 人民出版社 Renmin chubanshe).

Chapter 6

Non-family 'Social' Letter Writing II:
Letters of Gōng Wèizhāi 龔未齋

In this chapter we continue the study of historical Chinese non-family 'social' letters through the analysis of three letters written by 龔未齋/龚未寨 Gōng Wèizhāi (1738–1811; Gōng's personal name was 萼 È). Gōng, in a similar way to Xǔ Jiācūn, was one of the Shàoxīng literati who spent his life working in Northern China as an office clerk. Not much information is available about Gōng's life: he led the modest life of office clerks, and he was a kind of senior figure of the Shàoxīng circle, admired by his younger colleagues, such as Xǔ. However, even though Gōng is insignificant as a historical figure, within the field of Qīng Dynasty letter writing he is a considerably important author: although such a 'value' is unavoidably subjective, it can be argued that he was one of the best historical Chinese epistolary experts. His letters differ from that of ordinary expert letter writers: while epistolary experts, such as Xǔ, mastered all the stylistic and rhetorical requirements of letter writing, Gōng often went beyond these requirements, making considerable refinements, without becoming artificial or even too artistic. Due to this characteristic of his work, his letter collection 雪鴻軒尺牘/雪鸿轩尺牍 Xuěhóng-xuān chǐdú (*Letters from Snow Swan Retreat*) became one of the most renowned epistolary model books, and so his writings are useful for the present book to enquire into the refined features of 'social' letter writing, beyond what we have studied in the previous chapter.

In the present chapter we will study Gōng's three relatively brief letters, written to Xǔ Jiācūn. Despite the brevity of these works, they are not easy to read due to the fact that they apply a complex inventory of epistolary tools. These letters are interesting sources for the student of letter writing because they carry out discussion on epistolary art. In fact, the topic of letter writing occurs in each of these works and in the discussions of Letter 17 and, in particular, 18, it becomes a central notion; thus, these letters show the way in which epistolary experts treated this art. It should be noted, however, that these are not 'specialized' but 'social' letters, that is the discussion on epistolary arts has a practical purpose, namely, the enforcement of the relationship between the author and the recipient.

Letter 16

Section 1

與許葭村

病後正不能搦管而一息尚存又未敢與草木
同腐平時偶作詩詞祇堪覆瓿惟三十餘年客窗酬
應之札自攄胸膈暢所欲言雖於尺牘之道去之千
里而性情所寄似有不忍棄者遂於病後錄而集之
内中惟僕與足下酬答爲獨多惜足下鴻篇短製爲
愛者攜去僅存四六一函錄之於集借美玉之光以
輝燕石并欲使後之覽者知僕與足下乃文字之交
非勢利交也

New words/expressions

1. 搦管 *nuòguǎn*: lit. 'grasping the stalk [of writing brush]', to take up the brush and write (literary synonym for 'writing correspondence')

2. 一息尚存 *yī-xī-shàng-cún*: as long as one still has breath left within him (idiomatic expression)

3. 覆瓿 *fùbù*: lit. (a writing can only be used) to cover the jars (in which men store sauces), that is one's writing is worthless (honorific self-denigrating expression)

4. 客窗 (客窗) *kèchuāng*: lit. 'window of an inn', here: in service far from home

5. 酬應 (酬应) *chóuyìng*: to socialize with; 酬應之札 *chóuyìng-zhī-zhá* means private correspondence

6. 攄 (抒) *shū*: to express

7. 胸膈 *xiōnggé*: feelings

8. 暢所欲言 (畅所欲言) *chàng-suǒ-yù-yán*: lit. '[speaking] freely what one wants to say', that is narrating one's feelings with artless words (idiomatic expression)

9. 酬答 *chóudá*: letter of exchange/response

10. 鴻篇短製 (鸿篇短制) *hóngpiān-duǎnzhì*: lit. 'wild goose essay, short work', outstanding letters of various length (honorific addressee-elevating form; 鴻 *hóng* is often used in honorific expressions: wild goose is a 'large' bird, and so *hóng* becomes a synonym for 'greatness')

11. 四六 *sì-liù*: lit. 'four-six', that is letter written in a traditional prosaic style (having four and six character-long sections)

12. 美玉 *měiyù*: lit. 'fine jade', refined works (honorific elevating form)

13. 燕石 *yānshí*: lit. 'stone of Yān[shān]', that is fake gem, here: worthless collection (rarely applied self-denigrating form, see more below)

14. 文字之交 *wénzì-zhī-jiāo*: literary friendship (formulaic expression)

15. 勢利 (势利) *shìlì*: snobbish and greedy

Translation

To Xǔ Jiācūn

During my convalescence I was unable to take up my brush and write. Yet, as long as I still have breath left within me [I will not] die slowly in the manner of plants [i.e. without leaving anything behind]. The poetic and lyrical works that I have casually written during my life are worthless. Nevertheless, for more than thirty years, in service far from home, I [have written extensive] private correspondence in which I narrated my feelings with artless words. Although these writings are a thousand miles distant from what one would call the 'art of letter writing', they record my various dispositions, and I feel reluctant to throw them away. Therefore, after recovering from my illness I have copied and collected my correspondence. Within my correspondence, letters of exchange between this humble servant and yourself, sir, are by far the most numerous. It is regretful to me, however, that most of your outstanding letters of various length have been taken away by [others who also] admire [your work], and I have only one letter written in traditional prose left, which I have copied into my collection. Thus, I would like to ask you, sir, to lend me [your refined works and let them illuminate my worthless collection], like shiny jades enlightening worthless stones. In this way the readers of my work will know that the relationship between you, sir, and my humble self is a true friendship between men of letters and not the snobbish and greedy connection [of some of the literati].

Section 2

許子之不憚煩也

以奉告容錄出一番另請教削知

因足下素有嗜痂之癖故書

New words/expressions

1. 嗜痂之癖 *shìjiā-zhī-pǐ*: 'addiction to eating scabs', that is eccentric taste (self-denigrating form, see more below)

2. 奉告 *fènggào*: lit. 'informing deferentially with two hands', to humbly inform (honorific verbal form)

3. 容 *róng*: to allow someone to do something (deferential epistolary verbal form)

4. 請教削 (请教削) *qǐng-jiàoxuē*: lit. 'asking teaching and cutting (errors)', to fulfil one's humble request to correcting a document (honorific verbal form)

5. 不憚煩 (不惮烦) *bù-dàn-fán*: to spare no effort

Proper names

1. 許子 (许子) Xǔzǐ: 'Master Xǔ', that is 許行/许行 Xǔ Xíng (his exact dates are unknown), an ancient Chinese thinker (see more below)

Translation

As I know sir that you have an eccentric taste [and find some pleasure in my badly written work] I write [the present letter] in order to humbly inform you about the matter [i.e. the author's plan to publish his work]. If you allow me to send a copy [of the work to you], and fulfil my humble request by correcting it, I will know that you, sir, like Master Xǔ of old, do not try to spare yourself effort.

Brief overview

This letter, written after the illness of Gōng Wèizhāi (cf. Letter 15 in the previous chapter), is an important source for scholars with interest in Gōng's life because it records Gōng's plan to publish *Letters from Snow Swan Retreat*. Although it is a relatively brief work, it contains several noteworthy stylistic and rhetorical elements that are typical to Gōng Wèizhāi's letters (see more below).

Rhetorical, pragmatic and sociocultural features

1. This letter has the following chain of thought:

Section 1: Reference to the author's illness (indirect explanation for the delay in writing to the recipient) → Expression of the author's wish to leave something behind (introduction of the main theme) → Claim that the author is not skilful at writing poetry (one of the most important genres for historical Chinese literati) → On the other hand, he is an experienced letter writer and has saved (copies of) the letters that he wrote during his lifetime → Polite claim that these letters are of low quality but the author is attached to them, hence his goal to publish them in a collected form → Request for the recipient to lend his letters written to the author and thus the author will be able to publish them with his own letters.

Section 2: Polite denigration of the author's skill as a letter writer → Request for the recipient to read and evaluate the author's selected letters before they go to print.

Although this is a relatively brief letter, it has two objectives. Section 1 informs the recipient about the author's decision to publish the *Letters from Snow Swan Retreat* and requests the recipient to lend his letters, and Section 2 requests the recipient to review the manuscript. The first request is probably symbolic, not only because usually edited collections of letters did not include the works of other authors, but also because the manuscript of the *Letters from Snow Swan Retreat* was ready at the time of this letter as it becomes evident from the text. Thus, the 'real' request of this letter is made in Section 2.

2. It is a typical feature of Gōng Wèizhāi's 'social' letters that they frequently make use of different 'unusual' self-denigrating and recipient-elevating expressions. The label 'unusual' means that these expressions are somewhat unconventional as deferential forms. In the present letter, examples include 燕石 *yānshí* (lit. 'stone of Mountain Yān', that is 'a fake stone') and 嗜痂之癖 *shìjiā-zhī-pǐ* (lit. 'addiction to eating scabs', that is eccentric taste). The former one originates in the 51st (闞子 *Kànzǐ, Master Kàn*) chapter of the Sòng Dynasty encyclopaedia 太平御覽/太平御览 *Tàipíng-yùlǎn* (*Imperial Reading of the Tàipíng Era*), in which a crazy man finds a worthless stone that looks like a jade (this jade-like stone is called *yānshí* in the source) and he appreciates it very much; when warned by a guest that the stone is not worth more than ordinary tiles and bricks, he becomes furious and assiduously guards the stone thereafter. In later texts, *yānshí* became a literary synonym for worthless items, but it is quite rare that it is used in a self-denigrating sense. It should be noted that the author's use of this expression is noteworthy because it is used in a semantic parallel with the deferential recipient-elevating form 美玉 *měiyù* ('fine jade', your refined works).

The second expression *shìjiā-zhī-pǐ* originates in the 42nd chapter (劉穆之傳/刘穆之传 *Liú Mùzhī zhuàn, The Biography of Liú Mùzhī*) of the 宋書 *Sòngshū* (*History of the Southern Sòng Dynasty*), which records the following anecdote about 邕 Yōng (his dates of life are unknown), son of the man of letters Liú Mùzhī 劉穆之 (?–419):

邕性嗜食瘡痂，以爲味似鰒魚。

> Yōng's addiction was to eat his own scabs: he argued that their taste was like that of the abalone.

In later texts *shìjiā-zhī-pǐ* often occurs as a literary synonym for 'depraved taste' but it rarely occurs in honorific contexts.

3. Wordplay is a rhetorical tool of 'social letters', which is particularly frequent in Gōng Wèizhāi's letters. In the present letter, an example for wordplays is the closing section:

知許子之不憚煩也。

I will know that you, sir, like Master Xǔ of old, do not try to spare yourself effort.

Here the author makes a literary reference to *Mencius* (滕文公上 *Téng Wén-gōng shàng*, *Duke Wén of Téng, 1st part*, section 4), which contains the following section:

何爲紛紛然與百工交易？何許子之不憚煩？

[Mencius said:] 'Why does he [i.e. 許行 Xǔ Xíng] have a confusing exchange with the craftsmen? Why does he not try to spare himself effort?

Here the author makes an implicit playful analogy between Xǔ Xíng of old and the recipient Xǔ Jiācūn, who both have the family name Xǔ 許.

Interpreting such wordplay can be rather problematic, even though they are important parts of the inventory of 'social' letters. Although there is no definite way to deal with wordplay, a point that may help is that many of them are frequently based on personal names.

Letter 17

Section 1

答許葭村

登堂望遠極目蒼涼正

切秋水伊人之想適接瑤章如

同晤對即滿浮三大白不負茱

萸令節也

New words/expressions

1. 極目 (极目) *jímù*: as far as the eye can see

2. 蒼涼 (苍凉) *cāngliáng*: desolation

3. 秋水伊人 *qiūshuǐ-yīrén*: to be reminded of an old friend by the autumn scenery (see more below)

4. 瑤章 (瑶章) *yáozhāng*: lit. 'fine jade writing', esteemed letter (honorific elevating form)

5. 滿浮 (满浮) *mǎnfú*: to empty a full cup with one swallow

6. 大白 *dàbái*: a full cup of wine

Proper names

1. 茱萸 Zhūyú: lit. *Cornus officialis* or 'Dogwood'; it is a literary reference to the Double Ninth Festival or 重九 *Chóngjiǔ*, when the Chinese climb high mountains, drink chrysanthemum wine and wear the *zhūyú* plant in order to purify themselves

Translation

Reply to Xǔ Jiācūn

I ascended to the great hall [of our tribunal] and looked upon the horizon: I beheld desolation as far as the eye could see. This autumn scene stirred in me a longing for you, my old friend. Yet, your esteemed letter reached me at this time, and reading it was like meeting you in person. [My spirits were buoyed] and I decided after all not to defy the Double Ninth Festival, and I drank three large cups of wine, each with one swallow.

Section 2

并發縱倚馬　地而又百函　應酬最繁之　足下處

之才無難揮灑而中書君
疲於奔走將有未老先生
禿之慮相知以心初不以
筆墨間課疏密也

New words/expressions

1. 應酬 (应酬) *yìngchou*: to have social intercourse, social appointments

2. 倚馬之才 (倚马之才) *yǐmǎ-zhī-cái*: lit. 'the talent of writing on a horse', that is to possess an outstanding literary talent, in a similar manner with the men of old who could write even while in the saddle (idiomatic expression)

3. 揮灑 (挥洒) *huīsǎ*: lit. 'to sprinkle', to write freely without any difficulty

4. 中書君 (中书君) *zhōng-shū-jūn*: a literary synonym for writing brush

5. 疏密 *shū-mì*: density

Translation

You, sir, are labouring in a bustling area [which necessitates] a great deal of administrative work, yet you find time to send me countless letters. However, even if [you possessed outstanding literary talent, akin to the men of old who could] write even while in the saddle, and could write letters without any difficulty [i.e. in a minute], I am much afraid that your brush would be tired from your swiftness and its hair would fall before it would become old [i.e. before its time]. We are true friends and we do not need to count [i.e. our bond does not depend on] the frequency of our correspondence.

Section 3

金粟如來墮落塵世爲聲色
香味觸法所擾久已拖泥帶水受
一切苦厄足下具大智慧早已觀
自在菩薩矣尚向舍利子求揭帝
之咒哉

New words/expressions

1. 墮落 (堕落) *duòluò*: a heavenly person being banished to a mundane place

2. 聲色香味 (声色香味) *shēngsè-xiāngwèi*: music, women and gluttony, that is worldly temptations (Buddhist term)

3. 觸法 (触法) *chùfǎ*: to break the law ('law' means here 'proper behaviour' or 'dharma')

4. 拖泥帶水 (拖泥带水) *tuōní-dàishuǐ*: to be muddled (formulaic expression)

5. 一切苦厄 *yīqiè-kǔ'è*: lit. 'an *aeon* of suffering', that is to suffer all manner of distress (see more below)

6. 揭帝之咒 *jiēdì-zhī-zhòu*: lit. 'the *mantra* of gate', here: your teaching (see more below)

Proper names

1. 金粟如來 Jīnsù-Rúlái: lit. 'Golden Grain Tathagata Buddha', that is Buddha

2. 觀自在菩薩 (观自在菩萨) Guānzìzài Púsà: Guānzìzài Bodhisattva, that is Avalokiteśvara or 觀音 (观音) Guānyīn Goddess of Mercy

3. 舍利子 Shèlìzǐ: Śariputra, a disciple of Buddha; in Chinese Buddhist texts Śariputra is often represented as an untalented disciple, and thus it functions as an honorific self-denigrating expression in the present text, hence its translation as 'stupid disciple' (see also below)

Translation

[I am like] a Buddha that was banished to this mundane world, and I grieve because I cannot follow the right path as it is strewn with worldly temptations – I have long been muddled and suffered all manner of distress. You have, sir, great wisdom, and long ago [became as perfect as] Guānyīn Bodhisattva. I wonder how long you will consent to enlighten me, your stupid disciple, with your teaching!

Brief overview

This brief work is a typical 'social' letter that serves the enforcement of social relationship between the correspondents: Gōng Wèizhāi praises Xǔ's epistolary skill, which would have been important to Xǔ who respected Gōng as an epistolary master, hence the social function of the text. In fact, the present letter is more significant than could be assumed from its content: it is one of the most perfectly written works of Gōng Wèizhāi, which contains noteworthy rhetorical elements (see more below).

Rhetorical, pragmatic and sociocultural features

1. This letter has a relatively simple chain of thought:

Section 1: Description of the author's longing for the recipient → Reference to the arrival of the recipient's letter, which made the author, thereby encouraging him, to celebrate the Double Ninth Festival.

Section 2: Appraisal of the recipient's skill as a letter writer → Symbolic request to the recipient that he should write less in order to avoid overwork → Reinforcement of the friendship between the author and the recipient.

Section 3: Description of the author's unfortunate situation (stereotypical complaint) → Appraisal of the recipient → Symbolic request for the recipient to give advice to the author on how to improve himself and find a way out of his unfortunate situation.

One issue that may cause difficulty for the reader is the role of the complaint in Section 3: the author's switch of topic seems to be random. However, this section has an important role in the conveyance of the 'social' message of this letter:

after praising the recipient in Section 2, the author in this section strengthens the bonds between the recipient and himself by symbolically requesting the recipient to suggest a way out of the unfortunate life of an office clerk. This is a conventional theme in the letters of the Shàoxīng literati, and in the present context it serves the reinforcement of the relationship between author and recipient by referring to their common background; furthermore, it provides an opportunity to the author to further praise the recipient as a person who is more skilful than himself.

2. In the previous chapter (Letter 14) we discussed the notion of 'literary frame'. Usually, these frames only manifest themselves in the citations and references made in brief sections of 'social' letters. However, in the works of expert letter writers, such as Gōng Wèizhāi, it is a frequent phenomenon that a frame determines the way in which a whole section/paragraph, or even the whole text, is phrased. In the case of such larger frames, it is usually necessary for the reader to become acquainted – at least to some extent – with the source referred to by the authors.

In the present text, such a major 'literary frame' can be observed in Section 3, which is centred on a Buddhist allegory. That is, the author uses different Buddhist terms and expressions, such as 觸法 *chùfǎ* ('to break the law'), cited from the famous Buddhist *Heart of Prajñā Pāramitā Sutra* (般若波羅蜜多心經/般若波罗蜜多心经 *Bānruò Bōluómìduō Xīnjīng*); also the rhetoric of this section is based on this work. In other words, this Sutra functions as a 'literary frame' for Section 3. Some of the expressions and names cited from the Sutra – such as 一切苦厄 *yīqiè-kǔ'è* (lit. 'an *aeon* of suffering', that is to suffer all manner of distress) and the elevating reference to the recipient as 觀自在菩薩 Guānzìzài Púsà (Guānzìzài Bodhisattva) – can be interpreted without familiarity with the original work. However, this literary frame also manifests itself in the specific way in which the author shapes some of his thoughts, and so some acquaintance with the original source is necessary in order to properly interpret this section; the most representative example for this is the last sentence of the letter:

尚向舍利子求「揭帝之咒」哉！

Still try [to teach] the '*mantra* of *gate*' to Śariputra! (word-by-word translation)

I wonder how long you will consent to enlighten me, your stupid disciple, with your teaching!

This sentence can be interpreted only if one is aware that in the Sutra Avalokiteśvara addresses Śariputra who was an ignorant disciple of Buddha;

furthermore, a central concept of the Sutra is the so-called *mantra* of *gate* (lit. 'gone'), which is a mystical syllable. Thus, in the present context, Śariputra functions as a self-denigrating expression (in contrast with Guānyīn, which functions as a recipient-elevating expression), and '*mantra* of *gate*' represents the recipient's tuition of the author.

3. In the previous letter we met the phenomenon of wordplay. While the wordplay studied previously was relatively simple, the present text contains a considerably more complex example. That is, in Section 1 the author uses 秋水伊人 *qiūshuǐ-yīrén* ('to be reminded of an old friend by the autumn scenery') in order to describe his longing for the recipient, and thus also to indirectly describes the recipient as his 'old friend'. *Qiūshuǐ-yīrén* is a literary reference to the 詩經 *Shījīng* or *Book of Odes* (I.11.129), which contains the following line:

所謂伊人，在水之涘。

The man of whom I think is on the bank of the river.

By using this popular literary expression the author makes a wordplay that cannot be properly translated: the expression *qiūshuǐ-yīrén*, word-by-word, is also an implicit reference to Xǔ whose studio name was 秋水軒 *Qiūshuǐ-xuān* ('Autumn Water Retreat').

In order to be able to interpret this type of more complex wordplay – which is nevertheless based on a name in a similar way to the previous one – it is useful to check the studio, literary, etc. names of the recipient and author of a letter. It is necessary to be aware that a historical Chinese person can have many names, such as school name, courtesy name, and different pseudonyms; most of these are usually included in biographical entries (if available) of specialized encyclopaedias.

4. We previously discussed the phenomenon that in historical Chinese letters addressee-elevation and self-denigration are often conveyed through the author's comparison of the recipient and himself to historical persons. In the present letter, a more complex version of this phenomenon can be observed, which could be labelled as 'implicit deferential historical reference'. When using such a reference, the author elevates the recipient and denigrates himself without explicitly naming the historical/legendary persons involved. Thus, the use of such a reference presupposes that the recipient has a strong command of Classical literacy.

In this letter, an example of 'implicit deferential historical reference' is 百函 并發 *bǎi-hán-bìng-fā* (lit. 'hundred letters are sent one after the other', trans. 'send me countless letters'), which is a reference to the 42nd chapter (劉穆之 傳 *Liú Mùzhī zhuàn, The Biography of Liú Mùzhī*) of the 宋書 *Sòngshū* (*His-*

tory of the Southern Sòng Dynasty), which remarks that the man of letters Liú Mùzhī (cf. the previous letter) had an outstanding skill in letter writing and once managed to write hundred letters in a half day:

自旦至日中，穆之得百函…

From dawn to noon Mùzhī wrote hundred letters . . .

By using this reference the author not only praises the skill of the recipient as a letter writer, but also implicitly compares him to a renowned historical epistolary expert, that is he implicitly elevates the recipient.

Although a letter can usually be correctly translated without identifying such implicit citations, it is necessary to be aware of their existence.

Letter 18

Section 1

答許葭村

陳遵尺牘名震當時然高自

位置惜墨如金不肯輕投一札足

下殆亦有此癖

New words/expressions

1. 輕投 (轻投) *qīngtóu*: lit. 'to send lightly', that is to send a letter when it is not necessary

2.   癖 *pǐ*: mania; here: conceit

Proper names

1.   陳遵/陈遵 Chén Zūn: (his exact dates are unknown) a Hàn Dynasty man of
     letters who became renowned for his great skill in letter writing; the 92nd
     chapter (陳遵傳/陈遵传 *Chén Zūn zhuàn, The Biography of Chén Zūn*) of
     the 漢書/汉书 *Hànshū* (*The History of the Western Hàn Dynasty*) contains
     the following passage that records Chén's skill in epistolary arts: 性善書，
     與人尺牘，主皆藏去以爲榮。 ('He was born with dexterity in letter writ-
     ing; people who received his letters carefully stored them with honour.')

Translation

Reply to Xǔ Jiācūn

Chén Zūn [of old] gained a great reputation among his generation [for his expertise in] letter writing. However, he formed an overtly high opinion of himself and
he spared his ink as if it were gold, unwilling to send a letter to anyone if it were
not necessary. [I wonder], sir, whether you are not on the brink of falling into
[the error of] his conceit?!

Section 2

之事得不易有之書也

今則喜若人巧爲其能以莫須有

能自惜其墨焉僕始怪若人之愚

足下忘其癖而洋洋焉灑灑焉不

今有人焉以莫須有之事使

New words/expressions

1. 莫須有 (莫须有) *mò-xū-yǒu*: lit. 'not-must-have', that is fabricated/unjust accusation (formulaic expression; see more below)

2. 洋洋灑灑 (洋洋洒洒) *yángyáng-săsă*: lit. 'voluminous and magnificent', abundant words and long lines (formulaic expression)

3. 若人 *ruòrén*: an imagined person

Translation

[Let us suppose that] there is a man who makes an unjust accusation [against you], which makes you, sir, forget your conceit and [reply to him with] abundant words and long lines, unable to spare your ink. Although in the beginning my humble self would be surprised at that supposed person's foolishness [for accusing you], later I would praise him for his wiliness in being able to elicit an otherwise unobtainable letter from you, by means of false accusation.

Section 3

而近亦因足下之書恍然得所解蓋
足下握三寸之管若決江河一波未平一
波復起跡之字裏行間則悄然無風也若
人之波不必欲有風而始起始見得足下
削簡之法乎使若人而見足下之書必且
詡然曰一枝未借尺璧先來失在彼而得
在此夫亦可無憾

New words/expressions

1. 三寸之管 *sān-cùn-zhī-guǎn*: lit. 'stalk of three inches', literary synonym for writing brush

2. 決 (决) *jué*: a river burst its banks

3. 字裏行間 (字里行间) *zìlǐ-hángjiān*: between the lines (formulaic expression); here: a synonym for 'letter'

4. 悄然 *qiǎorán*: quiet

5. 削簡 (削简) *xuējiǎn*: lit. 'cutting document', that is the art of letter writing (this expression originates in the ancient Chinese custom of carving letters into pieces of bamboo and wood, before the invention of paper)

6. 詡然 (诩然) *xǔrán*: joyously

7. 一枝 *yī-zhī*: lit. 'branch', a literary synonym for letter

8. 尺璧 *chǐbì*: lit. 'round flat piece of jade of one inch with hole in middle', that is precious jewel (deferential reference to the letter of the addressee)

Translation

Recently I observed your letters and suddenly understood [your reason for abstaining from writing correspondence]. When you, sir, grasp your writing brush [and compose a letter], [your talented words flow like] the flooding Yangtze or Yellow Rivers bursting their banks, the unceasing waves foaming one after another. Nevertheless, reading your letters one finds stillness. As the flow of your words is not induced by a windstorm, it becomes obvious that it is produced by your outstanding skill in the art of letter writing, sir. Now, should the supposed person receive and read your letter, he shall exclaim with pleasure: "My letter has not yet been sent, and I have already received such a precious jewel, [why should I reply to him?] He has incurred a loss and I have gained profit, who should feel regret for this?"

Section 4

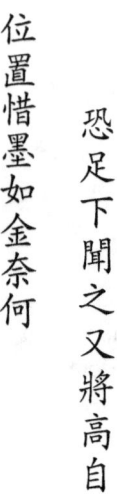

恐足下聞之又將高自位置惜墨如金奈何

Translation

I am afraid that when you, sir, hear these words you will form an overtly high opinion of yourself and spare your ink as if it were gold. But I can do naught against this!

Brief overview

This work belongs to a noteworthy group of Gōng Wèizhāi's letters, in which he focuses his discussion on the art of letter writing. These works are not 'specialized' letters due to the fact that they have definite social goals. For example, the present work is a eulogy in which Gōng acknowledges the expertise of his younger friend in the art of letter writing. It should be noted that along with its topic the present work is noteworthy also because it makes use of many difficult stylistic-rhetorical features (see more below).

Rhetorical, pragmatic and sociocultural features

1. This letter has the following chain of thought:

Section 1: The author makes a reference to the epistolary expert Chén Zūn and describes his behaviour (there is no historical evidence that Chén was indeed conceited, and so it can be supposed that this is a rhetorical exaggeration of the author) → He compares the recipient to Chén.

Section 2: Description of a hypothetical situation in which someone makes a false accusation in order to obtain a letter from the thus infuriated recipient → This would be a clever move because in this way that person could obtain a letter from the recipient.

Section 3: The author politely claims that the recipient's reason for being reluctant to write letters is that he is greatly talented and so he is afraid that if he writes to another person, that man will not answer his letter as he has already obtained his precious letter and thus gained 'profit'.

Section 4: Symbolic worry that upon reading these words the recipient will form an even higher opinion of himself and thus will not write to the author.

Although this letter has a relatively simple chain of thought, it is based on a complex rhetorical concept, which may be confusing for the reader: there is an apparent contrast between the author's commendation of the recipient and the symbolic criticism. The reason for this contrast is that the present work was written as part of the discourse between Gōng and Xŭ on the delay of Xŭ in writing a letter during Gōng's illness (see Letters 15 and 16), and so this letter functions as a symbolic reprimand for Xŭ, but in fact it is a eulogy.

The author's symbolic criticism could be defined as 'mock impoliteness'.[1] That is, the author makes several statements, such as "[I wonder], sir, whether you are not on the brink of falling into [the error of] his conceit?!", which on the surface have impolite meanings but in fact convey politeness. For example, in the case of the cited sentence, although the author seems to claim that the recipient is conceited, through this statement he implicitly compares the recipient with a renowned epistolary expert, that is this claim expresses a polite discursive meaning.

Such forms of 'mock impoliteness' belong to the more refined inventory of 'social' letters and they do not frequently occur in other epistolary genres.

2. In the previous chapter we learnt about parallel writing. Although it is often not too important to analyze the parallel features of a text in depth, in some cases it is necessary to take parallel textual features into account in the analysis of some textual features, in particular in cases when wordplay is used by means of parallel writing. In some 'social' pieces the authors first use formulaic expressions, and then create expressions, which make parallels with the previous formulaic expressions.

This phenomenon can be observed in the following part of Section 2:

… 以莫須有之事，得不易有之書也。

… to elicit an otherwise unobtainable letter from you, by means of false accusation.

莫須有/莫须有 *mò-xū-yǒu* (lit. 'not-must-have', that is fabricated/unjust accusation) and 不易有 *bù-yì-yǒu* are used in parallel here. However, the former is a formulaic expression and a historical reference, while the latter is created by the author. In fact, *mò-xū-yǒu* originates in the 35th chapter (岳飛傳/岳飞传 *Yuè Fēi zhuàn, The Biography of Yuè Fēi*) of the 宋史 *Sòngshǐ (History of the Sòng Dynasty)*. According to this source, the renowned general 岳飛/岳飞 Yuè Fēi (1103–1142) and his son 岳雲/岳云 Yuè Yún (1119–1142) were imprisoned by the corrupt minister 秦檜/秦桧 Qín Huì (1090–1155) under the false accusation of writing a letter in which they plotted rebellion against the imperial court. When the retired general 韓世忠/韩世忠 Hán Shìzhōng (1089–1151) heard about this, he became furious and visited Qín in order to protest against the imprisonment of Yuè and his son. Qín did not pay attention to the general and replied with the following impertinence:

飛子雲與張憲書雖不明，其事體莫須有。

Although it has not been proven as to whether Fēi and his son Yún wrote a letter [of treason] to Zhāng Xiàn, it is needless to discuss this matter at all.

In later texts *mò-xū-yǒu* became a synonym for 'false accusation'. Thus, as this description demonstrates, *mò-xū-yǒu* is a strictly formal expression and an implicit historical reference.

Usually, such parallel language wordplay is applied in 'social' letters in order to express humour.

3. In the present text, a phenomenon can be observed, which could be defined as 'mixed citation'. This notion refers to the technique whereby the author connects citations of different origin, in order to express a longer chain of thought.

Such a 'mixed citation' can be found in Section 3 of the present letter where the author makes use of the allegory of the Yangtze and the Yellow Rivers, in order to describe the recipient's talent:

蓋足下握三寸之管，若決江河，一波未平，一波復起。

When you, sir, grasp your writing brush [and compose a letter], [your talented words flow like] the flooding Yangtze or Yellow Rivers bursting their banks, the unceasing waves foam one after another.

In this section, 若決江河 *ruò jué Jiāng Hé* is cited from *Mencius* (盡心上/尽心 上 *Jìnxīn-shàng [The Exhausting of the Heart, first part]*, section 16), which contains the following section:

> 及其聞一善言，見一善行，若決江河，沛然莫 之能禦也。

When he [i.e. the legendary ruler 舜 Shùn, r. 2255–?2195 BC] heard a good word, or saw a beneficial action, he became similar to a stream or a river bursting its banks and flowing out in an irresistible flood.

On the other hand, 一波未平，一波復起 *yī-bō wèi-píng, yī-bō fù-qǐ* is cited from 楊載/杨载 Yáng Zài's (1271–1323) essay 七言古詩/七言古诗 *Qīyán-gǔshī* (*Old Style Poem of Seven Words*), which contains the following section:

> 須是波瀾開合，如江海之波，一波未平，一波 復起。

[A poem] should 'wave'[2] from its beginning to its end, in the manner of rivers and seas, the unceasing waves of which foaming one after another.

As it can be seen, the author connects two different sources in this literary description of the recipient's skill, in order to adequately describe the ways in which the recipient writes a letter, thus elevating him.

In a similar manner to some other refined epistolary tools of 'social' letter writing, it is usually not necessary to analyze whether a 'mixed citation' occurs in a certain letter or not, but it is important to be aware of the existence of this phenomenon. Furthermore, in some cases, such as the present letter, 'mixed citations' may have additional goals besides their literary function. For example, if one analyzes the aforementioned 'mixed citation', it becomes evident that the second citation *yī-bō wèi-píng, yī-bō fù-qǐ* not only complements the first one but also serves as a basis for another 'parallel wordplay' in Section 3. That is, at the end of the section when describing the imagined person's alleged words, the author uses the following words:

> 一枝未借，尺璧先來

My letter has not yet been sent, and I have already received such a precious jewel.

This section forms a playful parallel prose along with *yī bō wèi píng, yī bō fù qǐ*.

Further Reading

Readers with interest in Gōng Wèizhāi's letter writing may consult the book *Model Letters in Late Imperial China: 60 Selected Epistles from 'Letters from Snow Swan Retreat'* (2009, München/Newcastle, Lincom) by the present author.

In Chinese, a discussion on Xǔ's epistolary activity can be found in 趙樹功 Zhào Shùgōng's 中國尺牘文學史 *Zhōngguó chǐdú wénxuéshǐ* (*History of Chinese Epistolary Literature*, 1999, Shijiazhuang, 河北人民出版社 Hebei renmin chubanshe, 575–578).

For readers with an interest in reading Gōng's work in Chinese, one of the best sources is the 1985 edition of the work by 上海書店 Shanghai shudian (this is a joint edition of the works of Xǔ and Gōng). Two other reliable sources are the 1976 綜合出版社 Zonghe chubanshe edition (Tainan) and the 1994 廣文書局 Guangwen shuju (Taipei) edition.

Readers with an interest in the rhetorical epistolary strategies of Gōng Wèizhāi may consult the paper 'Exploring the historical Chinese polite denigration/elevation phenomenon', by the present author, to be published in the volume: Jonathan Culpeper and Dániel Z. Kádár (eds.) *Historical (Im)politeness* (2009, Berne, Peter Lang).

Joint Exercise for Chapters 5 and 6

Task: Translate the following two brief Letters 19 and 20, written by Gōng Wèi-zhāi and Xǔ Jiāxūn; these works are closely related because Letter 20 was written in response to Letter 19. In the course of completing this exercise the reader is required to work in an independent way: it will be the reader's task to punctuate and translate the text. Even though in Appendix I these letters are available in a punctuated and edited form, and also at the end of this section the English translation of the texts analyzed can be found, the reader is advised not to make use of these aids as far as is possible. In order to aid the reader's work, the Chinese texts of the studied letters are followed by synopses.

Letter 19

與許葭村

重九後數行覆候起居知邀青照

小陽佳日舞彩調琴天倫至樂遠

勝蓬瀛而玉麟早已投懷何竟祕而不

宣勞遠人揣度乎

阮君書來道其夫人有如達之喜

因思是月也雀入大水故敝署五產而

皆雌今來函又改於十月娩身其得蛟

龍也必矣第親自造作者竟不知其月抑又

奇也

舍姪甘林得館之難正如其伯之得

子豈其東家尚未誕生也

今年曾寄寓信計六十餘函足下陰

行善事不厭其煩何以報之惟有學近日官

場念金剛經萬遍保佑足下多子耳

Synopsis

This social letter addresses various topics, but its main theme is that the author foretells that the recipient will "father a son"; as in old China sons were more valuable than daughters, such a prediction in fact was a symbolic good wish.

The main contents of the letter are as follows: In Section 1 a reference is made to a letter of response that the author previously sent to the recipient. In Section 2 the author describes the presumed joy of the recipient after his son was born, as imagined by the author, and also symbolically reprimands the recipient for not informing him about the birth of his son swiftly enough (in reality, the author did not know whether the recipient's child was already born, and so it is sure that this is a symbolic reprimand).[1] In Section 3 the author shifts topic by mentioning the fact that 阮錫侯 Ruǎn Xīhóu, a mutual protégé, makes unfounded predictions: as Ruǎn does not even know the time of his child's birth for sure, it is impossible to predict whether it will be a boy or a girl. In Section 4 the author complains about not having a male heir (despite the fact that he is able to foretell the gender of others' babies) and also for the continuous failure of his beloved nephew 龔甘林 Gōng Gānlín (his exact dates are unknown) in his career. Finally, in Section 5, the author expresses his gratitude to the recipient for helping him by forwarding his family correspondence back to Shàoxīng, and wishes he may be blessed with many other male children in the future.

List of difficult words/expressions

1. 候起居 *hòu-qǐjū*: to wish serenity

2. 青照 *qīngzhào*: to condescend to read one's work (honorific verbal form)

3. 小陽 (小阳) *xiǎoyáng*: synonym for the Tenth Lunar Month

4. 舞彩調琴 (舞彩调琴) *wǔcǎi-tiáoqín*: lit. '(preparing) the abundant colours (of the festival) and tuning the musical instruments', that is to meet for merry celebrations

5. 天倫之樂 (天伦之乐) *tiānlún-zhī-lè*: the joy of one's family harmony (formulaic expression)

6. 蓬瀛 *péngyíng*: the land of immortals

7. 玉麟 *yùlín*: lit. 'jade unicorn', revered son (honorific elevating term of address)

8. 投懷 (投怀) *tóuhuái*: here: the birth of the recipient's son

9. 如達 (如达) *rúdà*: literary synonym for pregnancy

10. 雀入大水 *quèrù-dàshuǐ*: technical term of divination for periods when only girls are born

11. 敝署 *bìshǔ*: humble office (self-denigrating form)

12. 蛟龍 (蛟龙) *jiāolóng*: lit. 'flood dragon', literary synonym for one's son

13. 舍姪 *shèzhí*: lit. 'home nephew', that is one's own nephew (deferential self-denigrating form)

14. 東家 (东家) *dōngjiā*: master

Letter 20

與龔未齋（慰其姪失館）

手書疊至謂四月駕池夢蘭可卜弟非神乎技者方自

笑其鳩拙安所得珠而藏之櫝耶

昔侯夫人逾月而娩以其時攷之宜爲震之長男而爲

巽之長女良由當局者自失其期遂令旁觀者難神其算也

令姪館事屢謀屢失降而就副未免大才小用靜以待

之自有碧梧千尺耳

寓函往復何足云勞而仁人用心祝以多子則兄之善

頌善禱積福尤宏不更當老蚌生珠耶

Synopsis

This work is a response to Letter 19. In Section 1, the author makes an intertextual reference to the recipient's prediction that the author's child will be a boy; then he deferentially states that he does not possess such a talent for divination; finally he politely states that his son has not been born yet, by claiming that he would never dare to hide this fact from the recipient (who possesses the art of divination). In

Section 2, the author reflects on the recipient's previous statement on the Ruǎn family, by agreeing that it would be difficult to foretell whether their child will be a boy or a girl if the parents do not even know the estimated time of birth (the Ruǎn family's child was a girl). In Section 3, the author encourages the recipient with regard to his nephew's career by stating that in the long run his nephew will be able to find an appropriate position. Finally, in Section 4 the author first politely dismisses the recipient's previous acknowledgment of his labour, and then encourages the recipient that he still has a chance to become a father as a result of his charitable deeds.[2]

List of difficult words/expressions

1. 疊 (叠) *dié*: several, repeatedly

2. 鴛池 (鸳池) *yuānchí*: literary synonym for fathering a son

3. 夢蘭 (梦兰) *mènglán*: pregnancy, to become pregnant

4. 神乎技 *shénhu-jì*: the art of divination

5. 逾月 *yúyuè*: to pass over to the next month

6. 震 *zhèn*: here: to foretell (*zhèn* is originally a divine trigram of the 八卦 *bāguà* symbol, hence its contextual meaning)

7. 巽 *xùn*: here: as a result, as an outcome, by means of fortune (its origin is similar to that of *zhèn* above)

8. 當局者 (当局者) *dāngjú-zhě*: lit. 'authorities', here: those to whom something occurs

9. 神 ... 算 *shén-suàn*: foretell

10. 就副 *jiùfù*: here: to serve as an office assistant

11. 碧梧千尺 *bìwú-qiānchǐ*: lit. 'the green parasol tree [grows to] thousand *chǐ* length', that is to attain an outstanding position (formulaic expression)

12. 善頌善禱 (善颂善祷) *shànsòng-shàndǎo*: lit. 'love to praise and pray (for the blessing of another person)', that is charitable deeds (idiomatic expression)

13. 積福 (积福) *jīfú*: to have happiness accrued as a result of someone's charitable deeds

14. 老蚌生珠 *lǎobàng-shēngzhū*: to have a son born in one's old age (idiomatic expression)

Translation of Letter 19

To Xǔ Jiācūn

After the Double Ninth Festival I sent you a short letter of response in order to wish you serenity, and I am sure that you have already received and condescended to read it.

During the joyous days of this, the Tenth Month, [your family] is meeting for merry celebrations and your harmony is far greater than [that of the immortals in their] paradise. Moreover, your happiness was heightened when your respected son was born, but I do not know why you withheld this news from this secluded person in far-off lands leaving him to guess about this?

Young Ruǎn informed me by letter of the happy news of his wife's pregnancy. I thought that in this month only girls were born – this would explain why all five children born to [the wives of the members of] our humble office would prove to be girls. However, in his letter [Young Ruǎn told me that although his child is] unexpectedly to be born in the Tenth Month, he claims to know that it will be a boy. I think this is a strange statement, all the more so as he does not even know for sure the month [when the child will be born].

[Unfortunately, it seems that] it is as difficult for me to have a son as it is difficult for my humble paternal nephew Gānlín to gain official status: it is hard to tell whether their master was already born.[3]

In this year you have helped me by sending more than sixty family letters; you, sir, aided me magnanimously without uttering a word of complaint, and I wonder how I could repay you for this?! I think I can only follow the custom of the officials of our days and chant the *Diamond Sutra* one thousand times in order to bless you, sir, with many male children!

Translation of Letter 20

To Gōng Wèizhāi (consoling him for his maternal nephew's loss of official service)

I received your letters in which you stated that it can be foretold from the [time of the] pregnancy [of my wife] that in the Fourth Month I will father a son. This younger brother of yours does not possess the art of divination, and I can only laugh at my clumsiness, [which is similar to that of a] turtledove. Thus, how [would I dare to be so bold as] to [intentionally] hide [the information that I have fathered a son, like hiding] a treasure in a box?

Ms. Ruǎn's child was born one month after [the expected time]. On the basis of this timing one could have foretold whether they were going to have a son or a daughter. It is evident that if those to whom [the joyous matter of childbirth occurs] cannot tell its time, then it will be difficult for the bystander to predict [the gender of the child].

[As regards] the matter of your revered maternal nephew's career [you mentioned that] whenever he attempts [to attain an appropriate position] he always fails. However, if he lowers [his expectations] and becomes a clerk he will squander his great talent; but, if he waits with a calm heart, he will attain an outstanding position.

How would the handling of your family correspondence mean labour for me? You, my benevolent friend, who wish the blessing of many male children, will have an amazing amount of happiness accrued as a result of your charitable deeds, and should you not all the more [have the chance to] father a son in your old age?

Part IV

Political Letter Writing

Chapter 7

Political Letter Writing: A Long Letter
of Yuán Shìkǎi 袁世凱

In this chapter we examine the genre of historical Chinese private[1] political letters, that is letters written by high-ranking officials with the aim of informally discussing political events with their colleagues and/or to convincing them of something and thus attaining certain political goals. From some perspectives political letter writing is the most complex historical Chinese private epistolary genre. First, in political epistolary discourse the relationship between the author and the recipient can be fairly complex and authors of such letters often have secondary or hidden goals, which can only be understood through historical research. Secondly, political letters are important historical documents, and they often become subject to ideological debates; readers with interest in letter writing per se often meet such debates. Thirdly, the authors of political letters usually discuss many contemporary events without explicitly explaining them.

Illustration 3 Yuán Shìkǎi's portrait as the Emperor of China

In order to illustrate these points, let us cite a brief telegram, which was written in the style of traditional letters in 1913 by 袁世凱/袁世凱 Yuán Shìkǎi (1859–1916), the author studied in this chapter. This telegram occurs here in an unpunctuated fashion (Appendix I includes this document in a punctuated form).

明教何日稅駕渴盼德音

但祈還輈祖國絕不敢強以所難敬具蒲輪鵠候

先生不願從政而有意主持名教舉國想望風采

薄俗針砭欽仰無似凡河汾弟子京洛故人均言

去國念年困心衡慮大著發抒政見足爲

轉須磨別莊康長素先生鑒

民國二年八月二日

袁世凱　　冬

2nd Day of the Eighth Month of the Second Year of the Republic [1913]

[Telegram] sent for inspection to the Respected Kāng Chángsù [i.e. 康有爲 Kāng Yǒuwéi] at his temporary residence in Suma [Kobe, Japan]

Since you left the country and studied abroad you have devoted all your energy to thinking. Your great book expresses your views on politics, it is a remonstrance against bad practices, and I admire and esteem it as an unparalleled work. Your distinguished disciples and old friends left behind in the capital say without exception that you, sir, do not wish to be engaged in politics but only want to devote yourself to your outstanding teaching. The whole nation is anxious to see your elegant demeanour, and I only beg you to turn the shaft of your cart and return to your homeland, and by no means would anyone force you to be engaged in what you would find uncomfortable [i.e. politics]. I respectfully prepare bulrush [to cover] the wheels [of your cart to make your journey hither comfortable], and I [eagerly] await your wise teaching as a swan [cranes its neck]. [As regards] the day you will stop [i.e. arrive] hither, I will anxiously await your kind reply.

Yuán Shìkǎi   Stop

In the course of translating this telegram, written to the renowned scholar 康有為/康有为 Kāng Yǒuwéi (1858–1927), one should be aware that this is not a simple invitation to an intellectual living abroad (in Japan), but is in fact a political document, the author of which had the hidden objective of gaining the recipient's support for his own policy. Furthermore, as it is an important historical document, if the reader intends to study it from the point of view of sinological literature they will unavoidably meet ideologized statements, such as it is an 'insincere document' (as the author wanted to 'lure' Kāng back to China), in Chinese Marxist works. Finally, certain references within this work can be properly interpreted only if the reader is aware of the political discourse of the time: for example, the label "great work" refers to Kāng's 大同書/大同书 *Dàtóng-shū* or *Book of Great Harmony*, which was his seminal political treatise. In a nutshell, the translation of this political document requires some preliminary investigation.

In this chapter we will analyze a long political letter – the longest one included in this book – written by the renowned military official and politician Yuán Shìkǎi who held important ranks during both the Qīng Dynasty and the early Republican era. Yuán started his political career as a military official, and after rising in rank he became the Imperial Resident in Korea, which was then a protectorate of the Qīng Dynasty. He first gained fame as the commander of the Chinese stationary forces in Korea during the First Sino-Japanese War (1 August 1894–17 April 1895); he managed to avoid the humiliation suffered by the Chinese army as he was summoned back to Peking before they were routed. After the war he gained even greater military power: as an ally of the great politician 李鴻章/李鸿章 Lǐ Hóngzhāng (1823–1901); he was appointed as commander of the so-called New Army. In 1898 he became a supporter of the Hundred Days Reform (戊戌變法/戊戌变法 Wùxū Biànfǎ), which aimed to change politics and education in China, but later he suddenly changed sides and helped the Dowager Empress Cíxǐ (慈禧, 1835–1908) to crush the reform movement. Later, in 1911, he played a prominent role in the abdication of the child emperor Pǔyí 溥儀/溥仪 (1906–1967), and became the Provisional President of the Republic of China. In

1915 he tried to restore the monarchy and proclaimed himself as the emperor of China; however, this attempt failed and soon Yuán died of uraemia.

Yuán has been chosen as the subject for this chapter as he is a controversial figure in Chinese history, his letters being subject of ideo-political debates. Furthermore, another reason for this choice is that Yuán was an eminent letter writer and had a strong command of Classical Chinese literacy despite being a military official.

The letter studied in this chapter was written in 1897, before the Hundred Days Reform, to 翁同龢 Wēng Tónghé (1830–1904), the tutor of the Emperor Guāngxù (光緒/光绪, 1871–1908) who was the leader of the reformists. This long letter describes the reasons that necessitate reform and suggests a pragmatic approach by means of which they should be carried out. From the perspective of this book this is a suitable document because it represents the aforementioned problematic features of political letter writing:

(i)   This work served the author's hidden political ambition to gain the trust of Wēng and also to influence the Emperor Guāngxù through his tutor;

(ii) It is subject to scholarly and moral debates: while Yuán is often claimed to be a 'traitor' of the reform movement, this document seems to suggest that at least at the time of the writing he had rather elaborate and serious ideas on the way in which the reformation of Chinese political life should be carried out. Some Marxist scholars give rather subjective accounts on this letter, in order to downgrade its value;

(iii) Finally, the present document contains different information that can be interpreted only with the contemporary foreign political issues (e.g. the First Sino-Japanese War) in mind.

Before beginning the examination of this work it should be noted that from a calligraphic perspective this is the most difficult chapter: the Chinese text is not only unpunctuated but it is also written in a calligraphic style. The reader is advised to individually punctuate and translate the text before consulting Appendix I, which contains the text in a punctuated and non-calligraphic form, or the translation at the end of this chapter.

Letter 21

Section 1

上翁同龢變法說帖　光緒二十三年二月初七日

謹陳管見

竊維自古之天下不能無非常之變遇非

常之變徒諰諰焉慶額疾首詬厲時數之適然而

日聽其陵夷衰微不肯破膠固拘墟之成見急起

變法以應之恐卒至於束手待斃而不可救藥也

Synopsis

In this section, after formally opening the letter, the author introduces the general theme of the letter, that is the need for political reform during times of urgency.

List of difficult words/expressions

1. 維 (维) *wéi*: to think something

2. 數 (数) *shù*: fate

3. 陵夷衰微 *língyí-shuāiwēi*: decline (formulaic expression)

4. 束手待斃 (束手待毙) *shùshǒu-dàibì*: to wait helplessly for death (idiomatic expression)

5. 不可救藥 (不可救药) *bùkě-jiùyào*: incurable (idiomatic expression)

Section 2

今之時局可謂極非常之變矣德人以三巨艦闖入膠澳据爲己有設巡撫以鎮之又遺其親王濟師是不倂顯無退志恐彼親王到後更不知有何變局山東濱海要地介居南北洋之中使他族逼處則海道有隔絕之患我之海軍勢將永不克振

Synopsis

Here the author describes the concrete political problem that makes the reform inevitable, that is the German invasion of the Jiāo Bay (膠澳/胶澳 Jiāo'ào) in November 1897, which led to an increasing German influence in Shāndōng Province. Furthermore, the author describes the reason why the German influence in this region is dangerous: Shāndōng is a crucial territory for the Chinese Navy.

List of difficult words/expressions:

1. 巨艦 (巨舰) *jùjiàn*: large warship

2. 巡撫 (巡抚) *xúnfǔ*: governor

3. 濟師 (济师) *jìshī*: garrison

4. 隔絕 (隔绝) *géjué*: to be completely blocked

5. 勢將 (势将) *shìjiāng*: certainly will . . .

6. 克振 *kèzhèn*: here: to effectively combat

Section 3

論者謂中國貧窮不堪用武亟宜陰嗾他國興師助我
當可驅逐德人抑或商準各國開口通商即可公處膠澳此恐
未能嗾群雄之斗飽群夷之欲也 何者俄法向有密約英倭近
復締交四國各有黨援勢若分成兩敵以德之中立也於是彼
四國者莫不視其向背以爲輕重夫彼方重之即安得而背之
雖俄人與我關係較重睦誼較敦然惟利是視又豈肯舍公法
局外之例愛我仇德使德英合謀增樹劫敵以自詒伊戚也哉
是成有以知其必不然矣且也俄儻然認東北數省入其版興

英復隱然視大江南北在其掌
握倭窺浙閩法圖滇桂鷹瞵虎
耽各奮得時則駕之志德人既
難於先諸國將效尤於後沓來
紛至群起而我爲難數年前西
人有瓜華之謠并具圖説遍傳
五洲以今日時勢揆之任此謠
不爲無因此誠可危之甚也

Synopsis

In this section the author discusses a topic that generated active debate at the time of this letter: the possibility of making an alliance with another colonizing power, by means of which the Germans could be driven out of Shāndōng. The author overviews the reasons why such an alliance would be impossible, that is none of the colonizing countries is interested in risking a conflict with the others, especially because there is a balance of power among them, and also they have a scheme according to which they want to divide China. The present section is concluded with a negative prediction that the occupation of China is on the horizon.

List of difficult words/expressions

1. 論者 (论者) *lùnzhè*: those who argue for something

2. 陰嗾 (阴嗾) *yīnsǒu*: to secretly negotiate

3. 興師 (兴师) *xīngshī*: to dispatch troops

4. 開口通商 (开口通商) *kāikǒu-tōngshāng*: to open a port for free trade

5. 群雄 *qúnxióng*: the colonizing powers

6. 公法 *gōngfǎ*: international/public law

7. 增樹 (增树) *zēngshù*: to increase

8. 自詒伊戚 (自诒伊戚) *zìyí-yīqī*: to seek disaster for oneself (idiomatic expression)

9. 版輿 (版舆) *bǎnyú*: territory

10. 倭 Wō: archaic name for Japan

11. 浙 Zhè: abbreviated name for Zhèjiāng Province

12. 閩 (闽) Mín: brief form of Fújiàn Province

13. 滇 Diān: brief form of Yúnnán Province

14. 桂 Guì: brief form of Guǎngxī Province

15. 鷹瞵虎耽 (鹰瞵虎耽) *yīnglín-hǔdān*: hawks and tigers stare with hungry look (modified idiomatic expression)

16. 效尤 *xiàoyóu*: to follow a bad example

17. 沓來紛至 (踏来纷至) *tàlái-fēnzhì*: to come one after the other

18. 瓜華 (瓜华) *guā-Huá*: to divide China

Section 4

且夫我之忍尤含詬降心俯首以相從者不爲不至矣而人初不之憐也既力過勢禁之不能復理論情動之不可若復踞蹐常習故不知變計拱手坐視聽客所爲彼亦公然不讓擇肉而食長蛇封豕肆其貪殘吞噬之餘所存有

海疆日蹙而關稅之征鹽漕之入
向所資以裕帑藏充度支者一旦
攘奪殆盡而舉不復為我所有區
區彈丸何以立國雖曰積薪厝火尚
未及燃而切身之災固日憂其近
矣

Synopsis

In this section the author criticizes those politicians who oppose the reforms. As he argues, such behaviour is unacceptable because the colonizing powers will not stop until they occupy the whole country. By gradually loosing territory China will surely face an economic crisis: the loss of land means a reduction in taxpayers, and once such a large-scale loss occurs it will not be possible to rebuild the country. The author concludes this section by discussing his worry that this disaster is imminent, even if it has not happened yet. Here he refers to those politicians who do not worry about the situation and oppose the reforms, believing that the foreign influence will not affect their own power; the author predicts that these catastrophic events will influence everyone personally.

List of difficult words/expressions

1. 忍尤含詬 (忍尤含诟) *rěnyóu-hán'gòu*: to endure offence and humiliation (idiomatic expression)

2. 降心俯首 *jiàngxīn-fǔshǒu*: humble and submissive (formulaic expression)

3. 力遏勢禁 (力遏势禁) *lì'è-shìjìn*: to stop an army by military force

4. 理諭情動 (理谕情动) *lǐyù-qíngdòng*: to convince someone with argumentation and move him with emotions

5. 蹈常習故 (蹈常习故) *dǎo-cháng-xí-gù*: to follow old ways and practices (idiomatic expression)

6. 拱手坐視 (拱手坐视) *gǒngshǒu-zuòshì*: lit. 'to sit and watch with hands cupped in front of one's chest', that is to obediently sit and watch without doing anything (formulaic expression)

7. 長蛇封豕 (长蛇封豕) *chángshé-fēngshǐ*: lit. 'long snake and big pig', that is a cruel and greedy person (idiomatic expression)

8. 之餘 (之余) *zhī-yú*: after . . .

9. 海疆 *hǎijiāng*: coastal areas and territorial seas

10. 帑藏 *tǎngzàng*: state treasury

11. 度支 *duózhī*: estimated expenditures

12. 區區彈丸 (区区弹丸) *qūqū-dànwán*: a tiny piece of land

13. 積薪厝火 (积薪厝火) *jīxīn-cuòhuǒ*: lit. 'to place a fire on a pile of firewood', that is imminent danger (idiomatic expression)

Section 5

自甲午軍興以後朝野士庶凡識
時務之輩莫不爭以變法為言陳事者
條說甚詳而飭下各行省邊辦者亦復
指不勝屈乃因仍遷就迄未有實而見
諸施行者廟堂亦憂容勛舊不加督責
任此變法恐終未有其期然而事變迭
乘人不我待痛切於剝膚厄甚於倒
懸何可不幡然振厲以圖挽回補救於
萬一

Synopsis

In this section, the author refers first to the First Sino-Japanese War, which ended with the humiliating defeat of the Chinese army, and notes that this event has made many recognize the need for political reform. Then, he refers to his famous 12,000 word-long petition, submitted to the Guāngxù Emperor in 22 August 1895, in which he described the need for reform and the practical measures that should be made, and he describes the alleged reasons for the failure of this petition, that is (i) its overtly detailed nature and (ii) the court's inability to force provincial administration into implementing the changes suggested. The author finally claims that reform cannot be attained in such a powerless way and emphasizes the need for said reform.

List of difficult words/expressions

1. 甲午軍興 (甲午军兴) Jiǎwǔ-jūnxīng: the outbreak of the Sino-Japanese war in the Jiǎwǔ Year (1894)

2. 朝野士庶 *cháoyě-shìshù*: the leaders and the public, scholars and ordinary people (formulaic expression)

3. 識時務 (识时务) *shí-shíwù*: to take note of a situation

4. 指不勝屈 (指不胜屈) *zhǐ-bùshèng-qū*: numerous (idiomatic expression)

5. 遷就 (迁就)/牽就 *qiānjiù*: to make compromises

6. 勛舊 (勋旧) *xūnjiù*: meritorious officials of the court

7. 迭乘 *diéchéng*: to be replaced by something else

8. 痛切於剝膚 (痛切于剥肤) *tòngqiè-yú-bāofū*: lit. 'with an intense pain in one's skin', that is extremely painful/critical situation

9. 振厲 (振厉) *zhènlì*: to exert oneself and make a determined effort

Section 6

易曰窮則變此其時矣第於積重之秋驟行變法之政兹事體大猝難畢舉而究其所

異時徐圖恢復之計

我出猶可多存數千里土地人民以為

抗拒群雄保我全局而畫疆自守政自

護持根本二三年間可望自立從後不能

革汰其宿弊矯其積習用以培養元氣

瞬刻不容稍緩誠就斯三者而實力變

最要者如用人理財練兵三大端實屬

Synopsis

The author emphasizes the need for the reform by citing a section from the Confucian Classic *Book of Changes*. Then he offers a pragmatic solution to carry out reforms (such a pragmatic approach is needed because his complete list of suggestions failed): the court should implement only the most important points of the author's reform plan, which are 用人 *yòngrén* ('to reform the employment [i.e. to employ proper persons for the proper task]'), 理財/理财 *lǐcái* ('to reform finance'), and 練兵/练兵 *liànbīng* ('to reform military training'). By reforming these areas, China can regain its former strength within a few years, or even if this will not be possible the situation will be much better than it would be without reform.

List of difficult words/expressions

1. 第 *dì*: however

2. 茲事體大 (兹事体大) *zīshì-tǐdà*: This is an important matter! (idiomatic expression)

3. 大端 *dàduān*: salient feature, main aspect

4. 畫疆自守 (华疆自守) *huàjiāng-zìshǒu*: here: to defend one's country (idiomatic expression)

Section 7

世凱雖至愚戇亦略知忌諱何
敢妄肆狂瞽之舌故作不祥之論第念
覆巢之下詎有完卵棟折榱崩孰免傾
壓情急勢迫敢不盡言

Synopsis

In this section the author deferentially emphasizes the fact that he does not intend to make negative predictions without reason, and that his reason for discussing facts in such negative a manner is his alarm at the critical situation.

List of difficult words/expressions

1. 愚戇 (愚戆) *yúgàng*: stupidly honest

2. 略知 *lüèzhī*: to know something about . . . (polite expression downgrading one's own skill)

3. 忌諱 (忌讳) *jìhuì*: to avoid a taboo

4. 妄肆 *wàngsì*: absurdly and wantonly

5. 狂瞽 *kuánggǔ*: arrogant and superficial

6. 覆巢之下，詎(讵)有完卵 *fùcháo-zhī-xià, jù-yǒu wánluǎn*: lit. 'Under an overturned nest how could an intact egg exist?', that is How could anything escape destruction in an unfortunate situation?

7. 棟折榱崩，孰免傾壓 (栋折榱崩，孰免倾压) *dòngzhé-cuībēng, shú-miǎn qīngyā*: lit. 'When the ridgepole is broken and the rafter falls apart, how would it possible to avoid the collapse [of the house]?', that is When the country is in a state of ruin, how could it be possible to avoid collapse?

8. 勢迫 (势迫) *shìpò*: critical situation

Section 8

臨
穎
涕
泣
伏

乞
留
意
幸
甚

Synopsis

In this brief section the author concludes the letter in a conventionally emotive way, by using different epistolary formulas.

List of difficult words

1. 伏乞 *fúqǐ*: lit. 'to beg with prostration', that is to humbly beg (honorific verbal form)

2. 幸甚 *xìngshèn*: 'it would be a great honour' (deferential epistolary closing form)

Translation of Letter 21

Letter discussing the political reform, sent with due respect to Wēng Tónghé

(On the 7th Day of the Second Month of the Twentieth Year of the Guāngxù Era)

I hereby solemnly explain my humble opinion:

I believe that from time immemorial the world has not been able to exist without extreme changes. When encountering an extreme change, if people become worried, knit their brows in anguish, curse the fate of their time and let themselves decline, unwilling to smash obstinate and narrow views thereby bringing about a sudden political reform to cope with it [i.e. the challenge caused by the extreme change], they can but wait helplessly for death, without the chance of ever being helped.

Our current political situation can be called an extreme change. The Germans entered the Jiāo Bay with three large warships, they have claimed it as their own and have appointed a governor to rule it. Furthermore, they have sent their king's garrison. These [facts] not only demonstrate that they do not plan to leave but also one further worries about the crisis that may follow when their king arrives. Shāndōng is a strategic point bordering the sea; it is located between our Southern and Northern Seas. If another national conquers it, then our sea route will be disastrously cut and our navy will certainly be unable to fight effectively.

Some argue that China is in a poor condition, it is unable to use its own forces [to defend itself] and as soon as possible we should secretly negotiate with other countries to dispatch troops and help us, and in this way we will be able either to expel the Germans or reach an agreement whereby the Jiāo Bay would be an open port through which every country could freely conduct trade, and thus all countries would settle there. But I am afraid that we can neither make the [colonizing] powers fight each other, nor can we fulfil the wish of the barbarians [in the latter fashion]. What is the reason for this? Russia and France have a secret agreement and England and Japan have recently formed a political relationship. All of these four countries have their own ally; they seem to be divided into two enemy camps, the Germans being neutral between them. Consequently, these four countries treat their relationship with [Germany] in light of that of [the others]. If the other side has a good relationship with them [i.e. the Germans] why would this side enter into conflict with them? Although the Russians have a relatively good relationship with us and our friendship is sincere, they also pursue their own interest, and also why would they want to abandon the regulations of international law and aid us in taking revenge against the Germans, thus making the Germans and English plot together? This would only increase the number of their powerful enemies and thus they would merely make trouble for themselves. So, it can be clearly known that they would not agree to act thus. Furthermore, the Russians, as well as [the others] hope that many of our North Eastern provinces will become their territory, the English visualize the territories at the South and North of the Yangtze as their prize, the Japanese hope to seize Zhèjiāng and

Fújiàn Provinces, and the French plan to obtain Yúnnán and Guǎngxī Provinces. They are like hawks and tigers preparing to kill their pray, all eager to act as soon as the opportunity arises. The Germans have already started, and the others will follow this bad example, [pouring into our country] one after the other, rallying together, and we will find ourselves in an unbearable situation. A few years ago the Westerners whispered about the division of China, and also drew up maps [for this division], which became known everywhere in the world – on the basis of our current situation it seems that these whispers did not lack foundation. This is an extremely perilous [situation].

Now, those among us who swallow the shame and humiliation, yield to the situation and thus become servants [of the barbarians], may indeed see [this peril], but in the beginning they do not mind this. [They say that] since it is impossible to stop it [i.e. the enemy] with force, convince it with argument and move it with emotion, they return to the old ways and ignore the plans for reform. They obediently sit and watch, they follow that which is dictated by the guest [i.e. the intruders], despite the fact that he openly defies [the rules of the host, that is the laws of the country], takes the meat he desires [i.e. take whatever they want] and behaves arrogantly and violently. But, due to his wanton greediness and cruelty, what will remain after he has swallowed everything [i.e. all the territories]? In my humble opinion it is terrifying that our coastal areas and territorial seas gradually decrease, and the collection of the customs and taxes, the surrender of the salt and grain, which hitherto have been the sources of the state treasury and [by means of which] the expenditures have been covered, will be almost completely seized and will not be ours anymore. How then would it be possible to build a country from a tiny piece of land? Therefore, I say that [the danger is imminent] as if one placed fire on a pile of firewood that did not yet catch alight, and I worry unceasingly about the approaching disaster that will strike us.

After the war in the Jiǎwǔ Year, the leaders and the public, scholars and ordinary people, everyone in our generation who recognized this situation, argued for political change. The points of [the memorandum of] this person discussed [the necessary steps for the reform] in a detailed way, but when the provincial administration was ordered [to carry out my points], they [i.e. these points] proved to be too numerous, and finally everything was followed as before and compromises were made, and until now there has been no one who has put these points in practice. The Imperial Court looked fearfully upon its meritorious officials without reprimanding them [for this failure]. I am afraid that a reform carried out in this fashion will never be realized. But, disasters will come again in a new form, others will not wait for us [to modernize our country], and in such an extremely painful situation when the peril is at its worst, how can we not swiftly make determined efforts, and thus redeem a small part [of the catastrophe]!?

The *Book of Changes* says: "An extreme [situation] gives rise to [a desire for] change." This is that time. However, in such a period when bad habits are strong, the swift implementation of the policy of reform – which is a serious large-scale matter – cannot fully succeed. But the work on its [the reform's] most important aspects, such as the three salient points of 'employment reform', 'financial reform' and 'military training reform', should not cease for a moment. If we succeed in these three points and make a real change, washing away long-standing malpractices and removing inveterate habits, and use [these principles] in order to train our vitality and shield and sustain the essence [of our culture], in two or three years we can expect to stand on our feet again. And even if we cannot resist the foreign powers and defend our overall situation, we will be able to defend and govern ourselves and at least keep the population of a [land of] few thousand miles through this intentional planning to regain our power.

Although Shìkǎi is stupidly honest, he at least knows how to avoid unpleasant themes, and thus how would he dare [to have] an absurd and senseless tongue and intentionally make ominous prophecies. Instead, I [uttered these words] as I am afraid: how can anything escape destruction in our unfortunate situation, and how can we avoid collapse when the country is in ruin?! Frustrated by great distress at the [tragic] circumstances, [how could I] dare not to speak out all [that is in my heart]?

While writing [my letter] I weep [in despair], I humbly beg you to pay heed to [my words]. This would be the greatest honour to me.

Further Reading

Yuán Shìkǎi is usually not included in native works on Chinese letter writing due to his controversial political role.

For those who are interested in reading Yuán's letters in Chinese, perhaps the most reliable collection is 袁世凱函牘/袁世凱函牍 *Yuán Shìkǎi hándú* (*The Correspondence of Yuán Shìkǎi*), published by 越麓書社 Yuelu shushe (Changsha) in 2005. Another important collection is 袁世凱家書 *Yuán Shìkǎi jiāshū* (*The Family Letters of Yuán Shìkǎi*), published by Academia Sinica (Taipei) in 1990.

Readers with interest in Yuán's life may consult Jerome Chen's monograph *Yuan Shih-K'ai; 1859-1916* (1961, Liverpool, George Allen & Unwin).

Postscript: What Next?

This book has provided the reader the opportunity to develop a basic skill in historical Chinese letters. If the reader has become interested in this corpus, it is possible to continue her/his inquiries into the epistolary corpus. In what follows, a few recommendations are given on how to proceed.

It is obvious that the best way to further develop one's skill in working with the epistolary corpus is to read as many letters as possible, and also to gradually widen the scope of readings by non-private epistolary genres, as well. However, selecting appropriate texts is important when dealing with such a large corpus. In general, the best way to find an author or several authors for study is to consult some works on Chinese epistolary literary history, predominantly published in Chinese. Perhaps the most authoritative work on this is that of 趙樹功 Zhào Shùgōng (cf. Preface); another, more basic, source is 林軒/林轩 Lín Xuān's 書信文化/书信文化 *Shūxìn wénhuà* (*Epistolary Culture*, 2006, Shanghai, 科學普及文化出版社 Kexue puji wenhua chubanshe). It may be feasible to select an author on the basis of what is written in such works, but when using these sources the reader should be aware they may be ideologically biased and may evaluate certain authors on the basis of moral, political or other principles. Another useful way to find a material for further research is to consult the Issues 41 and 42 of the journal *Renditions* (*Classical Letters, Anniversary Double Issue of Renditions*, edited by Anders Hansson, 1994, Hong Kong, The Chinese University of Hong Kong). This work contains selected letters of historical Chinese authors from various eras, and it is an excellent source from which to overview the history of Chinese letter writing and to find an author of interest for the reader. A similar collection can be found in the reader 歷代書信名篇的智慧/历代书信名篇智慧 *Lìdài shūxìn míngpiān de zhìhuì* (*The Wisdom of Famous Historical Letters*), edited by 黃玉峰 Huáng Yùfēng and 周唯 Zhōu Wéi (2003, Hong Kong, 萬里 Wanli); this is an excellent selection that contains systematically arranged letters and their modern Chinese translation.

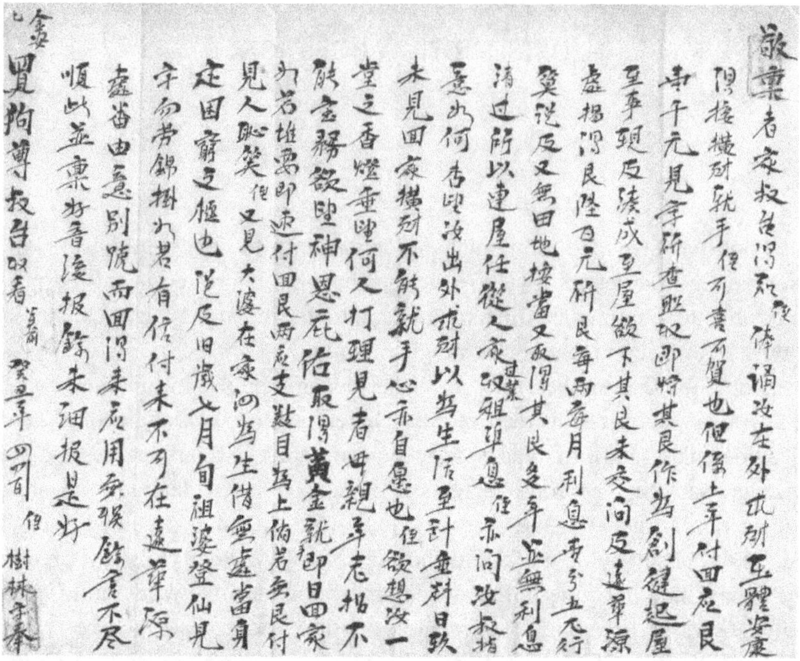

Illustration 4 Text of a late imperial Chinese letter from the Yip Sang correspondence (Courtesy of the City of Vancouver Archives)

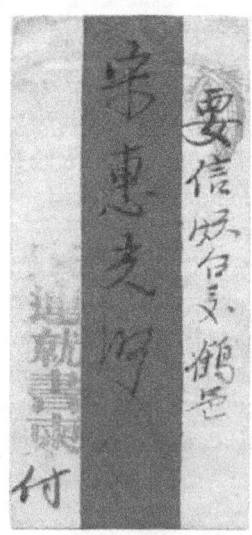

Illustration 5 Envelope of a letter from the Yip Sang correspondence (Courtesy of the City of Vancouver Archives)

In advanced studies on historical letter writing, along with developing one's skill in individually translating letters it is also important to gain expertise in reading letters in their original form. As Illustrations 4–5 (the text of a late imperial Chinese letter from the so-called 'Yip Sang correspondence' and the envelope of another one) and Illustrations 6–7 (an early Republican official letter and its envelope sent to a missionary temple) demonstrate, in order to be able to work with original or reprinted letters and envelopes one must become acquainted with Chinese calligraphy, as well as other aspects of epistolary arts, such as seals (cf. Illustration 4) and certain paper types (e.g. the text of Illustration 6 is written on an official letter paper). There are many excellent textbooks available on Chinese calligraphy, such as Lei Lei Qu's *The Complete Guide to Chinese Calligraphy* (2007, London, Cico Books); also, many research works are available on this subject, such as Zhongshi Ouyang and Shizheng Wang's *Chinese Calligraphy* (2008, New Haven, Yale University Press); furthermore, the reader is advised to consult T. C. Lai's *Chinese Seals* (1976, Washington, University of Washington Press). On the whole, there is a lack within the literature of reliable works specializing in historical Chinese epistolary arts. Yet, one monograph is available on this topic: this book 明清尺牘/明清尺牍 *Míng-Qīng chǐdú* (*The Epistolary Art of the Ming and Qing Dynasty*, 1995, Taipei, Recreation Press), written by 顧音海/顾音海 Gù Yīnhǎi, is an authoritative work that not only introduces the reader to some basic issues of historical Chinese epistolary art but also overviews the history of Chinese letter writing and illustrates it using a large number of photographs of original letters and envelopes. Unfortunately, this is not a textbook and it may be rather difficult for many Western readers to read it without preliminary training in Chinese calligraphy. Thus, in general, the reader is advised first to briefly study Chinese calligraphy and then work with reprint/photographed historical Chinese letters. In approximately 2012 the author of this book will publish an advanced textbook on this subject.

In general, it is difficult to obtain original letters, which are historical documents and so their use requires access to the archives of major (predominantly) East Asian libraries and collections. A much easier way to read original works is to acquire collections of photographed letters; in recent years, several of such documents have been published in China (see, for example, some related books of 上海書畫出版社 Shanghai shuhua chubanshe).

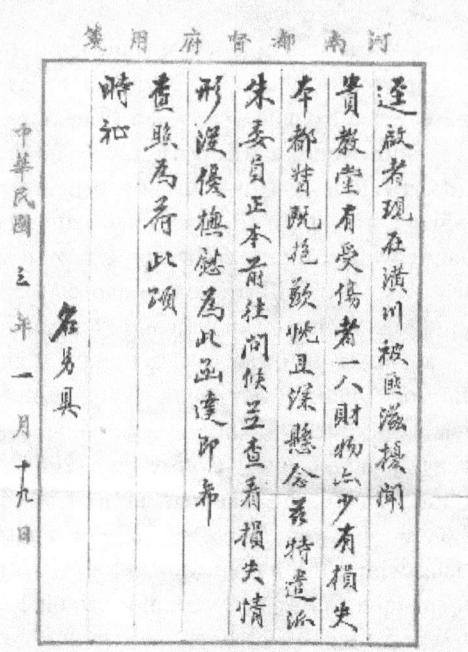

Illustration 6 Text of an early Republican official letter sent to a missionary temple (Courtesy of Mrs. Deborah Blumer)

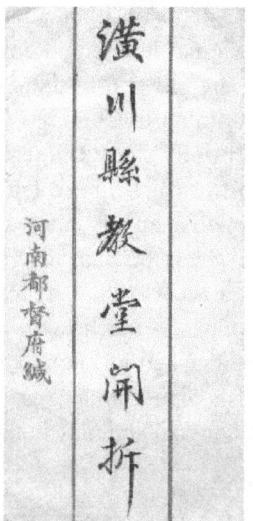

Illustration 7 Envelope of an early Republican official letter sent to a missionary temple (Courtesy of Mrs. Deborah Blumer)

When one starts to individually work on historical Chinese letters, it is advised to obtain some specialized reference books, due to the fact that Classical Chinese dictionaries alone may not interpret some honorifics and epistolary expressions. Thus, the use of the following three books or other reference works is recommended:

(i) 吉常宏 Jí Chánghóng's 漢語稱謂大辭典/汉语称谓大辞典 *Hànyǔ chēngwèi dàcídiǎn*, *A Comprehensive Dictionary of Chinese Terms of Address* (2001, Shijiazhuang, 河北教育出版社 Hebei jiaoyu chubanshe);

(ii) 洪成玉 Hóng Chéngyù's 謙辭敬辭婉辭辭典/谦辞敬辞婉辞辞典 *Qiāncí jìngcí wǎncí cídiǎn*, *A Dictionary of Chinese Honorific Elevating-Denigrating Terms and Euphemisms* (2002, Beijing, 商務印書館 Shangwu yinshuguan);

(iii) 蔣竹蓀 Jiǎng Zhúsūn's 書信用語辭典/书信用语辞典 *Shūxìn yòngyǔ cídiǎn* (A Dictionary of Epistolary Expressions (2003, Shanghai, 上海辭書出版社 Shanghai cishu chubanshe).

Modern Chinese letter manuals, usually defined as 應用文/应用文 *yìngyòng-wén* (lit. 'practical writing') textbooks, are also useful. Although they cannot be used as reference material, familiarity with the rules and lexicon of modern letter writing can aid one in reading historical letters, in particular because these books usually record the norms of Taiwanese letter writing, which is traditional in style. There are many *yìngyòng-wén* textbooks available, a good example being 蔡狄秋 Cài Díqiū's 應用文標竿/应用文标杆 *Yìngyòng-wén biāogān*, *Standard Practical Writing* (1999, Tainan, 文國書局 Wenguo shuju).

Finally, when beginning the study of historical Chinese letters it is recommended that the reader enquire into linguistic – in particular historical pragmatic – studies on this topic. In general, it is worth reading research that deals with letter writing in historical European cultures: as a matter of fact, from an intercultural perspective there is a lot in common between letter writing in the East and West, and knowledge gleaned from European epistolary cultures may be of use in understanding some features of historical Chinese letters. The reader may find the following works particularly illuminating:

(i) Susan Fitzmaurice's *The Familiar Letter in Early Modern English: A Pragmatic Approach* (2002, Amsterdam & Philadelphia: John Benjamins);

(ii) *Letter Writing* (2007, Amsterdam & Philadelphia: John Benjamins), edited by Terttu Nevalainen and Sanna-Kaisa Tanskanen.

On Chinese letter writing and its comparison with the Western epistolary culture an excellent work, 'The arrangement of letters: Hierarchy or culture? From

Cicero to China' (*Journal of Asian Pacific Communication*, Vol. 17/2, 245–285), was written by Andrew Kirkpatrick.

Along with works on letter writing, it may be worth reading some linguistic studies on Chinese politeness, which plays an important role in Chinese letters. Readers with interest in historical Chinese honorifics may consult the work of the author of this book, *Terms of (Im)Politeness – On the Communicational Properties of Traditional Chinese (Im)Polite Terms of Address* (2007, Budapest, Eötvös Loránd University Press); on modern Chinese politeness, the most authoritative work is Yuling Pan's *Politeness in Chinese Face-to-Face Interaction* (2000, Stamford, Ablex).

Notes

Preface

[1] The label 'private' does not mean that every letter studied in this book was addressed to one person only: privacy was interpreted in historical China in a different way to, for example, contemporary Europe or North America. For example, as will be discussed in Chapter 2, some private letters written to a single recipient were intentionally designed to be read by a wider audience. Thus, instead of describing a relationship between the author and the recipient, 'private' means that the works studied in this book were not *official documents* (usually defined as 公文 *gōngwén* in Chinese), such as petitions to the throne, but 'letters' in the strict sense of the word.

[2] It should be noted that in this book the label 'pragmatic' refers to the communicational features of the historical Chinese letters studied.

[3] That is, every text is printed by using the same standard font type, and also proper names are underlined, following a manner that was popular in China during the Republican Era.

Chapter 1

[1] It should be noted that in the present textbook the order of the three letters differs from their original order in *The Family Letters of Zhèng Bǎnqiáo* where they are arranged in chronological order and 'Letter 1' of this book is followed by 'Letter 3'. However, in the present work Letter 1 is followed by Letter 2 due to the fact that both of them deal with the same business transaction.

[2] In traditional Chinese society maternal relatives are more distant than paternal ones.

Chapter 2

[1] 文正公 Wénzhèng-gōng (lit. 'a lord with proper writing') was a posthumous name and rank offered by the Imperial Court to Zēng. It should be noted that this was one of the highest posthumous ranks, which was given only to two persons during the time of the Qīng Dynasty.

[2] While on many historical Chinese envelopes the sender's name and other details also appeared, in edited collections envelope texts, if they appear at all, do not contain the name of the sender.

Chapter 4

[1] Although the word 人 *rén* ('man') in the title of the *Yǔ-rén-shū* group literally means 'man', these letters were arguably written to an anonymous friend(s) or fellow scholar(s) of Gù, and so in the English translation *rén* occurs as 'my friend'. It should be noted that in historical Chinese letter collections there is a large number of letters written to anonymous recipients.

Chapter 5

[1] It should be noted that in the Chinese sinological literature the label Shàoxīng-shīye sometimes describes Shàoxīng literati in general and not the circle of Shàoxīng literati who worked in the capital during the second half of the Qīng Dynasty.

[2] Although the exact dates of Xǔ are unknown, it can be deduced from his correspondence with Gōng Wèizhāi that he was younger than Gōng.

Chapter 6

[1] On 'mock impoliteness' more information can be found in Jonathan Culpeper's paper 'Towards an anatomy of impoliteness' in the *Journal of Pragmatics* (1996, Vol. 25, 349–367).

[2] The expression 'waving' 波 (*bō*) is used in historical Chinese texts as an allegory for 'twists and turns in a high-quality piece of writing'.

Joint Exercise for Chapters 5 and 6

[1] When reading this section, an important point is that the recipient's son was unborn at the time of writing this letter, that is this is an imaginary description and the author in fact foretells that it will be a boy, on the basis of the planned date of the child's birth (the Tenth Month).

[2] According to Chinese Buddhist beliefs, charitable deeds manifest themselves in one's fortune. It should be noted that in this section when referring to the recipient's 'old age' the author is in fact polite: in traditional Chinese culture being old is an honour.

[3] Here the author makes a play on words. The rhetorical question "it is hard to tell whether their master was already born" on the one hand refers to the fact that he does not have a male child, and so it cannot be told whether the future chief in office of his child has been born or not. On the other hand, this question refers to the fact that his paternal nephew cannot gain office, and so it is impossible to know whether there is anybody born to be his chief in office.

Chapter 7

[1] The word 'private' should be emphasized here again because this genre should be differentiated from the genres of 'formal' political letter writing, such as 呈文 *chéngwén* or 'memorandum'.

Appendix I

The Chinese Texts
(Printed in a Punctuated Form)

Letter 1

范縣署中寄郝表弟

墓地風水，原屬堪輿家藉以惑人利己之言，不足取徵者也。語云：「墓地好，不如心地好。」苟子孫心地惡，祖宗雖葬好地，不興發，子孫心地好，祖宗葬壞地，亦得興發。故范文正公見五絕之地，不忍遺禍他人，安葬其父母，竟得飛黃騰達，位至宰相，足見好心地可以移轉惡風水。於其登山涉水，踏破鐵鞋，覓不到牛眠善地，不如清夜捫心，自省方寸間之心地，對於父母無愧怍，對於自己無暴棄，對於世人無欺詐，即可將父母之靈魂安葬心田，其遺骸盡可隨意處置，但求入土爲安。故先嚴先慈之遺柩，即葬於刹院寺老墳。

貴莊舊有墓田一塊。先嚴生前滿擬購置，旋因田中有孤墳一座，不忍平人之塚以作己塚，因是中止。然而此地既主出售，價值十二兩，又極克己。世人未必盡若先嚴，都存不忍鏟墓之心，必然貪廉爭購，至今未識有主與否？如未賣去，願出十二金得之，以作愚夫婦之壽穴。留此孤墳一角，以作牛眠常伴。生前預結鬼鄰，死後不虞寂寞，亦屬狂生之韻事。當自撰碑記，刻石示子孫，於祭掃時，多備一份厄酒麥飯，奠此孤墳，永著名例，以竟先君仁厚之意。

專此拜託，佇盼復音。

Letter 2

范縣署中寄郝表弟

台駕不來，好音先至，亦足以稍慰予懷。墓田既被捷足者先得，誠屬愚兄疏忽之咎。

至於該田風水，四面環河，後靠土山，不等堪輿家言，一望而知為牛眠佳地。我本不信風水，自先父母安葬後，閱三年即登賢書，成進士，出宰此邑，殊令人不能不信風水之得力也。

貴莊墓田，既為農家所得，至今仍事種植，固可設法收買。但田價須溢出兩倍，比較舊時價格，雖覺昂貴，然而物價早晚不同，何況相隔已閱十餘年，滄海桑田，變遷無定，漲價又屬居奇慣例。既目為奇貨而卻得之，三十六金自不能短期分毫。

老表弟既有來范之約，請挈同田主偕來，當場敘券。倘田主吝惜川資，即煩老表與之立券交易，墊款容後歸趙。

Letter 3

范縣署中寄郝表弟

范縣風俗惇厚，四民各安其業，不喜干涉閒事，因此訟案稀少。衙署多暇，間來唯有飲酒看花，醉後擊桌高歌，聲達戶外。一般皂隸聞之，咸竊竊私相告語，謂：「主人殆其儳乎！」語為雛婢所聞，奔告内子，旋來規勸曰：「曆來只有狂士掃生，未聞有狂官。請勿再萌故態，滋騰物議。從此杯中物，必待黃昏退食，方得略飲三壺。」受此壓制，殊令人不耐。繼思勸我少飲，是屬善意，遂與之相約，每晚罄十壺而後睡。次晨宿醒已解，從政自無妨礙矣。然而較之在焦山讀書時，每飯必得暢飲，其苦樂迥不相同。所以古人不肯為五斗米折腰，良有以也。我今直視靴帽如桎梏，奈何，奈何！

老表是我酒友，惠然肯來，欣甚慰甚，當下榻相迎，共謀痛飲也。

臨穎不勝佇望之至。

Letter 4

諭紀瑞　　十二月四日

字寄紀瑞侄左右：

前接吾侄來信，字跡端秀，知近日大有長進。紀鴻奉母來此，詢及一切，知侄身體業已長成，孝友謹慎，至以為慰。

吾家累世以來，孝弟勤儉。輔臣公以上吾不及見，竟希公、星岡公皆未明即起，竟日無片刻暇逸。竟希公少時在陳氏宗祠讀書，正月上學，輔臣公給錢一百，為零用之需，五月歸時，僅用去二文，尚餘九十八文還其父。其儉如此！星岡公當孫入翰林之後，猶親自種菜收糞。吾父竹亭公之勤儉，則爾等所及見也。

今家中境地雖漸寬裕，侄與諸昆弟切不可忘卻先世之艱難，有福不可享盡，有勢不可使盡。「勤」字工夫，等一貴早起，等二貴有恆。

「儉」字工夫，等一莫著華麗衣服，等二莫多用僕婢雇工。凡將相無種，聖賢豪傑亦無種，衹要人肯立志，都可以做得到的。侄等處最順之境，當最富之年，明年又從最賢之師，但須立定志向：何事不可成？何人不可做？願吾侄早勉之也。蔭生尚算正途功名，可以考御史。待侄十八九歲，即與紀澤同進京應考。然侄此際專心讀書，宜以八股試帖為要，不可專恃蔭生為基，總以鄉試會試能到榜前，益為門户之光。

紀官聞甚聰慧，侄亦以「立志」二字，兄弟互相勸勉，則日進無疆矣。順問

近好。

滌生手示

十二月十四日　（同治二年）

Letter 5

致歐陽夫人　　　　　五月初五日午刻

歐陽夫人左右：

自余回金陵後，諸事順遂。惟天氣亢旱，雖四月二十四、五月初三日兩此甘雨，稻田尚不能栽插，深以為慮。科一出痘，非常危險，幸祖宗神靈庇佑，現已全癒發體，變一結實模樣。十五日滿兩個月後，即當遣之回家，計六月旬可以抵湘。如體氣日旺，七月中旬赴省鄉試可也。

余精力日衰，總難多見人客。算命者常言十一月交「癸運」，即不吉利，余亦不願久居此官，不欲再接家眷東來。夫人率兒婦輩在家，須事事立個一定章程。居官不過偶然之事，居家乃是長久之計。能從勤儉耕讀上做出好規模，雖一旦罷官，尚不失爲興旺氣象。若貪圖衙門之熱鬧，不立家鄉之基業，則罷官之後，便覺氣象蕭索。凡有盛，必有衰，不可不預爲之計。望夫人教訓兒孫婦女，常常作家中無官之想，時時有謙恭省儉之意，則福澤悠久，余心大慰矣。

余身體安好如常。惟眼矇日甚，說話多則舌頭蹇澀。左牙疼甚，而不甚動搖，不至遽脫，堪以告慰。順問近好。

國藩手草

五月初五日午刻（同治六年）

Letter 6

稟父母　　七月初四日

男國藩跪稟父母親大人萬福金安：

六月二十八日接到家書，係三月十四日所發。知十九日四弟生子，男等合室相慶。四妹生產雖難，然血暈亦是常事。且此次既能保全，則下次較爲容易。男未得信時，常以爲慮，既得此信，如釋重負。

六月底，我縣有人來京捐官王道隆。渠在寧鄉界住，言四月縣考時，渠在城內并在彭興岐雲門寺、丁信風兩處面晤四弟、六弟。知案首是吳定五。男十三年在陳氏宗祠讀書，定五纔發蒙作起講，在楊畏齋處受業。去年聞吳春岡說定五甚爲發奮，今果得志，可謂成就甚速。其餘前十名及每場題目，渠已忘記。後有信來，乞四弟寫出。

四弟、六弟考運不好，不必掛懷。俗語云：「不怕進得遲，只要中得快。」從前邵丹畦前輩甲名　四十三歲入學，五十二歲作學政，現任廣西藩臺。汪朗渠鳴相　於道光十二年入學，十三年點狀元。阮芸臺元　前輩於乾隆五十三年縣、府試皆未取頭場，即於其年入學、中舉，五十四年點翰林，五十五年留館，五十六年大考第一，比放浙江學政，五十九年升浙江巡撫。些小得失，不足患，特患業之不精耳。兩弟場中文若得意，可將原卷領出寄京。若不得意，不寄可也。

男等在京平安。紀澤兄妹二人體甚結實，皮色亦黑。

逆夷在江蘇滋擾，於六月十一日攻陷鎮江，有大船數十只在大江游弋。江寧、揚州二府頗可危慮。然而天下降災，聖人在上，故京師人心鎮定。同鄉王翰城繼賢，黔陽人告假出京。男與陳岱雲亦擬送家眷南旋，與鄭莘田、王翰城四家同隊出京鄭名世任，給事中，現放貴州貴西道。男與陳家本於六月底定計，後於七月初一請人扶乩另紙錄出大仙示語，似可不必輕舉妄動，是以中止。現在男與陳家仍不送家眷回南也。

同縣謝果堂先生興嶢來京，為其次子捐鹽大使。男已請至寓陪席。其世兄與王道隆尚未請，擬得便亦須請一次。

正月間俞岱青先生出京，男寄有鹿脯一方，託找彭山屺轉寄。俞後託謝吉人轉寄，不知到否?又四月託李昂岡榮燦寄銀寄筆，託曹西垣寄參，並交陳季牧處，不知到否?

世兄與王道隆尚未請，擬得便亦須請一次。

前父親教男養鬚之法，男僅留上唇鬚，不能用水浸透。色黃者多，黑者少。下唇擬待三十六歲始留。

男每接家信，嫌其不詳，嗣後更願詳示。

男謹稟

七月初四日 〔道光二十二年〕

Letter 7

與張原田

予昔曾謂，水滸勝似史記。人都嗤爲妄，即如足下，平日于弟一切深信者，亦竟疑之。然予作此說，並非狂妄不稽，亦自是從讀書中領悟出來。其實史記是以文運事，水滸是因文生事。以文運事，是先有事。生成如此如此，卻要算計出一篇文字來。雖是史公高才也，畢竟是喫苦事。因文生事即不然，只是順著筆性去，削高補低都由我。史記不限于文，水滸不礙于事，即是水滸勝似史記處。

今爲此辭，足下當不復疑。

Letter 8

與王斲山

先生昔嘗爲予言：「不登泰山不知天下之高；登泰山不登日觀，不知泰山之高也；不觀黃河不知天下之深；觀黃河不觀龍門，不知黃河之深也。不見聖人，不知天下之至；見聖人不見仲尼，不知聖人之至也。」斯言耿耿，未嘗一刻忘之。今批水滸至設祭一篇，不覺拍案狂叫：「讀書不讀水滸不知天下之奇；讀水滸而不讀設祭，是不知水滸之奇也。」嗚呼！耐庵之才，固不可以斗石量也。

前奉呈之六卷，不知已讀竟否？亦有不愜意處否？須知我批此書，全是替古人做一件公事，並非聖嘆自己私事。儘管直直言之，彼中于客氣而説摸稜兩可話者，是生平所大惡。先生幸毋蹈此惡轍。

Letter 9

與王斲山

前雲衢聞予批點水滸傳，以爲不足浪費筆墨而批稗史，其見恰左。

聖嘆不問其書之爲正史稗史，只問其書之文章，做得好不好。即稗史亦不必不批。文章不好，即正史亦不必批。水滸一書，眞是天下

古今奇絕妙絕之文，奈何可以不批？吾非必願批是書，吾但覺不批是

書，中心殊不能自寬也。

足下書來，言曾一見此書，不見其佳處，特爲俗相蒙耳。夫水滸所

敘，敘一百八人之事。而此一百八人者，人有其性情，人有其氣質，人

有其形狀，人有其聲口。夫以一手而畫數面，則將有兄弟之形；一口而

吹數聲，斯不免再映。施耐庵以一心之所運，而一百八人，各自入妙，

此豈迂儒腐士所能爲，庸夫俗子所能領略者乎？予故謂水滸傳乃天下古

今之一部奇書，施耐庵乃天下古今一個才子。所批前六卷，已呈斲山先

生，不妨往索閱，定能如願，且證予言不虛也。

Letter 10

與人書十

嘗謂今人纂輯之書，正如今人之鑄錢。古人采銅於山。今人則買舊錢，名之曰廢銅，以充鑄而已。所鑄之錢，既已粗惡，而又將古人傳世之寶，舂剉碎散，不存於後。豈不兩失之乎。

承問日知錄又成幾卷。蓋期之以廢銅，而某自別來一載，早夜誦讀，反復尋究，僅得十餘條。然庶幾采山之銅也。

Exercise Text

與人書十九

彈琵琶佑酒，此倡女之所為，其識則然也。苟欲請良家女子出而為之，則艴然而怒矣。何以異於是？

Exercise Text

與人書二十

某君欲刻其文集，
以求名於世，此如人之
失足而墜井也。若更爲
之序，豈不猶之下石
乎？惟其未墜之時，猶
可及止。止之而不聽，
彼且以入井爲安宅也，
吾已矣夫。

Letter 11

與人書一

人之爲學，不日進則日退。獨學
無友，則孤陋而難成。久處一方，則
習染而不自覺。不幸而在窮僻之域，
無車馬之資，猶當博學審問，古人與
稽，以求其是非之所在，庶幾可得十
之五六。若既不出戶，又不讀書，則
是面牆之士，雖子羔、原憲之賢，終
無濟於天下。子曰：「十室之邑，必
有忠信如丘者焉，不如丘之好學
也。」夫以孔子之聖，猶須好學，今
人可不勉乎！

Letter 12

與友人論門人書

伏承來教，勤勤懇懇，閔其年之衰暮，而悼其學之無傳，其爲意甚盛。然欲使之效曩者二三先生，招門徒，立名譽，以光顯於世，則私心有所不願也。若乃西漢之傳經，弟子常千餘人，而位富者至公卿，下者亦爲博士，以名其學，可不謂榮歟？而班史乃斷之曰：「蓋祿利之路然也。」故以夫子之門人，且學干祿，子曰：「三年學，不至於穀，不易得也。」而況於今日乎！

今之爲祿利者，其無藉於經術也審矣。窮年所習不過應試之文，而問以本經，猶茫然不知爲何語。蓋舉唐以來帖括之淺，而又廢之。其無意於學也，傳之非一世矣。短綰緊之例行，而目不識字者可爲郡邑博士！惟貧而不能徒業者，百人之中尚有一二，讀書而又皆躁竟之徒，欲速成以名於世，語之以五經則不願學，語之以白沙、陽明之語錄，則欣然矣，以其襲而取之之易也。其中小有才華者，頗好爲詩，而今日之詩，亦可以不學而作。吾行天下見詩與語錄之刻，堆幾積案，殆於瓦釜雷鳴，而叩之以二

南、雅、頌之義，不能説也。於此時而將行吾之道，其誰從之？

「大匠不爲拙工改廢繩墨，羿不爲拙射變其彀率。」若徇眾人之好而自貶其學，以來天下之人，而廣其名譽，則是枉道以從人，而我亦將有所不假。

惟是斯道之在天下，必有時而興，而君子之教人有私淑艾者，雖去之百世而猶若同堂也。所著日知錄三十餘卷，平生之志與業皆在其中，惟多寫數本以貽之同好，庶不爲惡其害己者之所去，而有王者起，得以酌取焉，亦可以畢區區之願矣。

夫道之污隆，各以其時。若爲己而不求名，則無不可以自勉。鄙哉硜硜所以異於今之先生者如此。高明何以教之？

Exercise Text

與人書二十三

能文不爲文人，能講不爲講師。吾見近日之爲文人，爲講師者，其意皆欲以文名以講名者也。子不云乎：「是聞也，非達也。」、「默而識之。」愚雖不敏，請事斯語矣。

Letter 13

與龔未齋

客冬抱牘而來，既費錦心，并飲珍饌。別後馬首東指，承歡匝月，即又束裝。正擬探訪游蹤，適秦含章有札致弟，道足下依紅仍舊，高山流水，入耳同傾，既非彈之不調，何必碎之遽去耶？津鹽帶水，驛使時逢，折柳贈梅，勿虛所望。

Letter 14

與龔未齋〔譽其待人之厚〕

吾黨傾心丰采，幾如士仰荊州。平時嚮往有心，而天緣不假，奉教無從。今春因藹堂而得見先生，即荷忘年投分，垂愛逾常。頻飫郇氏之廚，屢醉公瑾之醴，銘心若篆，留齒猶芬。兼以藹堂之將入省也，而假以一塵安其片席，綢繆委曲，無微不至。先生之愛人以德，更於此想見一斑矣。

臨行雨絲風片。春到清明，不知路上行人，幾問杏花村酒。想此日琴裝已卸，坐東閣而對殘梅，雅興當復不淺也。

弟以鳩心之拙，謬作螳臂之當，彙筆素餐。正與南郭先生，齊門溷食，應不免為當道所嗤。惟望玉律之頒，藉獲金針之度，則此感豈有既耶。

阮昔侯於廿一日赴磁州。破題兒第一夜，鍾情如先生，當亦為之黯然也。

Letter 15

慰冀未齋喪妾并答遲慰

同志則相求，同病則相憐，此人之情也。弟謂同志者或有時而不求，同病者則無時而不憐。然憐於跡，究不若憐於心者為尤摯。

弟自去秋失恃，踉蹌而來。冬杪於冰天雪地中，捧檄赴都，途次為風寒所感，歸而病竟不止。履端後三日，仍腹藥，閱今一載，日與倉公、扁鵲為友。又不能舍此毛錐，靜加攝養，每念疾苦，竊自憐之。

春間足下病，繼又聞失寵。得耗之下，為足下憐，更有甚於為己憐者。蓋足下年居賜鳩，非人不適，何意好花易落，好月難圓。傷桃葉之遠摧，感朝雲之長逝，情之所至，其何能堪。況值衰病相侵，衾裯半冷，噓寒問燠，誰與為懽。此尤足下所悲從中來，不堪回首者。每欲致書慰問，恐足下當頤養之時，處煩惱之境，一紙相投，徒亂心曲。故未致尺書於左右，此正弟之略於跡，而憐於心也。

來書以弟無一函致慰，謂是愛之乎？怒之乎？弟竊以為子言過矣。夫君子有自反之道，無求人之理。愛之怒之雖在人，而所致愛致怒則在我，我而可愛，人必愛之，我而可怒，人必怒之。弟與足下相印以心，相要以久，愛之不暇，怒於何來。禮曰：「君子之交淡以成。」弟之所以落落者，竊有味乎淡交之義，而欲自附於君子之未也。

尺牘心折已久。付之梨棗，定當紙貴一時。以弟譾陋無文，亦蒙採入，恐因魚目而減夜光之價。削而去之，則為我藏拙多矣。

Letter 16

與許葭村

病後正不能搦管，而一息尚存，又未敢與草木同腐。平時偶作詩詞，祇堪覆瓿。惟三十餘年，客窗酬應之札，自攄胸膈，暢所欲言。雖於尺牘之道，去之千里，而性情所寄，似有不忍棄者，遂於病後錄而集之。內中惟僕與足下酬答爲獨多。惜足下鴻篇短製，爲愛者攜去，僅存四六一函，錄之於集。借美玉之光，以輝燕石，并欲使後之覽者，知僕與足下乃文字之交，非勢利交也。

因足下素有嗜痂之癖，故書以奉告。容錄出一番，另請教削，知許子之不憚煩也。

Letter 17

答許葭村

登堂望遠，極目蒼涼，正切秋水伊人之想。適接瑤章，如同晤對，即滿浮三大白，不負茱萸令節也。

足下處應酬最繁之地，而又百函并發，縱倚馬之才，無難揮灑，而中書君疲於奔走，將有未老先生禿之慮。相知以心，初不以筆墨間課疏密也。

金粟如來，墮落塵世，爲聲色香味觸法所擾，久已拖泥帶水，受一切苦厄。足下具大智慧，早已觀自在菩薩矣。尚向舍利子求「揭帝之咒」哉！

Letter 18

答許葭村

陳遵尺牘，名震當時。然高自位置，惜墨如金，不肯輕投一札，足下殆亦有此癖！

今有人焉，以莫須有之事，使足下忘其癖，而洋洋焉，灑灑焉，不能自惜其墨焉。僕始怪若人之愚，今則喜若人巧爲其能，以莫須有之事，得不易有之書也。

而近亦因足下之書，恍然得所解。蓋足下握三寸之管，若決江河，一波未平，一波復起。跡之字裏行間，則悄然無風也。若人之波，不必欲有風而始起，始見得足下削簡之法乎？使若人而見足下之書，必且詡然曰：「一枝未借，尺壁先來，失在彼而得在此，夫亦可無憾！」

恐足下聞之，又將高自位置，惜墨如金，奈何！

Letter 19

與許葭村

重九後，數行覆候起居，知邀青照。

小陽佳日，舞彩調琴，天倫至樂，遠勝蓬瀛。而玉麟早已投懷，何竟祕而不宣，勞遠人揣度乎？

阮君書來，道其夫人有如達之喜。因思是月也，雀入大水，故敝署五產而皆雌。今來函又改於十月娩身，其得蛟龍也必矣。第親自造作者，竟不知其月，抑又奇也。

舍姪甘林得館之難，正如其伯之得子，豈其東家尚未誕生也？

今年曾寄寓信，計六十餘函；足下陰行善事，不厭其煩，何以報之？惟有學近日官場，念金剛經萬遍，保佑足下多子耳！

Letter 20

與龔未齋【慰其姪失館】

手書疊至，謂四月鴛池，夢蘭可卜。弟非神乎技者，方自笑其鳩拙。安所得珠而藏之櫝耶。

昔侯夫人逾月而娩，以其時敂之，宜爲震之長男，而爲巽之長女。

良由當局者自失其期，遂令旁觀者難神其算也。

令姪館事，屢謀屢失。降而就副，未免大才小用，靜以待之，自有碧梧千尺耳。

寓函往復，何足云勞？而仁人用心，祝以多子，則兄之善頌善禱，積福尤宏，不更當老蚌生珠耶？

Telegram Written by Yuán Shìkǎi

民國二年八月二日

轉須磨別莊康長素先生鑒：

去國念年，困心衡慮。大著發抒政見，足爲薄俗針砭，欽仰無似。舉國想望風采，但祈還轅祖國，絕不敢強以所難。

凡河汾弟子，京洛故人，均言先生不願從政，而有意主持名教。

敬具蒲輪，鵠候明教。何日稅駕，渴盼德音。

袁世凱　冬

Letter 21

上翁同龢變法說帖　　光緒二十三年二月初七日

謹陳管見：

竊維自古之天下不能無非常之變。遇非常之變，徒諰諰焉，蹙額疾首，諉爲時數之適然，而日聽其陵夷衰微，不肯破膠固拘墟之成見，急起變法以應之，恐卒至於束手待斃，而不可救藥也。

今之時局，可謂極非常之變矣。德人以三巨艦闖入膠澳，据爲己有，設巡撫以鎮之，又遺其親王濟師，是不但顯無退志，恐彼親王到後，更不知有何變局。山東濱海要地，介居南北洋之中，使他族逼處，則海道有隔絕之患，我之海軍，勢將永不克振。

論者謂，中國貧窮，不堪用武，亟宜陰嗾他國興師助我，當可驅逐德人，抑或商準各國開口通商，即可公處膠澳。此恐未能嗾群雄之斗，飽群夷之欲也。何者？俄、法向有密約，英、倭近復締交。四國各有黨援，勢若分成兩敵，以德之中立也。於是彼四國者，莫不視其向背，以為輕重。夫彼方重之，即安得而背之。雖俄人與我關係較重，睦誼較敦，然以自詒伊戚也哉。是成有以知其必不然矣。且也俄儼然認東北數省入其版圖。鷹瞵虎耽，英復隱然視大江南北在其掌握，倭窺浙、閩，法圖滇、桂。德人既難於先，諸國將效尤於後，杳來紛至，群起而我為難。數年前，西人有瓜華之謠，并具圖說遍傳五洲，以今日時勢揆之，似此謠不為無因。此誠可危之甚也。

唯利是視，又豈肯舍公法局外之例，愛我仇德，使德、英合謀，增樹勍敵，以為難。

且夫我之忍尤含詬，降心俯首以相從者，不為不至矣，而人初不之憐也。既力過勢禁之不能，復理諭情動之不可，若復蹈常習故，不知變計，拱手坐視，聽客所為，彼亦公然不讓，擇肉而食，長蛇封豕。肆其貪殘，吞噬之餘，所存有幾？竊恐海疆日蹙，而關稅之征，鹽漕之入，向所資以裕帑藏

局，而畫疆自守，政自我出，猶可多存數千里土地人民，以爲異時徐圖恢復

用以培養元氣，護持根本，二三年間，可望自立。從不能抗拒群雄，保我全

端，實屬瞬刻不容稍緩。誠，就斯三者而實力變革，汰其宿弊，矯其積習，

體大，猝難畢舉。而究其所最要者，如「用人」、「理財」、「練兵」三大

易曰：「窮則變。」此其時矣。第於積重之秋，驟行變法之政，茲事

圖挽回補救於萬一？

然而事變迭乘，人不我待，痛切於剝膚，厄甚於倒懸，何可不幡然振屬，以

實而見諸施行者。廟堂亦憂容勛舊，不加督責。似此變法，恐終未有其期。

事者條說甚詳，而飭下各行省遵辦者，亦復指不勝屈，乃因仍遷就，迄未有

自甲午軍興以後，朝野士庶，凡識時務之輩，莫不爭以變法爲言。陳

積薪厝火，尚未及燃，而切身之災，固日憂其近矣。

充度支者，一旦攘奮殆盡，而舉不復爲我所有。區區彈丸，何以立國？雖曰

之計。

世凱雖至愚戇，亦略知忌諱，何敢妄肆狂瞽之舌，故作不祥之論。第念覆巢之下，詎有完卵，棟折榱崩，孰免傾壓？

Appendix II

Chronological List of Chinese Dynasties

夏 Xià .... *c.*2070–*c.*1600 BC
商 Shāng .... *c.*1600–*c.*1046 BC
周 Zhōu .... *c.*1046–256 BC
秦 Qín... 221–206 BC
漢 Hàn .... 206 BC–AD 220
    西漢 Xī Hàn ('The Western Hàn Dynasty')..... 206 BC–AD 8
    東漢 Dōng Hàn ('The Eastern Hàn Dynasty') .. AD 25–AD 220
三國 Sān'guó ('The Three Kingdoms') 220–265
晉 Jìn 265–420
南北朝 Nán-Běi Cháo
('Southern and Northern Dynasties')........................... 316–589
隋 Suí.. 589–618
唐 Táng.. 618–906
五代 Wǔdài ('Five Dynasties') 906–960
宋 Sòng.. 960–1279
金 Jīn 1122–1234
元 Yuán 1260–1368
明 Míng.. 1368–1644
清 Qǐng.. 1644–1911
The Republic of China
(Continuing in Taiwan) 1912–
The People's Republic of China................................. 1949–

Glossary of Epistolary Expressions, Honorifics and Grammatical Words

The present Glossary is limited to lexical items that very frequently occur in Chinese letters. For the sake of brevity, the Chinese characters occur in a traditional form only, and the words and expressions are not supplied with literal translation. Furthermore, the present Glossary includes a few simple but useful grammatical and formulaic words and expressions that are not mentioned in the glossary sections of the chapters.

A

安好如常 *ānhǎo-rúchǎng*: to be well as usual (formulaic epistolary expression)

B

拜託/拜托 *bàituō*: to request somebody to do a favour (honorific epistolary form)
頒 *bān*: to send a letter (honorific epistolary addressee-elevating verbal form)
比 *bǐ*: and, then
便 *biàn*: then
並 *bìng*: and; with
稟 *bǐng*: to send a letter to a higher-ranking person (honorific epistolary addressee-elevating verbal form)
並非 *bìngfēi*: definitely not

敝署 *bìshǔ*: humble office (honorific self-denigrating epistolary form)
不妨 *bùfáng*: might as well
不然 *bùrán*: not so
不失爲 *bù-shī-wéi*: may after all be considered as …

C

纔/才 *cái*: only then
藏拙 *cángzhuō*: to hide one's inadequacy (honorific self-denigrating epistolary verbal form)
呈 *chéng*: to submit (honorific epistolary verbal form)
承問 *chéngwèn*: to respectfully receive one's enquiry (honorific epistolary verbal form)
尺牘 *chǐdú*: letter (usually describes edited letters)

尺書 *chǐshū*: letter

酬答 *chóudá*: letter of exchange/ response

垂愛 *chuí'ài*: tender care (honorific epistolary addressee-elevating form)

此際 *cǐjì*: for the moment being

從此 *cóngcǐ*: henceforth

D

殆 *dài*: to be at the point of; almost

當 *dāng*: should

弟 *dì*: younger brother (deferential self-denigrating form of address)

對於 *duìyú*: towards

E

而況 *érkuàng*: all the more

而卻 *érquè*: however, but

F

煩 *fán*: to trouble someone with ... (polite expression)

方 *fāng*: only then

奉 *fèng*: to respectfully receive/ submit (honorific verbal form)

丰采/風采 *fēngcǎi*: elegant demeanour (honorific addressee-elevating expression)

奉呈 *fèngchéng*: to respectfully submit something to the recipient (honorific epistolary verbal form)

奉告 *fènggào*: to humbly inform (honorific verbal form)

奉教 *fèngjiào*: to respectfully receive the recipient's instructions (honorific recipient-elevating form)

伏承 *fúchéng*: to respectfully receive (honorific epistolary verbal form)

覆瓿 *fùbù*: one's writing is worthless (honorific epistolary self-denigrating expression)

父母親大人 *fùmǔ-qīn-dàrén*: honoured father and mother (honorific epistolary form of address)

伏乞 *fúqǐ*: to humbly beg (honorific verbal form)

夫人 *fūrén*: Madam, Lady (term of address used towards high-ranking ladies)

復音 *fùyīn*: letter of response

G

該 *gāi*: this, that, the given ...; ought, should

高明 *gāomíng*: brilliant person (honorific elevating form of address)

高山流水 *gāoshān-liúshuǐ*: to be close friends (idiomatic epistolary expression)

苟 *gǒu*: if

跪稟 *guìbǐng*: to humbly report (honorific epistolary verbal form)

貴莊 *guìzhuāng*: respected village (honorific addressee-elevating expression)

H

函 *hán*: letter

荷 *hè*: to respectfully receive something (honorific epistolary expression)

何況 *hékuàng*: moreover

鴻篇短製 *hóngpiān-duǎnzhì*: outstanding letters of various length
(honorific epistolary elevating
form; 鴻 *hóng* is often used in
honorific expressions: wild goose
is a 'large' bird, and so *hóng* became a synonym for 'greatness')

惠然肯來 *huìrán-kěnlái*: be so kind
as to come (honorific epistolary
formula)

J

既 *jì*: already; since; whereas, thus,
this being the case …

寄 *jì*: to send a letter

即 *jí*: then

漸 *jiàn*: gradually

譾陋 *jiǎnlòu*: shallow and ignorant
(honorific self-denigrating form)

教 *jiào*: to teach (honorific verbal
form, which refers to the recipient's comment on the author's behaviour or his advice for the author)

家書 *jiāshū*: family letter

家信 *jiāxìn*: family letter

皆 *jiē*: all

藉以 *jièyǐ*: by means of

即可 *jíkě*: acting in a certain way
should be appropriate…

僅 *jǐn*: only

謹稟 *jǐnbǐng*: to respectfully send
(honorific epistolary closing formula)

竟 *jìng*: finally

近好 *jìnhǎo*: blessing (formulaic
expression used in letter closings)

即如 *jírú*: as if

鳩心 *jiūxīn*: stupidity (epistolary
expression often expressing self-
denigrating meaning)

K

堪 *kān*: may

狂生 *kuángshēng*: this crazy person
(honorific self-denigrating expression)

L

來教 *láijiào*: honourable letter (honorific epistolary elevating form)

來信 *láixìn*: the recipient's letter

老表弟 *lǎo-biǎodì*: venerable
cousin (familiar honorific form)

曆來 *lìlái*: hitherto

臨穎 *línyǐng*: while writing these
words … (epistolary expression)

M

滿 *mǎn*: exactly

美玉 *měiyù*: refined works (honorific elevating form)

蒙 *méng*: to be granted by something (honorific verbal form)

嗚呼 *mínghū*: Ah! (onomatopoeic expression describing one's emotive cry out)

某 *mǒu*: I; certain, some

N

奈何 *nàihé*: 'What to do!' (rhetorical exclamation); 'Why?' (rhetorical question)

男 *nán*: your son (familiar self-referring form)

搦管 *nuòguǎn*: to take the brush and write (literary synonym for 'writing correspondence')

P

頗 *pō*: rather

破題兒 *pòtí'er*: the first … (epistolary expression)

僕 *pù*: this humble servant (honorific self-denigrating form of address)

Q

乞 *qǐ*: to beg (honorific verbal expression)

竊 *qiè*: humbly (deferential form, used before expressing one's opinion)

且 *qiě*: moreover

切不可 *qiè-bùkě*: be sure not to …

請 *qǐng*: please, beg you to…

請教削 *qǐng-jiàoxuē*: to fulfil one's humble request to correcting a document (honorific verbal form)

青照 *qīngzhào*: to condescend to read a work (honorific verbal form)

其實 *qíshí*: as a matter of fact

渠 *qú*: third-person pronoun

區區 *qūqū*: this trivial person (honorific self-denigrating form of address)

R

容 *róng*: to allow someone (deferential epistolary verbal form)

如釋重負 *rúshì-zhòngfù*: to feel relieved (formulaic epistolary expression)

S

尚 *shàng*: still, yet

矧 *shěn*: moreover (epistolary form)

舍姪 *shèzhí*: humble nephew (deferential self-denigrating form)

適 *shì*: just then

是以 *shìyǐ*: therefore

手草 *shǒucǎo*: respectfully write some words in haste (honorific epistolary closing expression, used towards one's inferior within the same generation)

手示 *shǒushì*: personally written instructions (formulaic expression used after the author's name

in family letter written to a
younger and less powerful family
member)

殊 *shū*: extremely

書 *shū*: letter

順問 *shùnwèn*: hereby wish (formulaic letter-closing expression)

嗣後 *sìhòu*: hereafter

遂 *suì*: thereupon

T

台駕 *táijià*: your honour (honorific addressee-elevating expression)

倘 *tǎng*: if

W

萬福金安 *wànfú-jīn'ān*: to wish wealth and happiness (honorific epistolary formula)

無文 *wúwén*: to lack literary talent (often used in self-denigrating contexts)

X

係 *xì*: copular verb

咸 *xián*: all

先慈 *xiāncí*: one's own deceased mother (honorific expression)

先君 *xiānjūn*: one's own deceased father (honorific expression)

先嚴 *xiānyán*: one's own deceased father (honorific expression)

下榻相迎 *xiàtà-xiāngyíng*: to personally greet as an honoured guest (formulaic expression)

幸甚 *xìngshèn*: it would be a great honour (deferential epistolary closing form)

欣甚慰甚 *xīnshèn-wèishèn*: to be extremely gratified (formulaic epistolary expression)

旋 *xuán*: soon; thereupon; to return

削簡 *xuējiǎn*: synonym for letter writing

Y

瑤章 *yáozhāng*: esteemed letter (honorific elevating form)

宜 *yí*: should

依 *yī*: still

以來 *yǐlái*: since

因 *yīn*: because

因此 *yīncǐ*: therefore

應 *yīng*: should

又 *yòu*: and; again

猶 *yóu*: even; still, yet

尤 *yóu*: more

猶當 *yóudāng*: all the more because

猶若 *yóuruò*: almost like

予 *yǔ*: first person pronoun

諭 *yù*: to inform a lower-ranking person (often used in the titles of family letters written to younger relatives)

餘 *yú*: more than …

與否 *yǔfǒu*: whether or not? (used at the end of sentences)

愚夫婦 *yú-fūfù*: myself and my wife (honorific self-denigrating expression)

於後 *yúhòu*: (t)hereinafter

玉麟 *yùlín*: revered son (honorific form of address)

玉律 *yùlǜ*: honourable letter (honorific epistolary elevating expression)

於其/與其 *yúqí*: rather than

愚兄 *yúxiōng*: this humble brother of yours (honorific self-denigrating expression)

Z

贈梅 *zèngméi*: revered letter (honorific epistolary form)

折柳 *zhéliǔ*: to present with a letter (honorific epistolary form)

珍饌 *zhēnzhuàn*: your wonderful delicacies (honorific form)

致 *zhì*: a letter written to … (formula used in envelopes/superscriptions written to rank-equals)

至於 *zhìyú*: as regards

之餘 *zhī-yú*: after …

專此 *zhuāncǐ*: sending this, hereby … (letter-closing formula)

佇盼 *zhùpàn*: to await (honorific epistolary form)

佇望 *zhùwàng*: to wish to see someone (epistolary form)

自 *zì*: self; from, since

字寄 *zì-jì*: words sent to … (letter-opening formula used before names)

總 *zǒng*: always; in sum

縱 *zòng*: even if

左右 *zuǒyòu*: honorific form used either after the recipient's name or as an independent form of address

足下 *zúxià*: sir (widely used form of address in letters written to rank-equals)

Index